Valuing the Closely Held Firm

Financial Management Association
Survey and Synthesis Series

The Search for Value: Measuring the Company's Cost of Capital
Michael C. Ehrhardt

Managing Pension Plans: A Comprehensive Guide to Improving Plan Performance
Dennis E. Logue and Jack S. Radar

Efficient Asset Management: A Practical Guide to Stock Portfolio Optimization and Asset Allocation
Richard O. Michaud

Real Options: Managing Strategic Investment in an Uncertain World
Martha Amram and Nalin Kulatilaka

Beyond Greed and Fear: Understanding Behavioral Finance and the Psychology of Investing
Hersh Shefrin

Dividend Policy: Its Impact on Firm Value
Ronald C. Lease, Kose John, Avner Kalay, Uri Loewenstein, and Oded H. Sarig

Value Based Management: The Corporate Response to Shareholder Revolution
John D. Martin and J. William Petty

Debt Management: A Practitioner's Guide
John D. Finnerty and Douglas R. Emery

Real Estate Investment Trusts: Structure, Performance, and Investment Opportunities
Su Han Chan, John Erickson, and Ko Wang

Trading and Exchanges: Market Microstructure for Practitioners
Larry Harris

Last Rights: Liquidating a Company
Ben S. Branch, Hugh M. Ray, and Robin Russell

Valuing the Closely Held Firm
Michael S. Long and Thomas A. Bryant

VALUING THE CLOSELY HELD FIRM

Michael S. Long
Thomas A. Bryant

OXFORD
UNIVERSITY PRESS
2008

OXFORD
UNIVERSITY PRESS

Oxford University Press, Inc., publishes works that further
Oxford University's objective of excellence
in research, scholarship, and education.

Oxford New York
Auckland Cape Town Dar es Salaam Hong Kong Karachi
Kuala Lumpur Madrid Melbourne Mexico City Nairobi
New Delhi Shanghai Taipei Toronto

With offices in
Argentina Austria Brazil Chile Czech Republic France Greece
Guatemala Hungary Italy Japan Poland Portugal Singapore
South Korea Switzerland Thailand Turkey Ukraine Vietnam

Published by Oxford University Press, Inc.
198 Madison Avenue, New York, New York 10016

www.oup.com

Oxford is a registered trademark of Oxford University Press

Library of Congress Cataloging-in-Publication Data

Long, Michael S.
Valuing the closely held firm/by Michael S. Long and Thomas A. Bryant.
p. cm. — (Financial Management Association survey and synthesis series)
Includes bibliographical references and index.
ISBN 978-0-19-530146-5
1. Close corporations—Valuation. 2. Business enterprises—Valuation.
3. Small business—Valuation. I. Bryant, Thomas A., 1953– II. Title. III. Series.
HG4028.V3L774 2006
658.15—dc22 2006007887

Credits and Acknowledgments

We want to thank numerous colleagues and reviewers for their inputs. Some of the reviewers have been anonymous; we want them to know that their inputs have been valued, even though we cannot acknowledge them by name. Our students and colleagues at Rutgers, Nicholls State, and Rowan have contributed in many ways. While we take full responsibility for the results, we are very thankful for their questions, ideas, stories, and assistance.

Special academic colleagues have taken a particular interest in this book and have helped immensely with their insights. Prof. John Lajaunie, Dept. of Economics and Finance, Nicholls State University, conducted a detailed review of a previous edition and has remained engaged with us on several issues. His input and support have been especially valuable. Dean Uric Dufrene, College of Business, Indiana University Southeast, has been an insightful supporter. Dr. John Pliniussen, professor of innovation, sales and emarketing at the School of Business, Queen's University, Canada, has also been a loyal supporter and constructive critic.

Other helpful readers and supporters have included: Joe Astrachan, Chris Cox, John Griffin, Richard Lambert, Zach Parker, Lynn Rebarber-Sherman, John Ryan, Alan Scharfstein, Ian Spraggon, Peter Stone, Myron Tuman, James Wakil, and David Whitcomb. The David and Henrietta Whitcomb Center for Research in Financial Services at Rutgers provided financial and data support. We thank and absolve them all.

The Financial Management Association has been a steady supporter of this project. We are especially grateful to original editors, Arthur Keown and Kenneth Eades and the current editors John Martin and James Schallheim of the FMA, Survey and Synthesis Series.

At Oxford University Press, Terry Vaughan, Catherine Rae, Ellen Guerci, Anne Enenbach, Christi Stanforth, and Laura Poole each helped in immeasurable—and measurable—ways. We are most grateful for their skills and support.

Finally, but not least, we want to thank our families. For Mike, wife Ileen Malitz, as a finance professor herself, got me interested in the importance of valuation many years ago and has dealt with this lengthy project almost ever since. Parents Stuart and Lauretta taught me right from wrong and provided the basis for my intellectual curiosity.

For Tom, wife Robin Reenstra-Bryant has been a colleague for more than thirty years and served as a patient sounding board for many of the ideas that were not good enough to include—as well as a constructive critic of many that were. Parents Joe and Mary have provided a lifelong commitment to good writing that has helped immeasurably, including many telephone discussions of the best uses of words and phrases. Children Dave, Alix, and Christine have bemusedly tolerated Dad's migrating work station.

Preface

Entrepreneurs work hard and provide invaluable services to our society. They get paid for that work, for the value they deliver, in two ways. Most draw a salary and other benefits as owner-managers of the firms they control, compensation for the ongoing value they bring to the office every day. For some, the big payoff comes when they sell the firm. At that point, they get paid for the ongoing economic value machine they have built.

We have each been involved with entrepreneurial communities most of our lives and independently came to the conclusion that most entrepreneurs don't see enough of those big payoffs. Many private firms are wrapped up, liquidated for pennies on the dollar, when the owners retire or pass away. Others are sold to other entrepreneurs or ongoing firms, and often at significant discounts. Given the agonies, stresses, and commitments the entrepreneurs go through to make their contributions to the greater welfare of our communities, those less than glorious outcomes strike us as unfair.

Trying to right that injustice, we have conducted various research projects over the last two decades. We are coming to believe that this discount has several sources and that it is not going to be simple to remedy the apparent wrong. Some of the problem lies with entrepreneurs themselves, operating their firms in ways that they find comfortable, perhaps, but that reduce their economic value to others.

The field of entrepreneurship research is relatively young, dated by many people from the late 1970s or early 1980s. There is much scholars have learned about best practices in this broad and complex field—and there is much we don't yet know. In 1980, no one could graduate from college, anywhere in the world, with a degree in entrepreneurship. There just wasn't enough formal knowledge to make up more than one or two courses. By 2005, entrepreneurship programs were available in nearly half of all U.S. colleges and universities, and Ph.D. programs were emerging at more than a dozen universities. Entrepreneurship has for several years been the fastest-growing field in business education; students see its value, and scholars find the knowledge gaps a worthy challenge.

While we had both been active in the field for several years, our paths had not crossed until Tom was appointed to a visiting position at the Rutgers Business School in 1998. Mike had joined the Rutgers faculty several years before. Although we were working in different departments, our shared interests in entrepreneurship brought us together.

For some time, Mike had been looking closely at that part of the entrepreneurial process where the owners of closely held firms transfer their accumulated equity to other owners. The sale of the firm is one point in the process at which the economic value to society of an entrepreneur's work can be measured with some precision. We had many conversations on this subject with entrepreneurs, their legal and accounting supporters, and with the special breed of investment banker or business broker who plays midwife to the exchanges. The overall consensus was that most entrepreneurs were selling their life's work at a significant discount.

We investigated further, with Mike focusing increasingly on the issue of valuation of the closely held firms, and Tom examining a host of related issues. Much is known about valuation—of publicly listed firms and other commonly exchanged private properties for which there is much public information, like real estate. Although much of that work does apply to closely held firms, unfortunately, much also does not.

For some time there have been several books and manuals available that purport to lead owners and their advisors through a series of formulas that help to value a firm. Our assessment is that those formulas may be good places to start, but they can also be quite misleading. Indeed, some investment bankers flatly refute many of the starting points those formula books use. This book does have formulas—but not ones that can be used to calculate the precise value of a firm. There are numerous formulas that play roles in the valuation process, and knowledge of them is important. Yet knowledge of markets, buyer psychology, seller psychology, and numerous other factors must be combined before anyone is likely to produce a fairly accurate estimate of the value of any given firm at a specific point in time.

Trying to sort out the best ways to fairly value closely held firms has turned out to be a significant task. In the end, we have drawn on many different sources and, we believe, some original thinking to stitch it all together. This book is the result of a long-term collaboration and of each author's diverse experiences and research. We hope that thoughtful owners and their advisors—and buyers, too—will find it useful.

Contents

Tables

Special Terms and Expressions

Note: For definitions, please see appendix 1 (Glossary).

Beta: A measure of systematic market risk
Bl: Beta for a levered firm
Bu: Beta for an unlevered firm
C: Cash
C_t: Cash at the end of year t
C_1/V_0: Expected free cash flow yield today
C-corp: Regular corporation
CEO: Chief Executive Officer
CF: Cash flow
CPA: Certified Public Accountant (U.S.)
D: Amount of debt (aka borrowed capital)
E: Amount of equity
E_t: Value of equity at the end of year t
EDGAR: Electronic Data Gathering, Analysis, and Retrieval system operated by the SEC
EPS: Earnings per share
EV: Expected value
FASB: Financial Accounting Standards Board (U.S.)
FCF: Free cash flow
FDIC: Federal Deposit Insurance Corporation (U.S.)
FIFO: First In, First Out (inventory flow method)
g: Expected growth rate in dividends

G: Growth in free cash flow
GAAP: Generally Accepted Accounting Principles
i: Inflation
INV: Inventory
IPO: Initial Public Offering
IRS: Internal Revenue Service (U.S.)
k: Required rate of return
LIFO: Last In, First Out (inventory flow method)
LLC: Limited Liability Corporation
LLP: Limited Liability Partnership
LP: Limited Partnership
MACRS: Modified Asset Class Recovery System (U.S. tax depreciation schedule)
MBA: Master of Business Administration (university degree)
MIT: Massachusetts Institute of Technology
MVA: Market Value Added
NASD: National Association of Securities Dealers (U.S.)
NASDAQ: NASD Automated Quotations (U.S. online trading system)
NFCF: Net free cash flow
NPV: Net Present Value
NRR: Nominal Required Return
NYSE: New York Stock Exchange
OEM: Original Equipment Manufacturer
P/E: Price/Earnings (ratio)
PV: Present Value
PVGO: Present Value of Growth Opportunities
R: Required Nominal Return
R&D: Research and Development
REIT: Real Estate Investment Trust
ROA: Return on Assets
ROCA: Return on Continuing Assets
ROE: Return on Equity
ROI: Return on Investment
S&P: Standard and Poor's
SBA: Small Business Administration (U.S.)
S-Corp.: Flow-through tax corporation, authorized by the IRS under Subchapter S

SEC: Securities and Exchange Commission (U.S.)
t: Marginal tax rate (chapter 6)
t_0: Time at the present (normally used as a subscript)
TAQ: Trade and Quote (data service for the U.S. Stock Exchanges)
tc: Corporate tax rate
V: Value
V_0: Value today
V_t: Expected value at end of year t
$(V_1 - V_0)/V_0$: Expected capital gains yield, from year 0 to year 1
WACC: Weighted Average Cost of Capital
WIP: Work in Process
WYSIWYG: What You See Is What You Get
\$$x$K: x thousand dollars
\$$x$M: x million dollars

Valuing the Closely Held Firm

What George Bernard Shaw said about a love affair is also apt for a business: Any fool can start one; it takes a genius to end one successfully.

—William D. Bygrave, "The Entrepreneurial Process," in William D. Bygrave and Andrew Zacharakis (Eds.), *The Portable MBA in Entrepreneurship* (3rd ed.)

1

Why Bother Valuing a Private Business?

Note to Readers

Each chapter opens and closes with a conversation between two business owners, discussing the kinds of practical questions we address in the middle part of each chapter. Although all the characters are fictional, these conversations reflect those of many business owners, their families, and their advisors. Through their eyes, we hope readers find it easier to grapple with the sometimes technical information required to answer those questions. We've tried hard to keep the whole book in a language that business people will tolerate, but there's nothing like a real one-to-one conversation. The first appendix is a glossary of the more technical terms used in the book.

Cast of Characters

Disclaimer: Each of these characters is fictitious. The two leading protagonists are modeled on hundreds of entrepreneurs we have met in the course of our careers, but they are not based on any single individual. We have given them our names, but they are not us, either; we simply felt it better to put our names on the characters than to put friends' names on them. These stories are developed for illustrative purposes only.

MIKE: Protagonist 1. Owner for the past fifteen years of a small manufacturing and distribution business, with gross annual sales recently in the $5 million range. Took the business over when his father died. Boat owner.

TOM: Protagonist 2. Owner for the past twelve years of a retail shop recently doing about $2 million a year in gross sales. Bought the business. Cottage owner.

THE PROFESSOR: Shadowy character; the voice of the middle part of each chapter.

PRISCILLA: Mike's wife

CELIA: Tom's wife

TRACEY: Tom and Celia's oldest child (age twenty-three); just starting her MBA.

ANDY: General Manager at Mike's company; hired employee with long service.

BILLY: Mike and Priscilla's oldest child (age nineteen).

MICHELLE: Mike and Priscilla's second child (age sixteen).

1.0 Mike and Tom Begin Their Quest

As they came out of the pro shop and started the hike up to the tall tee for the first hole, Mike asked his old friend Tom, "Hey, buddy, have you ever thought about what that business of yours is really worth?"

"What do you mean, 'What's it worth?' I'm not planning on selling it anytime soon, and I don't think you're proposing to buy it!" Tom wondered why Mike would even ask such a question, but Mike looked unusually thoughtful for this stage of their usually banter-filled weekly round of golf, so Tom's mind snapped back onto the topic. As he tried to answer his best friend's earnest question, he immediately faced a mess of different meanings. "Where would I start?" he asked. "It's most of my assets, and all of my real income. It's my number one hobby as well as my job. How do I put a value on that?"

"Well," replied Mike, "I was at that Chamber of Commerce session on Tuesday. We had a guest speaker, a professor from the university, who talked about how people figure out the value of private, owner-managed firms like yours and mine. It got me thinking a lot about my own company, and I find myself wondering about yours, too. We've been running these companies for more than ten years, and they provide a pretty good living for our families. Since I got through those messy first couple of years, I've never thought much about getting out. I've just been socking money into my retained earnings and assuming that's about all I can do. 'Course, we've paid off the house; that makes Pris happier—knowing that she can't be turfed out if the business screws up. I try to keep the insurance and college funds paid up—you know how that is. In good years, my accountant tells me how much I can put into our retirement funds, although some years there isn't enough to cover all of those things. But that speaker made me realize that the business is probably my most valuable asset, and I have no idea what it's really worth or how to maximize its value. Have you ever checked that out for your firm?"

"Why should I?" Tom shrugged. "I own the business. It provides a nice income for my family. Why should I worry about what the business is worth?

Except for taking care of my customers and employees, why bother with abstract things like where or how it creates 'value'? The question is theoretical anyway, since my will leaves the business to my kids when I die, so there is no need to worry about future value. The kids will take it over as is. It'll be nice and smooth for them. As the owner/manager, I have more pressing concerns and decisions to make."

"With that sort of mind-set, you will be lucky to make it to retirement!" retorted Mike "And your kids will probably have to sell the business to pay the estate taxes. The Professor convinced me, and the others at my table, that we need to frequently consider the value of our businesses. He even talked about various ways to estimate the value of a private firm—your firm, your retirement package—and your kids' inheritance. He gave some examples, and he's really got me thinking about this. It was a shock to realize how much I don't know. I suspect it's going to make a difference in not only when and how well Pris and I can retire, but also how I should be running the company.

"OK. Well, there's another thing that hit me. You know old Harry D.? Used to own the lumberyard?"

"Yeah, I've been at his table a couple of times at those Chamber lunches. He cashed out before the Big Boxes moved in, and seems to have turned into quite a philosopher in his retirement. Bit of a pain some days, if you ask me," mused Tom, "even though he's usually right when I stop to think about it."

"Well," said Mike, "he was at our table on Tuesday, and he pointed out something else that makes this important. He said that measuring the value of the business is the best way for an entrepreneur to know how well he's doing his job. We don't have to share the information, but *we* need to know if what we're doing is really using our time and resources as well as we can. Are we spending our time on the things that really make the positive differences? If the value of the business is declining, we're actually eroding the kids' inheritance. Harry's philosophy is that valuation is the entrepreneur's job performance indicator. It's our most important, Big Picture kind of feedback. If we don't know what will increase the value of the business, we don't really know what we're doing as owners. Ouch!"

"Sounds like that session really got your attention, Mike. Why don't you fill me in as we walk the course?"

They started talking about it that day, carried it over into the clubhouse, and quit when their heads began to hurt. It was a tough, complex subject, but the more they talked, the more they recognized its importance. Eventually, they hired the Professor to guide their discussions.

1.1 The Importance of Knowing the Value

This book is a primer on the valuation of closely held (i.e., private) firms. Most owners of closely held firms are in business to create wealth. Unless they know how to measure the value of their businesses, however, it is very unlikely that they will make decisions that consistently maximize that wealth. It's not a simple matter, however, to figure out which choices maximize their wealth creation endeavors. Corporate valuation formulas created for large public companies don't work for privately held firms (of any size). There is no simple answer, no magic prescription, yet the issues are vitally important to the health of the free enterprise economy and especially to the well-being of the entrepreneurs who drive it.

An owner's income is neither insured nor assured; his or her children's inheritance is tenuous. Owners must continue to change and innovate to maintain their incomes and assets. To stay ahead, they must make decisions that add value to their businesses. To do that right requires measuring the value of the existing business and then valuing new ideas for their investment potential. To be continuously successful in business, owners must understand both the basic concepts of valuation and the subtleties of the closely held firm. Only by understanding these concepts can they be sure to make the kinds of good decisions that increase their families' wealth.

The major problem with setting a value on a business is that no business operates in a vacuum. It has current competitors, which can probably be identified, and unknown potential competition from others wanting to provide the same (or better) goods or services. It is not a static thing that can be measured once, then updated with some simple adjustment. Many of the assumptions supporting any given valuation really will vary over time. In addition, owners and prospective buyers will bring different values to the table at different stages of their family and economic cycles, so a robust approach has to accommodate lots of room for revisions and updates.

The minor problem is that a naive approach will require sharing a greater portion of the business' profits with government tax collectors. We all know that it is not how much wealth we make but how much we keep that matters. That's why we try to minimize taxes when operating a business. An important consideration in the long run is effective planning for the transfer of the business so that we minimize the combined gift and inheritance taxes imposed in the United States and in many other countries. Planning for the future pays good dividends.

Valuing a closely held firm is much more difficult than putting a value estimate on a large public firm. We will see that there is more than just an information difference between a widely followed public firm and a comparable closely held business. Comparable public and private firms have different values, with the closely held (i.e., private) firms consistently valued below their public cousins. The differences are many, and their effects on valuation quite complex. One of the more important ones is the lack of liquidity of closely held firms; this factor does appear to cause many of them to be valued lower. The major difference between similar public and private firms is that there is no real separation between the owners and the managers of closely held firms. Almost by definition, control of a closely held firm leads to a focus on the owner/manager. That person (or small group of people) operates the business to maximize his or her (or their) personal well-being. The true meaning of personal well-being varies widely from owner to owner, with a range of personal, social, and family considerations.

1.1.1 *An Angel Investor's Dilemma*

One owner of our acquaintance runs several businesses in his "retirement." Let's call him Ronald. He saved enough in his first career to buy a pension for himself and his wife, but he decided that wouldn't be good enough. He wanted to earn more, so he could share more with certain charities of his choosing. He invested judiciously in commercial real estate and sometimes in tenant firms. Then he split the proceeds between his family needs and his philanthropic purposes. One of Ronald's additional objectives was to create a capital asset sufficient to secure the long-term future of one of his charitable beneficiaries, and that gave him a clear target for the asset value he needed to accumulate. He has laid out a twenty-year plan, during which time he intends to parlay his initial stake into both the current cash flows and the long-term assets he wants.

How can Ronald tell if his plan is on track? How can we tell if he needs to make changes? He could monitor the cash flows for current income, and he could get some information from the local real estate board about trends in commercial property values—many agents are trained and happy to provide such valuations. But his other investments require some way to value the small, privately held firms in which he is a shareholder. Those are critical parts of his portfolio, but how can he tell if they are really appreciating? If they aren't, what steps would turn that around? How could he tell if his changes resulted in improvements?

Different purposes lead to different operating strategies. Those variations in turn require substantial adjustments in the valuation process because existing methods were developed to value independent businesses—assuming each was being operated to maximize profits. Few owner/managers are pure profit maximizers, so potential buyers must adjust their valuation of the assets to try to factor out the personal peccadilloes of the present owners. At the end of the valuation process, the purchaser's valuator must try to say what the business would be worth if operated according to the purposes of the prospective new owner, not the current owner. Yet all the available data are based on the firm the way it is being operated by the current owner.

This dilemma means that the basic concept of valuation is important, although sometimes difficult in practice. Owner/managers must understand that it is a firm's future ability to generate cash flows that creates most of its value.

First and foremost, a firm is an investment vehicle—at least from a financial point of view. Value cannot be determined by looking backward at what was initially invested in the business and the accumulated earnings retained since then. (That approach is also important, of course, but it reflects return on past investments, not current value.) This book thoroughly develops the concept of discounting, or bringing back to the present, expected future cash flows. Note that all valuation is based on *expected* cash flows, because no one knows for certain what the future holds. To a large extent, estimates of future performance are based on recent past performance and expected competitive changes in a firm's marketplace. A major valuation difference between public and closely held firms is a matter of adjusting for the lack of separation between the managers and owners of the businesses.

Consider the following situation where a valuation was commissioned in the late 1980s. Five medical doctors had formed a Subchapter S corporation (let's call it MD5) to buy a partnership in a startup company (let's call it MRI-Chi). MRI-Chi was buying a recently introduced magnetic resonance imaging (MRI) machine and was going to run an MRI facility in a Chicago suburb. Each of the MD5 shareholders invested $100,000 in MD5, which in turn bought a partnership stake in MRI-Chi, putting up $500,000 of a $20 million total capital investment. The MD5 shareholders had an agreement that if any one of them died, an independent appraiser would value the business, and the others would buy out the deceased's share on the basis of that appraisal.

About two years after MRI-Chi was up and running, one of the MD5 shareholders died. A local finance professor was hired to value the business. He discussed this valuation with a couple of his university colleagues who did tax and legal work for small firms. One was an attorney; the other was an accountant. Both said to look at the amount invested and subtract 10% for the closely held nature of the firm, resulting in a $90,000 value. These advisors to closely held firms just looked backward at what had been invested in the business. Their only consideration of the future was to ask whether the firm was still operating.

The finance professor took a different perspective. The financial statements of both the MD5 corporation and the MRI-Chi partnership showed high levels of profits. Medical professionals will say that MRI stands for "Magnetic Resonance Imaging," but the professor discovered that in terms of business, it stands for "Money Reproducing Incorporated." Patients are pushed through the machine, and money is pulled out. Using the valuation techniques that will be presented in this book, he valued the widow's share as being worth $250,000. No complaints were heard from the other shareholders, so we can conclude that they felt the share was worth at least that amount. That outcome does not mean that the investment was necessarily that outstanding when the money was invested. Rather, the uncertainty of this new MRI process had been resolved favorably during the first two years of the business.

1.2 Specific Times That Require Valuation

Although many owner/managers commission outside valuations to ensure objectivity at critical times in their ownership, it remains important for owner/managers to understand the processes that create value. Valuation is a fundamental technique for keeping score, for assessing one's own performance as a manager of a closely held firm. If the value goes up, the owner/manager is making good decisions.

Most owners are in business to maximize the value of their firms, given their constraints, such as the supply of good ideas, managerial skills, capital, and outside competition. Unlike public firms, where the stock market evaluates the firm every day, owners of closely held firms will find that formal evaluations are most crucial when important decisions must be made. Let's review those situations.

1.2.1 *Decision-Making Reasons for Conducting a Valuation*

The first set of reasons for undertaking the valuation of a closely held firm deals with making wealth-maximizing decisions. Starting a business or evaluating investment proposals to expand an existing business requires a valuation—if we are going to get the best performance out of our investments. Given that the investment has not yet been made, these are probably the most important valuations to consider. Will a proposed new business create greater wealth than the investment needed to get it going? For a major expansion proposal, will it increase the firm's value by more than the additional investment? Rational managers should make only investments that are expected to increase wealth.

A similar set of criteria applies to decisions about buying an existing business. Such a choice requires considerable study when the acquisition target is a small closely held firm. Does an ongoing concern exist—as is almost always assumed with a larger firm—or is one merely buying a set of assets with which to organize a similar new business? This apparently small difference has a huge impact on how the purchase should be valued. An ongoing concern is valued as the present value of its projected future free cash flows. An asset purchase is valued as the replacement cost of the assets, both tangible and intangible. The latter value is compared with the cost of buying the same set of assets and starting from scratch. Differences between the two can be huge, more than an order of magnitude.

A potential buyer must also consider whether the purchase is strictly a financial investment or a strategic one. The former just considers costs and projected returns. The later considers how this purchase fits in with other current operations, expected changes in the competitive business environment, and other new value the purchaser can bring to the business.

The flip side of buying a business is selling the business either entirely or in portions. When an owner/manager decides that it is time to sell a business, a valuation estimate is needed.

> Any valuation is always an "estimate," since real market value is the price at which the business actually sells, and that won't be known with certainty until the deal closes.

What the estimate does, however, is give the owner a reasonable position on which to base an asking price. In an environment of unsolicited takeover offers, knowledge of the current value of the business can help an owner determine quickly whether or not an offer should be given serious attention.

1.2.2 *Entering the Securities Market*

A valuation is most important when a firm seeks outside funding or when its current owner/managers wish to sell a portion of their holdings. If the firm is overvalued, no one will invest. If it is undervalued, the current owner/managers will unnecessarily dilute their ownership position. When owner/managers set values low, to be sure they attract the funds they seek, they still have to ask at what price *they* are themselves willing to make the deal, and at what (too low) price they would not proceed. Differences of opinion about valuation estimates are some of the most acrimonious sources of conflict between entrepreneurs (especially inexperienced ones) and potential investors. Entrepreneurs and inventors tend to value their contributions highly—those are the "sparks of genius" that create the business opportunities. Later investors realize how much is still to be done, and how much more investment will be needed, so they tend to undervalue the founders' contributions. Successful deal making requires finding the acceptable compromise zone between those parties, and that is aided by accurate valuation.

Valuations are also undertaken by underwriting firms. The accuracy of those valuations is crucial to both ongoing businesses and ones coming to market for the first time, so it should not be surprising that underwriters are very well compensated. The underwriters' valuations help set the price at which firms can raise funds from public offerings of their securities.

One strategy is to take a firm public through issuing new shares and raising additional funds. Then, some time in the future, maybe six months or a year later, the owner/managers sell a portion of their own holdings in a secondary offering to diversify their financial assets.

A firm can also make a private placement of equity if additional funds are needed and it is either not ready or unwilling to go public—or thinks it can get a better valuation from a limited number of private investors. Again, the valuation is extremely important for the offering. Most potential investors in these situations will be experts in valuation and will undertake their own analyses to make sure they pay a price low enough to create an acceptable potential for the rewards they seek. By creating a minority ownership position for the new investors, the existing owner/managers may suffer a discount in the business' value or give up control of the business to outsiders. In the later case, the new investors may plan to take the firm public in a short time period or otherwise manage it for resale in the foreseeable future. They may also merge it into other existing business operations they control.

1.2.3 *Legal Reasons*

There are several legal reasons that require a business to be valued. Some are friendly; others get ugly. Some participants want a true value to result; others want a biased value (usually to avoid or minimize taxes or legal settlement costs). Let's start with those situations where a biased value is preferred.

Businesses must pay taxes. A common tax applies to property, both real and personal. The tax is determined from the current value of the property or its appraised value. Although this is not the same as valuing a going concern, it has many of the same elements. A firm with poor current profits and a poor future potential could argue that its specific assets are not as valuable as their book value would indicate. Conversely, a very profitable business will prefer to value its assets at their replacement cost (much lower than their income-earning value).

When ownership is transferred, a value must be determined, and transfer taxes paid on the amount of that value. At first glance, one might think that an unbiased value would be preferred. But look carefully—when ownership is transferred and not sold in an arm's-length transaction, it is usually a matter of gifting it to one's heirs or selling it to an insider. In these situations, the objective is to get the value as low as possible, thus minimizing the transfer taxes, without attracting the tax collector's attention, so that as much value as possible transfers to the new owners.

The portion of the business not transferred will eventually end up in the original owner/manager's estate (or the spouse's, depending on who dies first). Estate settlements definitely attract the tax collector's attention. The government wants the value of the firm set as high as possible to maximize its tax collections, while the heirs will of course claim the businesses is worthless to minimize taxes. Obviously, in these situations an objective valuation is necessary. Unfortunately, American courts, in trying to be objective, have developed rulings that give little regard to the real economic values.

Although the objectives are skewed in these cases, they are done under friendly conditions when compared to divorce cases. In most situations, when couples get divorced and a business is owned, it is considered as jointly owned for property settlements, even if only one member of the couple was actively involved in the business. The owner, wanting to keep the business, has many incentives to minimize its value and hence to minimize the buyout price. The departing spouse, on the opposite side, can be expected to try to significantly inflate its value. Settlement requires a valuation on which both parties agree.

The last specific case deals with other-than-married partners or joint owners of a business. There are two reasons for valuation requirements in these situations. If one of the owners dies and there is a buyout agreement, the value must be determined in order to pay the deceased owner's estate. This situation is like the MRI example discussed earlier. Second, to avoid the situation where the surviving owners have to come up with cash to pay off the deceased owner's estate, cross-insurance is often maintained. To have correctly sized policies, this technique requires a continuously updated and accurate value of the business. The agreement in these cases usually states that the insurance pays in full for the deceased's share of the business. In these cases, an objective value is desired.

1.3 How We Proceed

Now that the importance of knowing a firm's value and the specific times when it is required are understood, we proceed with ways to estimate that value. These estimates are based on a rational wealth-maximizing approach.

Valuations are only estimates, because the only true value is the price at which the business actually sells. A valuation tries to estimate what that price is likely to be.

The first thing we must undertake is to show why and how closely held firms differ from large public firms. These differences and additional tests will be discussed in the following chapters as we develop the details of the valuation process. The key difference is the lack of separation between ownership and management of closely held firms.

- Does an ongoing concern exist or is the business just an extension of the owner/manager?
- Does the owner/manager operate the business only to maximize wealth in the traditional sense, or does he or she extract from the business any benefits other than money, that is, nonfinancial value?
- What adjustments are required to determine a value that is independent of how the owner/manager chooses to take his or her compensation and nonfinancial benefits?
- How do we factor out those choices made to maximize the owner/manager's after-tax business and personal income?
- If the business is producing superior returns on its investments, is that because of the specific owner/manager or because of the business? In other words, how likely is it that the ability to earn attractive returns can be transferred to a new owner?
- Finally, how should value be adjusted for minority shareholders, given their dependence on the goodwill of the primary owner/manager?

How these questions are answered determines the value of the business, as developed in the following chapters. A fundamental assumption, and one we test in chapter 2, is that the firm is an *ongoing concern*. Is it worth more as a firm, with all its assets and relationships working together, or as a pile of assets, more valuable if broken up and sold to other users? In chapter 3, we deal with valuation of firms in the latter situation, ones that are not going concerns. With closely held firms, this option is extremely important because in many situations, no business exists separately from the current owner/managers. When they sell their businesses, they are really selling groups of assets. The key in valuation is what an outsider starting a similar business would have to pay to obtain the same set of assets. Both tangible (e.g., buildings, machinery) and intangible (e.g., reputation, relationships) assets must be considered.

Returning to the main theme, chapter 4 develops the key concepts used to estimate the value of going concerns. The core indicator is the present value of the future expected free cash flows. In simple terms, these cash flows equal the cash produced by business operations, minus new investments required to maintain that money-making potential. The key point is that the value estimate be based on what the firm can do in the future in producing cash flows and not on what it has done in the past. Chapter 4 considers value where a firm is earning only its required or opportunity cost rate of return on its real investments. This nongrowth situation applies to most small, closely held firms.

Chapter 5 proceeds to consider the situation where the firm is expected to earn above-average returns on its investments, that is, to grow. For public firms, this condition is normally required for shares to sell at a large price-to-earnings ratio. For all firms, it is necessary for the firm to create wealth. We discuss why most small, closely held firms cannot expect to make above-average returns on their future investments. Added-value returns usually exist during the startup stage. Once the initial idea is exploited, many firms earn only their required return on future investments. Even then, one must be careful not to get hit by "Wal-Mart Liquidator effect", where the competitive environment is changed quickly and drastically by an outside entry, radically changing the money-making equation, altering values, and sometimes sending previously sound businesses into liquidation.

Chapter 6 deals with the effects of inflation on both the real value of the business and the measurement of the value of the business. Because depreciation is calculated from historical costs, the value of tax savings created decreases with inflation. Although this phenomenon is well known, the next development looks at problems with measuring the value when using historical cost accounting statements. Adjustment factors are developed to handle situations where inflation rates as low as 3% per year can cause distortions in value of up to 30%, unless adjustments are made.

Chapter 7 examines ways to calculate an appropriate discount rate, one used to value the estimated future free cash flows. Closely held firms cannot go to the marketplace and estimate their required rates of return, as public firms do. Even when closely held firms measure their risk by comparison to similar public firms, they require an additional adjustment for their lack of liquidity. That adjustment makes the proper discount rates extremely difficult to estimate.

Chapters 8 and 9 deal first with additional considerations in buying an existing firm (chapter 8) and then selling or exiting the business (chapter 9).

The required valuation and other considerations are complex enough to require additional chapters to explain. The major point in buying a business is to understand what is being bought and what is required to keep the business running. Too often, new owners fail because they forget certain costs. The major point in exiting a business, whether selling to an outsider or passing it on to one's children, is to plan ahead. Obviously not all the points discussed are going to exist in every deal, but they bring up ideas to be considered in structuring purchases and exits from business.

In chapter 10, we summarize the key points arising from those detailed discussions in chapters 2–9. It reminds us what has been presented in this book, what we do know about the valuation of closely held firms—and what is still not well understood. It is our assessment of the state of the art in this evolving field. We have taken the liberty to suggest where we think both research and practice need to go from here.

Now that we have outlined where we are going, let's start looking at some of the adjustment factors that make closely held firms unique to their owners and such a challenge to value accurately.

1.4 Ah! I'm Beginning to See Why!

"So, what the professor is saying is that we can draw salaries and other benefits from our businesses, but a big chunk of the real value we get from being owners is tied up in the value of the business itself?" Tom asked. He and Mike were driving back from their first lunch meeting at the University Club with the Professor, and they were struggling with the concepts of valuation.

"Sort of. I think." Mike sounded uncertain. "The two kinds of value don't seem to have a lot to do with each other, though. Like, we can draw big incomes, and leave little or nothing in the company—or draw smaller incomes and leave more in the company. Maybe there's a trade-off." He really wasn't sure he understood this part of the Professor's discussion.

"You'd think so, eh?" Tom, on the other hand, saw this part clearly. "I mean, if we take all the profits out of the company, that means we're not reinvesting, so it won't grow."

"Yeah," Mike replied, "but some years there's nothing much worth investing in, in my business. Other years, there are some things I just have to buy in order to keep up with the industry. And then my wife sometimes wants me to take something extra out for a new house, or the kids' college funds, or—"

"I know what you mean!" interjected Tom. "And there were times I had to take money out of my own funds to put back into the company to keep its cash flow positive, to make payroll."

"Really? Are you still doing that? I just go in to see my friendly neighborhood banker, and we make some arrangements." Mike grinned at Tom to make sure he knew it was a tease.

"Not so much any more," Tom admitted, "but it was a real stretch the first couple of years. It took me a while to understand cash flow. Hey, that raises another question that's been nagging me. When you go to see your banker, I assume you have to show her your financial statements. Do you ever get any feedback, other than the loans, on how the bank sees your financial progress? I mean, does she ever make any suggestions, or comment on specific areas of progress? Other than the basic ratios, I wonder what they look for."

Mike chuckled. "Well, a couple of years ago, she suggested that I ought to consider some diversification of my assets and recommended I talk with one of the bank's brokers. That sounded like an in-house set-up to me, so I ignored it. I figure the best use of the profits from my company is either my family or reinvestment in the company."

"Yeah, that's the way I see it, too," agreed Tom, "but how do you really know what the best use is? I mean, at this stage, with our hard work starting to pay off pretty well, we need to start thinking about what our best investments really are."

2

Is It a Business, or Just a Pile of Assets?

Special Questions and Adjustments in the Valuation of Closely Held Firms

2.0 What's It Worth?

"So," said Tom, as the old friends began their golf round the next week, "I can't get this valuation thing out of my head. What do you think I'd get if I sold my business? Not that I'm planning on selling, of course, but our last conversation has me thinking about what I've earned by my investment of money and effort in this business. Have I been investing wisely? Have I made more this way than I would have done by taking a job and working for some company all these years? When I stopped to think, that was a good question and I really couldn't answer it. I know what I invested when I bought it, and I know what I take out each year, but I reinvest something every year, and I don't really know how that's adding up. To figure it out, I need to know what the business is worth now. I checked the financial pages last Sunday and the P/E ratio of some of the public companies in my industry is about 18. Do you think I should I just multiple my earnings by 18?"

"I don't know," replied Mike, "but I don't think it's that simple. The Professor said that private firms like ours seem to sell, on average, for about 15% less than their public cousins—but there's a wide range. I don't want to give up that discount. I've been thinking about this valuation stuff too, for the same reason—I want to know what I've earned, what value I've created. Is this the best way to provide for my family? I keep turning down those jobs the headhunters call about, and I can only smile at our high school reunions when the guys talk about their salaries. I figure I'm living better, paying fewer taxes, and increasing my equity—but does it match their pension plans?"

2.1 Differences in Valuation Methods between Public and Closely Held Firms

Valuing a closely held firm is a more difficult process than valuing a large publicly held firm, in part because closely held firms' financial data are not standardized and private securities are not frequently or publicly traded. As a result, experts in valuation produce a wider range of estimated values for small closely held firms than they do when assessing the value of much larger public firms. The problems only begin with a lack of verified financial data—because closely held firms do not usually produce audited financial statements. The problem is deeper than information asymmetry problems (when insiders know much more about the business than potential outside buyers), serious though those problems might be. There are several even more fundamental differences between closely held firms and public firms. Yet almost all business valuation tools have been developed to apply to properties that have either verified financial data, published comparable data, or both. Few of those assumptions apply to closely held firms, so the methodological tools of valuation have to be extensively modified. This chapter discusses the specific factors that affect the valuation of closely held firms and what methodological adjustments are necessary to value them accurately.

Four specific factors must be considered in valuing a closely held firm. None of the four is a serious consideration in valuing a public firm.

1. Does an ongoing firm exist? Would there be an ongoing firm if the current owner left suddenly? Only if the firm would continue to operate without the current owner can we conclude that a going concern is present. In many closely held firms, no entity separate from the owner/manager really exists, so the business must be valued for transfer as no more than the sum of its assets. Many times, when someone is buying a business, they are really buying just the assets to start their own business. This circumstance is particularly common with service businesses. If we conclude that a business *is* an ongoing business, however, the specific problems of valuing a closely held firm must then be addressed.
2. Closely held firms lack separation between the firm and the owner/manager. The owner/manager is much more likely than a public company CEO to make personal-utility-maximizing decisions than firm-value-maximizing choices. This tendency causes the value of a closely held firm to change with an owner/manager's personal objectives.

3. The owner/manager's compensation is usually set to maximize his or her wealth, after the firm's and individual's taxes have been paid. This strategy creates difficulty when a valuator tries to separate "salary" from "profits"—to create a restated estimate of total owner's compensation.
4. After the business is sold and has a new owner, will its profits continue? Is the firm generating the profits, or is it the personal work of the current owner/manager that creates the real value?

Each of these problems will be discussed in the following sections. We will show how valuations have to be adjusted, depending on the circumstances of each case.

2.2 Does a Going Concern Exist?

When valuing closely held firms, the first consideration is whether a separate ongoing firm actually exists. For a large firm, *ongoing* refers to whether or not a company is solvent and could continue to exist as it is currently structured. With a closely held firm, the emphasis changes from potential profitability to the independence of a business that could exist separated from its current owner/manager(s). Thus the appropriate question becomes whether the business could continue to function with a change in ownership.

In many cases, closely held firms are not entities separate from their owners. The business is merely an extension of the entrepreneurial person who developed the firm. It is most likely structured as a separate firm for legal and/or tax reasons. With a change in ownership, however, a different business is likely to emerge. Before the owner/manager is changed, it can be quite difficult to determine whether a separate business exists, but it is nonetheless a critical step in determining how the business should be valued.

The following two criteria, taken together, form an effective test for whether or not a closely held firm should be considered an ongoing entity, separate from its current owner/managers.

2.2.1 *What Happens If the Current Owner/Manager Is Replaced?*

First, will the firm continue to operate as it is currently structured if the current owner/manager is replaced? By this we mean, will the old business truly carry on, or is a new business going to be formed using the old assets? Many sales of small firms are really the restructuring of the old assets into new firms. People purchase a farm to become a farmer, a cab medallion to become a taxi driver, or a seat on the stock exchange to become a trader. These are all new businesses that require a person to obtain specific assets before entering the field. These assets are basically interchangeable items and do not by themselves represent specific ongoing businesses.

2.2.2 *Do the Customers Patronize the Business, or the Current Owner?*

The second test of a going concern considers the customers who deal with the business. Do the customers and other stakeholders view themselves as dealing with the *business* or with its current *owners*? If they will continue to deal with the firm even if the owners leave, then the firm is likely ongoing. If not, it is really a collection of assets, being used by the current owner, that will be reworked by new owners.

TWO KINDS OF ACCOUNTING FIRMS: AN EXAMPLE For example, consider an accounting business. An independent accountant usually has her firm's name on the door—something like "Small Business Solutions, Joan Smith, CPA." She probably has an office staff and several junior people working for her, yet her business is merely an extension of Joan. She might have valuable assets to sell when she retires, including preferred access to her current customers and an ongoing staff and organization. However, the buyer must establish herself as leading a new going concern. Most of Joan's clients would probably consider the buyer to be a new firm even if the same name, Small Business Solutions, is used.

Contrast that situation with a large firm. Assume that your accountant is part of the firm KPMG. Although you may deal with a specific individual, you know that if he or she leaves the firm, there will be a replacement of similar quality. Furthermore, the users of your financial statements look at KPMG, not the specific partner who signs the statements, to establish credibility. One reason that some people are willing to pay the higher rates of a big firm is because the users of their financial statements can identify and trust the reputation of the accounting firm and do not have to consider the quality and integrity of the individual accountant.

If the firm passes both tests, it should be valued as an ongoing business. Even though changes will be made in the firm after it is sold, the valuation process should start by assuming that current cash flows will continue, along with those expected to be generated in the future.

2.2.3 *Valuing the Assets Instead*

A firm failing to pass the two preceding tests is worth the value of the specific assets being sold. These assets can be both tangible and intangible. In rural areas, farm land is priced for its location and growing qualities (bottomland or upland, black soil or sandy loam, for example). Those are tangible assets, because the buyer is paying for the direct economic value of the thing being purchased. Intangible assets, however, are often worthless by themselves, but have economic value when used in certain situations. Identical intangible assets, such as cab medallions or seats on a security exchange, are often priced differently, depending on the location in which they can be used, the scarcity of alternatives, and so on. A cab medallion in one city will likely have a different value than a taxi license in another. Similarly, a seat on one stock exchange is likely to be worth a different value than the same seat at a different stage in the market cycle or a seat on a different exchange. Quite often, current prices of such common intangible assets are published in local newspapers. These are easily identifiable specific assets.

Conceptually similar, but more difficult to measure, is the value of a service business such as that provided by a doctor, lawyer, CPA, or plumber. What would a buyer get, besides taking over an existing office, staff, client records, and possibly some used equipment? A buyer gets the chance to see, and hopefully to impress, most of the current customers—once. If they do not like the new owner/service provider, they will shop elsewhere. The product is the owner's expertise, not the former operations, which is why we cannot normally value such businesses as going concerns. We will deal with the specific factors for this kind of valuation in chapter 3.

Consider the differences between the values of a business featuring a famous person as a speech maker versus one having a licensed dentist as its core service provider. Without the famous person, the first firm would have little to sell. The dental practice, on the other hand, is likely to continue after a change of ownership, if the transition from the old dentist to the new one is handled properly. Customers would prefer to continue in the same place with their records carried forward. In all such transitions, however, the new manager will have to perform well to retain his or her clients.

The dichotomies used here as examples are unusually easy cases. Real decisions about which firms are going concerns and which are not are often somewhat arbitrary. Ford Motor is obviously a going concern even though the Ford family controls 40% of the voting stock and the current Chairman of the Board, William Clayton Ford Jr., is the founder's great-grandson. Consider a newer firm whose founders' names are not on the door: Microsoft and Bill Gates. If Gates was suddenly and irreversibly unable to continue his roles, the value of Microsoft would probably suffer. Does this mean that Microsoft is not a going concern? Not really; it just shows that Gates is a highly valued key employee. What about Mike Bloomberg, who controls the privately held Bloomberg News Service? Although his temporary departure to serve as mayor of New York probably causes significant problems for his managers, one would still consider Bloomberg News Service a going concern. Moving along the spectrum to an even more personal relationship, consider Lutèce, a four-star restaurant in New York City, often rated as America's best in the 1980s, owned by chef Andre Soltner from 1961 to 1994. A valuation of Lutèce was undertaken prior to the sale. The valuation was done two ways, with and without Soltner continuing as chef. Because customers of a restaurant of this caliber view the chef as the major factor in its quality, it becomes very questionable whether a going concern exists without him. Thus the separate entity question involves more than the value of the current owner/manager to the business. It is really a matter of the extent to which the business is identified with that individual.[1]

One test that is not considered in determining a going concern is its legal organization. Owner/managers organize their firms legally to minimize their costs. These costs include transaction costs to establish the business, its potential liability exposure, and joint firm and individual tax exposure. Although most small proprietorships and regular partnerships would not qualify as going concerns under our definition, others would, including many limited liability companies (LLCs), or in some states, limited liability partnerships (LLPs). Most LLCs have a limited life (thirty-year maximum) and are reorganized if there is an ownership change. LLCs can be taxed as either corporations or partnerships. Some are going concerns under our criteria, while others are not. Conversely, many small corporations are merely extensions of their owner/managers' self-employment. Conceptually, the corporate form has a continuous life but, for valuation purposes, many small, closely held corporations are not going concerns.

Conversely, the firm being sold as ongoing need not be an actual separate firm. When large public firms sell off assets, they are almost always divesting themselves of specific ongoing divisions or sectors. For example, when Beatrice sold Samsonite,[2] it sold an ongoing luggage business and not just an inventory of suitcases and other assets. In cases like that, a piece of a larger business can be organized and valued as a going concern.

2.3 Closely Held Firms Lack Separation of Manager and Owner

Another important valuation problem faced by closely held firms is the lack of separation between the owners and the managers of such firms. With publicly held firms, we assume that ownership (shareholders) is separate from management (executives). Even when we know that the managers own a significant amount of the equity or even a controlling interest, the firm is an organization separate from its managers. It pays wages and benefits to its managers, pays its own taxes separate from those paid by the managers, faces liabilities for its actions separately, and can change all or part of the ownership group without a new organization being created.

[1] In this particular case, the answer turned out both ways! Lutèce was purchased by Ark Restaurants in 1994 and Soltner left soon after. The New York restaurant gradually declined without Soltner and was closed in 2004. But a Las Vegas version was opened in 1999 and continues to thrive—without Soltner's involvement. See the Associated Press report at www.cnn.com/2004/TRAVEL/02/11/lutece.closing.ap (accessed August 1, 2006).

[2] In 1987, as part of E-II Holdings Inc.

In simple accounting terms, it is an ongoing business, separate from its owners and managers.

With a closely held firm, the owners and managers are usually either the same group or person, or closely related. As they operate the business to maximize their personal utility or well-being, the elimination of distinctions between ownership and control becomes necessary. This combination of interests blurs the separation between the individual, maximizing his or her utility, and the firm that is used for that purpose.

2.3.1 *Maximizing What? For Whom?*

Maximizing one's utility or well-being is not necessarily consistent with an objective of maximizing wealth. Similarly, maximizing a firm's wealth or value is not necessarily consistent with maximizing an individual's wealth. The first paradox results from different desires and preferences of the owner/manager. These factors will vary between individuals and are difficult to quantify into a single value measurement. The second paradox results from the tax and legal environments in which a firm operates. How the owner/manager operates in these situations is usually consistent and can be quantified in the valuation process.

First, let's consider public firms. They are assumed to operate to maximize their owners' wealth. Much academic research undertaken in recent years shows that managers are rewarded for increasing wealth through both bonuses tied to short-term performance and executive stock from stock price appreciation. For those who do not respond to that "carrot," the stick exists in the form of a takeover. Research has found that firms that are not successful in maximizing wealth are more likely than average to be taken over and their managers fired. The incentive structure used by large firms is consistent with the normative objective of maximizing wealth. Furthermore, capital markets measure performance almost continuously. It is relatively accurate in the long run to assume that public firms are being operated to maximize investor value.

With a closely held firm, there is no capital market discipline to ensure that firms maximize value. One cannot assume that the owner/manager is operating the business to maximize wealth. He or she might obtain benefits other than financial wealth from this business. For example, an owner/manager might prefer farming land that has been in the family for generations to selling to a developer; it gives greater satisfaction, although the economic value may be much lower. This behavior is not necessarily irrational.

An outside evaluator must be careful to consider more than just the present and future incomes the business may produce. The evaluator must also consider the alternative uses of the firm's assets. This approach gives two values. One values the assets as they are currently used, and the second values them as if they were used to their maximum economic potential. The dual valuation allows the owner to see what is being foregone by not putting the assets to their most economically productive use. In an important sense, it allows a farmer to understand the price he is paying for holding on to the value of his heritage.

2.3.2 *The Value of Forgone Opportunities*

A more difficult valuation problem occurs when an owner/manager purposely limits the size of a business. Many self-employed people have difficulty delegating responsibilities. They can run organizations where everyone reports to them, but not ones where they have to delegate significant managerial control to subordinates. Such businesses may have many opportunities to increase wealth through expansion but the owners limit them, to keep the firms within their personal spans of control. The difference between such a constrained firm and one in which those additional opportunities are seized is an important consideration for a potential buyer (and hence for a potential seller).

It is quite difficult to quantify these lost opportunities. Yet if we are trying to value a business as it could be, if operated according to its potential, we would want to adjust our pro forma estimates of future operations to include at least some of those foregone opportunities. Remember that a business can be valued in two ways—as it is currently structured, and as it would be if maximizing its wealth potential by expanding with delegated managers and outside capital. To make the second option a realistic alternative probably requires a change in strategic management, and probably also a change in ownership. The current owner/manager has demonstrated a reluctance to delegate managerial tasks, so expansion through delegation will likely have to be accomplished by new owners. In those cases, the valuation of the present and potential businesses may be radically different.

Alternatively, an owner/manager might not want to deal with outside investors. Such a choice limits growth to what is possible with funding from internally generated cash flows. Many owners do not see this as a problem because most of the postponed investment opportunities do not earn excess rates of return. But for some firms, this policy will create a permanent capital rationing situation where they are unable to undertake all of their good investment opportunities due to a shortage of capital. With those firms, an estimate of the wealth foregone due to restricted investments must be made. Similar to the management delegation problem, this situation is difficult to quantify and will require careful research and estimation.

2.3.3 *The First Outside Bid as a Valuation Tool*

The one time that these values come out directly is when outsiders make an offer to buy the business. The owner/manager then needs only value the business as it is currently being operated to see the cost, in terms of foregone wealth, of maintaining the current operation. The owner/manager can then weigh whether the satisfaction from running the business is worth the foregone value. Note, however, that the first outside bid is usually a low estimate of the firm's value, and unsolicited bids are usually considerably below real market value. Thus, any calculation of the value of the firm based on a first bid should be considered a lowball offer.

It is difficult for an evaluator to get the data needed to value the business as it is currently operating and *then* to consider all the contingent approaches or options for using the assets. Recall the farmer. She might be farming only to preserve lower real estate taxes on the land, while waiting for an offer to sell the land. Thus a valuation of her business as a farm would be useless. The lesson here is that there is no valid cookie-cutter approach to valuation of closely held firms. The impossibility of separating the owner from the manager in a closely held firm almost always requires the evaluator to consider two values for the business—one as it is currently being run and the other at its best value-maximizing use in the hands of new owners.

2.4 Alternative Ways of Organizing a Firm: Adjustments for Taxes and Insider Compensation

Although the owner/manager's objective in running a business might be difficult to determine, the firm's tax status is much more straightforward. The business will normally be organized to provide the greatest after-tax return to its owner/managers, counting both business and personal taxes.

The problem an evaluator faces is to determine a reference point for the valuation. Valuation of a going concern requires that a reference position be determined. Is the firm to be valued as it is currently run and structured? Is it to be valued with proposed changes that a potential buyer might make? Should the firm be valued as it is currently run, but with tax and compensation adjustments based on a comparable small public firm?

We will review the pluses and minuses of each approach and show where the various approaches are applicable. We will then show how to estimate the value of a controlling interest in a closely held firm.

2.4.1 *"As Is" Cash Flow Basis*

The easiest approach to valuing a firm is on an "as is" basis. The owner's salary and benefits are taken as the correct opportunity cost for those managerial contributions. The remaining free cash flows are capitalized to determine the value. The tax status, whether it be as a regular corporate form, subchapter S, LLC, or LLP, is not considered, because a new owner may have a different preference. We simply add those cash flows together, project them into the future, and discount the sum of expected returns back to a present value. This method produces a simple (and misleading) estimate of the returns the firm will generate for an investor (owner). By comparing those returns to alternatives available to such investors, an approximate value can be obtained. But we should *not* do that!

For newer firms, this valuation will usually overstate value, since early stage owner/managers often take less personal compensation for their efforts, to retain as many resources as possible in the firm to support its growth. For more established firms, particularly if they are successful, the value is much too low as those owner/managers often take excess salary and perks to minimize their tax obligations. Hence, valuing a firm as is gives a meaningless result.

A firm's *true value* is what a willing buyer, with the same knowledge as the current owners, would pay. Given that no such buyer is ever likely to exist, this construct remains theoretical.

What we really need to find is the closest reasonable approximation to that value that is likely to occur. To do that, we'll need to know a lot more about the potential buyers, and what they see as value. It is unlikely that they will see the same value in the existing firm as the current owner. For that reason as well, the "as is" method is not a sufficient estimate of the value of a going concern.

The "as is" approach might prove useful, however, in justifying a specific value to use for estate and gift tax purposes, when transfers of ownership are being considered. We'll present a more detailed discussion of these issues in chapter 9.

2.4.2 *Another Owner's Return*

A second approach takes the position of someone buying the firm. In this situation, the value of the firm to the prospective buyer is determined after adjusting the "as is" value for proposed changes in the businesses. It considers how the business fits into a potential buyer's current or expected business and how it would make use of the potential buyer's unique talents and other assets. For example, a buyer would consider any economies of scale present when considering expansion by acquisition. Specifically, one owner/manager might be able to direct the affairs of what are currently two firms in the same business in neighboring towns. Consolidating that top management layer might permit the new owner/manager to draw the combined compensation of both pre-merger owner/managers. Other costs might also be reduced, for example, in bookkeeping, banking, and legal services. Larger buying power, additional product lines, more flexible facilities, and so on, might all be managed to produce economies in the combined firms.

By deducting the cash flows available from the new owner's existing pre-merger operations from the combined cash flows, one can identify the incremental gains from the acquisition. The marginal cash flows available to the new owner/manager are then capitalized to determine the value of the combined firm after the acquisition. This value represents the maximum amount that buyer would be willing to pay for the firm; the calculation gives the firm's economic value under that buyer's management.

Source	Buyer's Firm	Combined Firms	Increase due to Acquisition
Net Cash Flow	100	250	150

Adjustments would also be made to reflect the owner/managers' planned salaries and benefits. If the plan is to extract the ownership benefits in the form of excess salaries and perks in order to minimize corporate taxes, the annual cash flows should be adjusted upward to reflect the economic value being created. For example, business deductions that are really for personal benefit, such as the second business car or health benefits for grown family members, would require adjustments in the value. This approach requires grossing up the value of these items at the owner's marginal tax rate, since he or she would normally be required to make these payments from after-tax income.

Marginal Tax Gross-Up Formula
Value of benefits = (cash value/[1 − marginal tax rate])

These grossed-up amounts are then added back into the owner's pro-forma income estimates. If the firm is a "C" or regular tax-paying corporation, a higher (tax-deductible) salary would be paid instead of dividends, giving the same the adjusted value.

2.4.3 *Current Operations with Professional Managers*

The final approach values the business as if it were run by hired professional managers. This approach starts with the firm as it currently operates—*except* that adjustments are made for managerial salaries, benefits, and tax status. The process starts with the profit before taxes. The owner/managers' salaries and benefits are added back, including any extra amount for family members, friends, and others who are on the payroll for more than the market value of the services they contribute to the firm. The costs of hiring outside managers to replace the current owner/managers are then subtracted to get the modified profit before taxes. Taxes are then estimated, assuming a regular C corporation (see table 2.1).

The resulting modified net income is then used to determine the ownership value of the business, that is, the value that a new owner would be able to allocate as she sees fit. This approach separates the value of professional management from the value of ownership.

Careful adjustments must be made for the selling owner/manager's salary and perks when estimating the business value. The books should be carefully examined to identify any nonworking parents, spouses, or children who are drawing salaries or benefits. Some owners of small businesses continue to use their companies to pay their children's health benefits even after those

Table 2.1 Example of Adjustments to Replace Owner/Manager with Professional Managers

Current operations, profit before tax	$100K
Add back owner/manager salary	275
Add back owner/manager benefits and perks	100
Add back excess payments to relatives and friends	150
Add back others' special perks	50
Deduct salaries of professional managers	(200)
Deduct benefits of professional managers	(50)
Pretax restated income	425
Deduct corporate tax at 34%	(144.5)
Restated after-tax income available to owners	$280.5K

offspring are grown adults. There have been occasions when houses have been owned by a company for the discretionary use of the owner/manager. Nonproductive assets, that is, ones that are owned and maintained by the company, but do not significantly contribute to business operations, such as a company airplane, luxury cars, and so on, should be investigated and added to the restated books as part of the available owner's benefits. There is no end to the imagination of small business owners when it comes to tax avoidance, and proper valuation requires putting all those items back into the pro-forma profit to be reallocated as the new owner sees fit.

The market value of the manager's salary must be estimated and subtracted from the profits before taxes are determined. To estimate salary values, comparable small public firms should be selected. Their managers' salaries and benefits will be given in proxy statements to their shareholders. The U.S. Securities and Exchange Commission (SEC) requires these filings and posts them on the Web under EDGAR (www.sec.gov/edgar.shtml). Firms selected for comparison should be in similar industries and locations, if possible, and one should also try to select firms where the manager is not a major owner. Take at least three comparable values, and adjust the valuation estimate on the basis of the best extrapolation of their underlying criteria (size, profitability, location equals cost of living, etc.) to the subject closely held firm. Because even the smallest public firms are much larger than most private firms being valued, it may be necessary to adjust the salary estimate downward to acknowledge the reduced scope of managerial skill required in the smaller firm.

A simple version of such a comparison is shown in table 2.2. Two indicators of firm size are included (Annual Revenues and Number of Employees) as surrogate measures of the kinds of responsibilities and skills associated with their management. We have also included a location indicator, because location has some bearing on cost of living and does affect the top-line salaries needed to attract managerial talent.

In this fictitious example, our private firm is smaller than each of the three public companies. By itself, that would suggest that the $140,000 minimum paid in the smallest public company should be used as an upper

Table 2.2 Comparison to Three Public Firms

Firm	Annual Revenues	# of Employees	CEO Salary	Location
Public A	$25M	200	$140K	Rural Midwest
Public B	$75M	500	$225K	Eastern city
Public C	$115M	700	$185K	South
Subject (actual)	$15M	85	$275K	Midwestern city
Subject (est.)	$15M	85	$130K	Midwestern city
Deemed owner's premium			$145K	

estimate of the appropriate salary for the manager of our private firm. That public company is about twice the size of our private firm, but salaries are not directly proportional to scale, so the size measures suggest a salary over $100,000. With those two simple tests, we have established a range of $100,000 to $140,000.

Consider, finally, the impact of location/cost of living. The $140,000 salary is being paid to an executive in one of the lower cost areas of the United States, the rural Midwest. A comparable role in an eastern city seems to lead to a 50% premium (company B). Our private firm is located in a medium-cost area lying between those two extremes, so the location adjustment should be greater than that used in company A but less than that used for company B.

Put together, these three indicators lead us to a managerial salary estimate in the $120,000–140,000 range for the subject company CEO. If we use the midpoint, $130,000 per year, as our best approximation of the cost of obtaining alternative talent as the CEO, then the premium (excess return) being withdrawn by the current owner is $145,000 per year. In restating the books to show what it would be like without the current owner/manager's choices embedded in them, the $275K current compensation package for the current owner/manager would be removed from the Expenses incurred by the firm. Then, the $130K figure would be put on the Management Salaries line, and the $145K amount would be added to the Profit before tax.

Once all such adjustments have been made, the economic and financial performance of the firm, stripped of the current owner's choices, can be determined. Based on those restated books, the value of the firm as a standalone entity can be estimated. This adjusted number would represent the fair value of the business if it were being considered for sale.

2.4.4 *Value of Control*

With the adjustments outlined in the previous section, we can now determine the monetary value to the current owner/manager of his control of the firm.

This part of the value equation represents the additional amount that the owner/manager can take out of the business, over and above what he would get from the sum of his alternative uses of the same capital and talent. Knowing the economic value of the business, as defined in the preceding sections, we can then calculate the likely return on a similar risk investment if the business were sold and the cash placed into a managed investment vehicle. We have also defined the value of the owner's talent as a manager and can estimate its value in salary if the owner were employed elsewhere at a market wage rate. Put together, those two values show the best alternative (market) uses of capital and talent. When we subtract them from the owner's current total compensation, we are left with the premium (or discount) the owner is able to extract from her current business.

Estimating Alternative Returns to Capital and Talent:
(Cash Value of the Business) × (Investment Yield) + (Managerial Salary)
= Alternative Annual Income from Capital and Talent.

Example: Let's say the business could sell for \$2.5M. At a 6.5% investment yield, that capital would produce an annual income (before taxes) of (\$2.5M × 0.065) = \$162.5K. Add in a managerial salary equivalent to that identified in section 2.3.3 (\$130K), and we estimate the alternative use of capital and talent to produce an annual income of \$162.5K + \$130K = 292.5K.

$$(\$2.5\text{M}) \times (0.065) + (\$130\text{K}) = \$162.5\text{K} + \$130\text{K} = \$292.5\text{K}$$

This sum represents what the owner might face as an alternative income stream, after a sale, and hence a baseline from which we can assess the current firm. If the number is larger than the owner's current income, there's an economic advantage in selling and taking employment. If it's smaller, there's an advantage to not selling. And if the investment income alone is larger than the total current compensation, the owner is essentially paying to work at his own firm.

By having control of the firm, the owner has the right, within the limits of the law, to allocate the profit produced by the firm's economic operations as she sees fit. In many cases, that opportunity results in the owner receiving a set of benefits in excess of her managerial value. This additional benefit may come from several sources, including exploiting minority shareholders and exploiting tax laws, as well as a fair return for the risks undertaken and the creative talent applied.

For estimating the value of the firm, its worth, as it is currently operating, restated as it would look if sold to outsiders, should be used in most situations. If an outsider is making an actual bid for the business, that bid value should be used. The expected return is its required rate of return, R, times its value. If less than 100% is owned, an adjustment is made for ownership proportion. To this expected return is added the opportunity cost of what the owner/manager would earn working as a manager elsewhere. For most owner/managers, their best opportunity cost would be running a business similar to the one they own. Hence the amount should be what they must pay a manager to run their old business. The sum of these two items is what an owner/manager should expect to earn each year if he cashed out of the business and took similar employment at a market-rate salary.

We also must determine the firm's value if the current owner continues as owner and operator. Here, we consider the actual salary, plus any excess wages paid to family members, plus any perks deducted as business expenses. Examples of these deductions would include the annual benefit of the company's condo in Florida, probably the first (and most definitely the spouse's) company car, membership in country clubs, and so on. The sum is then grossed up by both the owner's marginal tax rate (i.e., amount/ [1 − marginal tax rate] and the firm's marginal tax rate if it is a C corporation. What we are trying to estimate is the total average annual value that this business provides to its owner as if those benefits had to be funded from outside, pre-tax income.

The difference between the two values represents the owner's annual benefit from controlling the business. If the most recent year were a typical one in the business, that annual excess benefit would be capitalized, assuming that the heirs will make use of it after the current owner/manager retires. Or, if the business were going to be sold on the owner/manager's retirement, one would take the present value of the control benefit until then. With either approach, the values would be discounted using the same opportunity cost used in determining the initial value, since these benefits have the same overall risk as the firm's rewards to owners.

Note that owning and operating one's business might provide intrinsic values, such as "being president," more flexible working hours, and other valued things that we cannot easily measure. Those kinds of psychological and emotional factors are sometimes very important, but their value lies outside the terms of this book, since we are dealing with the financial core of the valuation process.

2.4.4.1 MINORITY INTERESTS If minority shareholders exist, their ownership benefit may have a lower value if they receive no perks or excess salary. In those instances, the gain to the controlling shareholders comes at the expense of those minority shareholders by omitting them from the control benefits, and from governments by paying less in taxes for the benefits received. The best estimate of minority shareholders' ownership value would be to subtract the capitalized value of control from the value of the business. This lower value is what minority shareholders should view as the firm's value. Their shares would then be valued by taking their ownership percentage of that reduced value of the firm. As an approximation, minority shareholders usually face a 30–40% discount in value when compared to the total firm value. That discount may be significantly less when a purchase of the entire business is imminent, and the negotiating power of minority shareholders increases—or if the majority shareholders choose to be generous, as is often the case in family and community enterprises.

2.5 How Should "Excess" Returns Be Valued?

Under normal circumstances, we assume that the owner/manager reaps the greatest benefit from controlling the firm. In addition, that individual is usually the one most responsible for the firm earning "excess" or superior returns. This section reviews the concept of excess returns and how they are measured. One of the key issues is whether the superior returns are dependent on the firm or the manager, that is, how likely it would be for their value to continue without the current manager. To the extent they would continue, the value of the firm is ongoing. The value of a firm is clearly tied to the extent to which its ability to create those superior returns can be successfully transferred to a new owner.

2.5.1 *Creating the Excess Returns and Defending Them*

Firms earning rates of return on their invested capital that exceed their *required rates of return* are defined by economists as earning *excess returns* (sometimes also called *monopoly rents*).[3] The *required rate of return* is normally defined as the time value of money (commonly estimated as the long-term government bond yield) plus a risk premium for the specific industry, and an additional illiquidity premium for being invested in a closely held firm. (The details of specific methods used to estimate the required rate of return are covered in chapter 7.) To earn an excess rate of return, a business must possess some form of competitive advantage: either a new or different product, or a production process that is cheaper than that of its competitors. Firms that earn excess rates of return can expect competitors to enter their markets and eventually drive returns on new investments down to the required rate—unless the initial firms continue to re-create the source of their advantage, by continuous innovation, for example.

2.5.1.1 MAINTAINING EXCESS RETURNS Continuous excess returns are very difficult to maintain. The most effective way is to create barriers to entry for potential competitors. Common means of sustaining competitive advantages are through the use of licensing, advertising, patents, or legal rules. Coca-Cola is a good example of a firm using advertising to maintain continuous excess returns. Pharmaceutical firms use patents. For the most part, these strategies require large operations. Barriers are usually very difficult to produce for small, closely held firms, which means that

[3] The term "excess" is *not* an ideological statement, just a mathematical one. It means returns above a specific threshold, or superior returns. In the economics literature, the usual way of expressing the concept is "excess returns," and we follow that convention here.

large excess returns will last for a only short time until competitors recognize that excess returns are being made. One of the reasons some private business owners jealously guard their financial privacy is to reduce the risks of competitors discovering their bonanzas.

Another way smaller firms maintain excess returns is by providing great service in a local market. Dominance of a local market can be an effective advantage for a small firm, like a family-owned corner store. Other options for smaller firms include exclusive licenses for distributing special products, contracts to provide unique parts to an original equipment manufacturer's (OEM) supply chain, close personal relations with customers, and so on.

2.5.1.2 FUTURE OPPORTUNITIES The ability to undertake new investments that will earn excess rates of return in the future is similar to earning excess returns on current investments. For public firms, the present value of these future options is what allows growth firms to trade at large multiples of their earnings; the market expects their earnings to grow, at rates greater than their reinvestment rate, due to their "pipelines" of new projects.

How do markets—or, for closely held firms, valuators—estimate the value of these growth options? First, the current and projected overall growth rate of the general economy is considered. Then the specific industry in which the firm operates is analyzed for its recent growth and foreseeable new products. For a regional business, the growth potential of the local market is considered. Finally, the individual firm is examined. The most commonly used initial approach is to look at the excess returns on existing investments and extrapolate those returns into the future for new investment opportunities. Similarly, because research and development (R&D) and advertising investments often generate future growth, their levels can be used to approximate growth opportunities (although they must be used with great caution, since effectiveness of R&D and advertising expenditures can vary widely from one firm to the next). Industries that indicate large growth opportunities will attract additional capital. For example, witness the large increase in the number of initial public offerings (IPOs) for Internet companies during 1998–2000.

Unlike public firms that publicize their breakthroughs well before they are commercially viable, a small, closely held firm can continuously earn excess returns by keeping its profitability a secret. Of course, if a store is always busy while its competitors are half empty, someone is going to stop in to see what that establishment is doing differently. For many well-organized, closely held firms, however, their competitors will never know how much better they are doing. After all, one primary reason for staying private is that one does not have to publish financial statements. Future investment opportunities at excess rates of return might be limited or even nil for some private firms, but secrecy may allow existing projects to earn excess returns indefinitely.

2.5.2 *Attribution Time: Who or What Is Earning Those Excess Returns?*

Now, assume that the closely held firm we are evaluating is earning excess returns. Who is responsible for generating those returns? Are they firm-specific, or do they result from some special ability of the owner/manager? This process of attributing the returns is the most important factor to consider in valuing a closely held firm for sale or transfer after the death of the key owner/manager. It is the ability to earn excess returns from, say, secret operating techniques that really separates the smaller closely held firm from a small public firm. The main difference and the difficulty in these valuations deals with who creates and controls those returns.

This matter is a somewhat more subtle extension of the earlier *going concern* discussion. It has already been determined that the business is a going concern. What the valuator must consider is the owner/manager's importance to the firm's ability to earn excess returns, on both current investments and future investment options. When a closely held firm earns excess rates of return, are they derived from parts of the business that are transferable or are they dependent on the current owner/manager?

It is quite likely that when Dad retires and Junior takes over, the profit level will drop. This phenomenon does not mean that Junior is a ne'er-do-well; rather, it is an indication of how good Dad had become in knowing the business and changing with the economy. One must look very carefully at the source of the returns. If they are manager-specific, they likely will not continue into the future; the rate of return will slowly decrease toward the normal investment rate once the person who created that special value has left. If, on the other hand, the firm earns excess returns from a well-known brand name or convenient location, its excess returns likely will continue under new ownership. And Junior may bring new ideas and energy, new networks and educational tools, to revitalize a tired business.

2.5.2.1 NEGATIVE EXCESS RETURNS AND THE MEAN REVERTING SITUATION Not all closely held firms can be expected to have positive excess returns. Many are in the opposite position, particularly in mature industries with excess capacity. Such firms no longer earn even the required return on their invested capital. Their value as going concerns is less than the investment in the business or its accounting book value. Perhaps the owner/manager is no longer keeping up with changes in the firm's primary markets. In this situation, one would expect new managers to increase the firm's performance to earn greater returns after some transition period.

Such an inversion of the before and after pictures is called a *mean reverting situation*. A "good" firm will sell for less than its current return would justify because a new owner would likely be unable to maintain the existing excess returns. A "poor" firm should sell for more than its earnings justify, as its new managers acquire both its current inferior earning potential and the option to turn the business around, increasing its future earning power. Value is driven by future earnings, under new management.

What the current owner/manager brings to the business must always be considered in valuing a closely held going concern, and those contributions may inflate or deflate the value of the business to a buyer. The value of the closely held firm without its key person can be substantially different than its current performance level would indicate.

2.6 An Adjustments Example

The following example is a real case of firm valuation, although the names of the company and individuals have been changed to protect confidentiality. Top Tool Company, LLC, is a tool and die company located in the Midwest. It is organized as a limited liability company with four partners: James Johnson Sr. (Jim) and his wife, Alice, and their three children: James Jr. (known as Jamie), Jane, and George. Jim is the principal partner who founded, built, and still runs the business. The firm has a reputation for extremely good products and prides itself on quick delivery. The fifty shop employees work very hard, putting in long weekend hours when necessary to meet deadlines. Jim rewards them well. In at least one instance, he purchased a house for an employee.

Total assets are $4.7 million, and partners' equity is $3.4 million. Over the past several years, revenues have averaged just over $9.1 million per year. The cost of goods sold has been averaging $6 million, selling expenses $630,000, and general and administrative expenses $1.65 million (see table 2.3). This performance leaves an average income from operations of $820,000. Top Tool, although very successful in its current operations, shows no real options for future growth.

Table 2.3 Top Tool Company LLC Annual Financial Statement (Pro Forma)

Total assets	$4.7M
Partners' equity	$3.4M
Average gross revenues	$9.1M
Expenses	($8.28M)
Cost of goods sold	$6.0M
Selling expenses	$0.63M
General and administrative expenses	$1.65M
Income from operations (before partners' draws)	$0.82M
Partnership draws	($0.80M)
Jim	$0.480M
Jamie	$0.090M
Jane	$0.100M
George	$0.130M
Reinvestment	$0.02M

As stipulated in their partnership agreement, Jim receives an average of $480,000 each year; Jamie receives $90,000; Jane is paid $100,000; George gets $130,000. The remaining $20,000 per year is reinvested into the business.

2.6.1 *Setting Up the Family Transfer*

The elder Johnsons (Jim and Alice), who are quite old, want to "sell" a substantial portion of the firm to their children. *Sell* is in quotation marks because they are really going to give each child $20,000 of the firm's equity each year until they no longer face estate taxes.[4] (Under U.S. law, such gifts are permitted without tax penalty.) A firm value is therefore needed to determine how many years of $60,000 gifts will be required.

Q1: IS IT A GOING CONCERN? The first step is to determine whether Top Tool represents an ongoing business or is merely an extension of Jim's ability to produce great tools. If Jim is replaced, can the firm continue or will it be reorganized? Although Jim is clearly the major force behind this firm's success, the business has grown in both size and organization to a point where it is more than merely an extension of Jim's toolmaking abilities. Also, customers identify with Top Tool as their supplier, rather than with Jim. With annual sales of over $9 million, it is not surprising that we find Top Tool is a going concern, no longer dependent on its founding partner. Note that the fact that the firm is legally organized as an LLC instead of a corporation should have no affect on its going concern status for valuation purposes.

Q2: FOR WHAT PURPOSE IS THE FIRM BEING OPERATED? Although the business lacks separation between Jim and Top Tool, he appears to operate the business to maximize wealth. Jim's main goal for the firm is to make money. For example, while buying a house for an employee might be considered unorthodox for a tool company, it was a value-maximizing decision. The employee, Bob, had marital problems and did not want his ex-wife to get the house. Rather than risk Bob's preoccupation with his personal problem, Jim determined that having Top Tool buy the house would improve Bob's immediate productivity and his long-run loyalty to the company. Not surprisingly, Bob and most other employees are extremely loyal and hard working.

Q3: WHAT ARE THE EXCESS RETURNS? Although Jim is an extremely hard worker himself, his children are overpaid and unproductive. Discussions with the firm's attorney and the firm's outside accountant revealed how bad the situation has become. From those conversations, it

[4] The gift tax is inflation-indexed; the 2006 allowance was $12,000 per person, or $24,000 for a married couple.

appeared that George is doing a job that would cost the firm about $60,000 per year if an outside replacement had to be hired. His siblings contribute nothing of value to the firm. (On the day the valuator visited, for example, only George showed up, and he arrived around 10 a.m.) By estimating direct benefits paid by the firm on their behalves at $5,000 per person, and adding in their excess draws, excess employee wages and benefits for these family members, an estimate of $270,000 per year was produced.

Jim's draw from his business appeared much larger than that of CEOs of comparably sized tool companies. To determine the appropriate salary for an outside CEO, executive compensation data were collected from three small, publicly held tool companies. Although they were the smallest public firms reporting compensation data, their average revenue was nine times that of Top Tools. However, the average CEO compensation was only $230,000 per year. Thus Jim, who was paid $480,000, received at least $250,000 more than his opportunity cost. By combining the excess wages and benefits paid for Jim's children with his own excess compensation, we arrive at an owner's excess benefit of $520,000 per year. This total excess compensation of $520,000 is an additional annual amount that would be available to a purchaser, over and above the apparent profits from the firm's operations.

Q4: WHAT IS THE REAL PROFIT-MAKING POTENTIAL OF THE FIRM? Top Tool's adjusted before-tax profit is the current $20,000 remaining after the partners' draw, plus the additional compensation of $520,000, for a total of $540,000. Because taxable income is between $335,000 and $10 million, the applicable tax rate is 34%. Top Tool's equivalent after-tax income is $356,400. This value should be capitalized at the appropriate discount rate to determine Top Tool's value. This value will be substantially different than the current profit-loss statement would project.

Top Tool's present financial statements show a profit that is understated by more than 95%, relative to the real profit-producing performance of the business. This discrepancy illustrates just how important it is to correctly restate the firm's operating performance before even attempting a financial valuation based on any investment-return model. The financial statements of a closely held firm should be treated as the outcome of the owner's tax and financial planning choices, at least as much as they are the outcomes of the business operations.

2.7 Just a Pile of Assets?

"So, let me get this right. If somebody says my business is *not* a going concern, then it's nothing more than a pile of secondhand furniture?!" Tom was clearly upset. "I can make a good living, take good care of my family, customers, suppliers—and then—poof! It's all worth next to nothing?!"

Mike didn't want to make things worse, but the message had to get through. "Unless that money machine can be transferred to someone else in such a way that the new owner can make good money too, then, yeah, I think that's what the Professor is telling us."

"How can that be?! I don't understand how a business that provides good livings for people can just be worth nothing."

"Well, that's not quite the way I heard him," Mike said in an effort to turn Tom's despair around. "What I heard was that it might be worth quite a bit to you—and it might be worth something to a buyer, but that those are two different assessments. Hey, we've each built businesses that work for us. The real question we have to start thinking about is whether we've built companies that would work for anyone else. If we have, then they are probably worth something as going concerns. If we haven't, then they will be just another pile of assets on the auction block when you or I retire. It's a scary thought, I'll admit."

Tom was still a bit frantic. "What you're telling me is that my business is not part of my pension plan, that I've been working all these years to create—nothing of real value, nothing I can sell, or my executor can sell to take care of my wife and kids."

"Easy, now, my friend!" Mike had to break this train of thought. "What he was saying is that would be the case if the business is not a going concern. If it is a going concern, then it is worth something more. What we have to do first is figure whether these things are going concerns. And that means thinking like a potential buyer of the business. We have to ask ourselves—Would I buy this used business? And then we have to ask—What would I pay for it? The answers will tell us a lot about what kind of asset each business is.

"By the way, did you catch that thing he said about our personal net worth statements? I started doing that in my head and realized that the business is probably my biggest asset—at least to me. What it's worth on the open market is a big factor in my personal net worth, and I realized I really don't have any idea what that number is.

"There has to be some range of estimates, I guess. At the bottom end is that 'pile of used assets' valuation. That's the minimum value. I started thinking about that, and it got pretty scary. The real estate is probably pretty valuable, but it's been a manufacturing site for a long time. Proving that it is clear of environmental liabilities is going to be tough, and that could tie it up for years, really punish its market value. After that, I've got a bunch of machinery we make work for us, but I sure wouldn't pay much more than scrap value for it at auction. And the rest—I don't know what our products or client lists are worth to anyone else. I just don't know! There's a lot about this stuff I don't know," Mike tapered off into his own fears.

The tables were turned, and Tom saw the need to get them both on a more positive agenda. "Well, old friend, I can see we have some homework in front of us. This is kind of like that health checkup I had a couple of years ago, a warning shot to do something before it's too late. It's pretty darn scary when you look at the downside, but let's not get fixated there, just motivated by it. You know it's possible to shoot a 15 on the sixth hole; if you focus on the worst that could happen, you tend to make it happen. Let's go the other way—find out what the real situation is, then make sure our businesses don't fall into that category."

There was a long pause as Mike shook himself, visibly pulling back from that abyss. "You know, it is possible that one or the other—or both—of our firms is going to be just a pile of assets. But even if that is the case, if we know that, then we can run the businesses to pull the profits out into other investments. Then we don't have to worry about sticking our families with the problem, since we would have planned for an orderly liquidation as a way to exit. The equity would be out of the business and into other things."

"That would be the way to manage a downside scenario," Tom concluded. "But, if they are valuable as going concerns, then we should probably make the opposite decisions—reinvest the profits in the business to grow that asset. I can see the difference between maintaining your machinery and buying state-of-the-art replacements. There's a big difference here, isn't there? So, our first step has to be to figure out which situation we're facing, and to what degree. Then we can start planning ways to deal with that."

Mike agreed, "We each need to know what we have before we can make those kinds of decisions."

"All right," said Tom, "let's get at it."

3

Valuation When a Firm Is Not a Going Concern

3.0 The Value of Assets

Friday night, while their wives were finding the ladies' room at the concert hall, Mike turned to his friend and asked: "All of these discussions we've been having about valuing our firms depend on them being 'going concerns.' While I'm sure both of ours are—at least I think they are—what would it mean if they were not?"

Tom replied, "I guess they would then be worth just what the assets are worth. But what are those assets worth? And what kind of markets would we use as references? There are some pretty big differences in the price you'd have to pay for some of these things, buying them new or at auction. And what's a customer list worth, anyway? Lots to me, but how would I figure out its value to someone else?"

"I don't know, but I think we should find out," continued Mike. "To really understand the value of what we've been building, we need to know if these companies are worth more as going concerns or as piles of assets—and which assets are the valuable ones. That way we'll be better able to decide where to make new investments, ones that will add value to our firms."

GOING CONCERN OR NOT? HERE'S THE PLAN Chapters 4 and 5 will discuss the key concepts in valuing a going concern. There, the emphasis will be placed on estimating the future free cash flows that can be generated by the ongoing firm and discounting them to find their present value. In accounting terms, we will be able to address those issues by considering only a modified income statement. Any valuable assets that a firm possesses, such as a useful brand name or a choice location, are recognized in the greater cash flows they allow the firm to generate, and those benefits will be reflected on that modified income statement.

Prior to that happy scenario, however, we must first deal with the dilemmas created by those (fairly common) situations where a firm *cannot* be valued as a going concern. In these cases, we consider the value of all assets, both tangible and intangible, being put to their most productive alternative uses. In this context, their earning power is assumed to be higher in some application other than the current business where they are employed, so we disregard their effect on the modified income statement. The consideration here in chapter 3 is strictly based on an extended Balance Sheet that includes all intangibles.

3.1 Valuing a Firm Both Ways

Before we delve into considering how to value these assets, let's review how a valuation should proceed. Many times, a firm should be valued both ways—as a going concern *and* as a non-going concern. By knowing both sets of values, both buyer and seller will be able to make better decisions.

If an owner/manager is considering retiring and selling the business, a non-going concern valuation is useful for most small firms, because the most common outcome is the organization of one or more new small businesses from the assets. Furthermore, even if the business is a going concern, the non-going concern value should also be considered as a lower estimate of the value of the business.

When the parts of a business are worth more than the firm as a whole, an economist might say it is time to liquidate. The key question in those circumstances is what the firm's assets are worth to someone else interested in starting another (likely very similar) business. This chapter presents all the different types of both tangible and intangible assets that must considered in valuing a non-going concern. It also covers the specific factors that influence the actual values of these assets.

3.1.1 *Redefining Going Concerns and Non-Going Concerns*

By definition, each firm that is not a going concern is a non-going concern. Let's begin by making sure we know what is required for a firm to be considered as a going concern when it is changing ownership. Then we can determine the circumstances that might reduce it to non-going standing.

3.1.1.1 GOING CONCERNS DEFINED Traditional accounting practice has questioned a firm's going concern status when it is in severe financial straits. "Can the business continue as a going concern, paying its creditors?" is the question being asked. The question is one of financial viability. If a firm can meet its financial obligations, it is deemed a going concern.

Closely held firms should approach the idea of being a going concern from a different angle. Sometimes called the entity approach, it asks the key question: "Does the firm exist as a separate entity, a going concern independent of its current owner/manager?" In chapter 2, we established two conditions for determining whether a firm is a going concern. First, could the firm continue to operate as it is currently structured if the current owner/manager were replaced? Second, do the customers and other stakeholders see themselves as dealing with the business and not just the current owner/manager? If both of these can be answered yes, then the firm should be considered a going concern.

3.1.1.2 NON-GOING CONCERNS DEFINED Most small, closely held firms will not meet these criteria. Rightly or wrongly, many owners of small businesses encourage their customers to call on them personally for the services provided by their firms. That's one of the advantages small firms have over "Big Boxes"—personal service. Customers want to know the owner and hold him or her personally accountable for the service and goods sold. That direct connection helps customers overcome the risks they take in choosing to deal with a small local firm, but it may have costs at the time of ownership transfer. Because the customer relationship is so personal, most customers put their trust in the current owner/manager. When that person leaves, the trust relationship is severed. With that break, a substantial portion of the firm's advantage, and its value, may also be lost. (There are important ways to transfer that trust, but that's an issue we'll address later. It may be the fundamental difference in the going/non-going determination—and a major factor in the transfer price.)

Owners of such firms use them to produce a livelihood, often a good one, but when they retire, they are usually selling assets, both tangible and intangible, that will be reorganized into a new firm. Without their personal involvement, their firms are just the sum of their parts; they are non-going concerns.

3.1.2 *Chapter Outline*

The issues considered in this chapter include how to value a firm in the situation where no going concern or separate entity exists or where the assets may be worth more than their going concern value. The chapter starts by discussing what is being purchased or sold other than the obvious tangible assets with the ownership transfer of a small closely held firm. The current owner must understand these other assets to obtain the highest possible price for the business.

Next, if the firm is not really a going concern, how are the various assets being valued? What do the markets say? What is a client list worth? What is a unique name or location worth? Then, as an example of a non-going concern approach to valuation, the modified book value is discussed.

Finally, the concept of total liquidation value is discussed as the extreme example of a non-going concern. This value represents the owner/manager's put option value for the business. When it is greater than the value of the firm as an ongoing concern, the owner/manager's economically rational, value-maximizing option is to exercise the put option by liquidating the business. That doesn't mean that all owners will liquidate such firms, but it does yield a financial baseline against which they can measure the value of their choices.

3.2 Valuing the Tangible Assets on a Balance Sheet

This discussion starts with the assets at the top of the Balance Sheet and works its way down. When we are finished with the tangible assets on the Balance Sheet, the potential intangible parts will be considered for the value they contribute.

3.2.1 *Cash and Marketable Securities*

Cash and marketable securities form the first asset. Cash value is the most standardized way of valuing assets, and the format into which we try to convert all the other assets wherever possible. With a non-going concern sale, the seller will most likely keep all the cash and assume all the liabilities while selling the assets. The transfer then leaves the accumulated cash and liabilities in the hands of the prior owner who created them, for him to dispose of. In valuing the business for other reasons, one must be sure to include the value of cash and marketable securities, along with the other assets, and remember to subtract the liabilities owed against them.

3.2.1.1 THE LIQUIDITY OF MARKETABLE SECURITIES The only special consideration on this line might be the value of investments in other businesses, both equity positions and loans. If the investments are not in the form of securities of publicly traded firms, their market values might be difficult to estimate. Probably more important is the extent to which these investments are liquid, that is, can be sold on short notice without a tremendous sacrifice in value. Liquidity is an important consideration with all closely held firms.

3.2.2 *Accounts Receivable*

If the firm sells its goods or services on credit, the receivables must be collected. Those collections can prove difficult. Consider: Why do firms pay their bills? They do it to ensure that they will receive future shipments and to maintain their credit rating for other shipments from other firms. Now, once it becomes known that the owner is leaving a supplier business, the recipients' first incentive drops to zero! The second incentive also drops, because they know that the owner will not have much incentive to report them delinquent if he is leaving the business. It is surprising how many owners sell their real assets but hold onto their trade credit accounts, when the new owners would appear to have a much better chance of collecting those accounts. Those creditors most likely want to continue to make sales to the new owners of recently purchased firms, whereas they expect to never make another sale to the departing owner.

We might think, therefore, that the new owners would be pleased to take on the accounts receivable. After all, those sales were created without their effort and represent a form of free money. However, new owners have incentives to *not* buy old receivables. In many cases, these negative incentives will outweigh the advantages of buying them. Let's consider the reasons.

Credit is granted as a form of product guarantee. The buyers get a product to inspect physically and, if for resale, to see their own customers' reactions to the product before having to pay their suppliers. A new owner does not want to guarantee the former owner's quality—particularly when the former owner, exiting the business, may have an incentive to produce lower cost work at the end of his term. Unless the deal is carefully structured otherwise, there is usually no financial incentive for the departing owner to maintain a business' reputation. If the receivables are sold, this situation is compounded. The new owners must correct any product defects and then collect for the products sold in that warranty-receivable period. If responsibility for those goods stays with the owner under whose control they were manufactured, poor-quality concerns are eliminated for the new buyers, because the departing owner will have incentives to maximize quality and hence minimize postdeal responsibilities.

The other reason to extend credit is financing. Goods purchased on credit do not require third-party (bank) financing until they are paid for. A common method to expand sales is to sell with looser credit terms: allowing a longer time before receivable collections are expected and selling to financially weaker customers who are more likely to default on their payments. An owner/manager getting ready to sell a business has an incentive to expand sales using easier credit terms. A casual observer would view the firm as having more growth and might therefore value the business higher, because purchase price is often based at least in part on some multiple of sales. Buying the entire business would cause a double whammy to the purchaser who first overpays for an illusory growth of (bad) customers and then must spend extra effort to collect shaky receivables from those customers. Buying only the physical assets minimizes this problem. The seller is less likely to sell to marginal customers just to increase growth if she has to collect those accounts herself.

Another factor is money—not the amount that is expected to be collected by the seller but instead the capital available to the buyers. Most of the time it is quite limited. A seller may be able to get a deal done by keeping the receivables and selling the rest of the firm for a lower cash price. From a buyer's point of view, this is usually nothing more than a short-run cash savings. Once sales are made, the new owners will have to find a way to finance their own receivables. If they feel, however, that they can line up outside financing for receivables or additional equity capital after they have started to operate the business, then they may prefer a purchase without receivables.

Countering these arguments for excluding accounts receivables from the sale is the idea of business continuity. The buyers should pay more than just the expected amount of receivables to be collected for an ongoing firm. Maintaining continuity with current customers is usually quite valuable as new owners start to build their business. The maintenance of those relationships is made easier when the least disruption occurs between sellers and buyers. This intangible asset must be valued and included as part of the price. It is part of the seller's human capital for this business (a subject we will cover in more detail later in this chapter).

Ignoring the straight financing motives, a preference about selling a business with or without receivables is going to come down to the type of business being sold. A key consideration is the firm's control over product quality. A straight retail or wholesale operation would want to sell the receivables; the continuity of relationships between the firm and its customers would outweigh any quality problems, because the producer or manufacturer determines the product quality. A manufacturing firm or a service firm might find it preferable to sell the firm's assets without the receivables, because the liabilities attached to those receivables would outweigh the benefit to new owners from continuity. Both choices may depend on the quality of the transition agreement between seller and buyer and on their trust in each other's integrity. It may also depend on the extent to which the buyer plans to continue to serve the prior owner's customers.

3.2.3 *Inventory*

Moving down the Balance Sheet to "Inventory," we find that similar valuation problems occur. This time, however, the main problem is more of a straight valuation difference than an adverse incentive problem. There are three main issues to deal with:

- Value of the inventory to a buyer of the going concern
- Liquidation values
- Choosing the right discount for the inventory valuation method

3.2.3.1 VALUE OF INVENTORY TO BUYER AND SELLER

If all the assets were sold to someone who is going to operate a similar business, that buyer will probably be willing to purchase the old firm's inventory at replacement cost. That's what she would have to pay to stock the business with its opening inventory anyway. Thus, she is likely to be indifferent at that price level and to actively resist any premium over that level.

A buyer of the entire business is going to look at the inventory to assess what the new business will need. Such a buyer is unlikely to pay more for the useful items than would be required to buy them from an outside supplier—and will probably pay nothing for the rest of the inventory, because it is deemed to be useless to the new firm. The rest of the inventory is likely to be discarded or auctioned. The costs of getting rid of it may even exceed the value the new owner might expect to receive, so he will give it a much lower value (perhaps even a negative one).

Thus, an inventory should be valued as the sum of the replacement cost of that portion which is being usefully added to the new firm and a deeply discounted value for the rest. This situation may also be one in which the portion of inventory not being transferred may stay with the departing owner, who may be able to liquidate it at a higher price.

To get as close as possible to the replacement value, the seller must not appear to be in any hurry to sell the business. In the situation of a deceased owner/manager, the trustees and heirs have a much weaker bargaining position to get a top price—especially if they are not prepared to operate the firm themselves. Potential buyers are likely to know that the inheritors are under pressure to sell quickly, if only to settle estate taxes, and certainly to minimize any further loss of intangible values. Such sellers must hope that several parties are interested in the firm so that its value is bid up in an auction market. This is another reason that owner/managers should plan for the future and make early arrangements to sell. The ability to walk away from an inferior offer and the time to devote to generating a better one put a seller in a much stronger negotiating position.

3.2.3.2 ORDERLY LIQUIDATION OF INVENTORY If the assets are sold piecemeal because the business is no longer profitable, they will likely change hands at a much lower liquidation value. A liquidation approach to inventory valuation gives two values: an orderly liquidation, such as a firm should undertake, and a fast liquidation that a creditor might take. With an orderly liquidation, the firm might receive more than its carrying cost on inventory. How many times have you seen stores announcing a "final liquidation sale" or "we are going out of business"—only to see the firm well and prospering sometime in the future? Like the growing factory outlet stores that sell items their regular mall stores don't want to carry, businesses in liquidation frequently buy additional merchandise, usually of lower quality, to liquidate. (They have no need to maintain a reputation for quality if the firm is actually liquidating.) The items being liquidated in these stores are often sold for more than cost. Although the profit margin might not be at the normal level, it is still positive. Operating costs are still being incurred, so gross margins need to remain above overall break-even levels.

The exact value of the inventory is going to vary with the specific assets being carried. Usually a firm does not consider total liquidation if it has been making wise inventory decisions in the past. Liquidations occur when the inventory is obsolete. Fewer people want last year's styles, which is why retail stores often discount their merchandise at the end of its season. It is better to get something for it now than incur the certain costs of storage until next season when it might not fetch any money at all. Therefore, it is important to assess inventory with an impartial eye, which might be difficult, because the selling owner chose those items. In the vast majority of cases, expect to sell it at less than its undepreciated book value.

A recent innovation, now widely used, is online auctions. The largest one, eBay, and its industrial siblings help owners liquidate their unwanted inventories in a controlled manner.[1] They also provide useful benchmarks for the likely auction value of existing inventory. By checking these Web sites for current selling prices, an owner can come up with much better estimates of liquidation values.

3.2.3.3 FAST LIQUIDATION Fast liquidation should never be a serious consideration in valuing your own business. An owner/manager, including heirs not wanting to continue in the business, should liquidate inventory in such a way as to obtain its maximum value. This maximum value process is rarely achieved with a quick liquidation.

Financial institutions, however, in repossessing inventory for lack of loan payments, for example, have a different incentive. They know little about the particular business or the items in its inventory. The longer they hold it, the more of it will be stolen or deteriorate. Therefore, they need to liquidate it as quickly as possible to close their books and recognize their losses on the loan. Investing more valuable time and carrying costs by trying to manage the business are not going to be effective ways of increasing the value to them of the collateral assets. They are likely to hire an auction company for a percentage of the sales and rid themselves of the inventory over a weekend. Fire-sale auction prices are often only 10% of book value, however; after the costs of the auctioneer are deducted, there is often little left for other creditors. Lacking the expertise that an owner/manager would have on these items, bankers use this process to get their maximum recovery value in a loss-minimizing situation, that is, make the best of their bad situation. It usually infuriates or depresses the former owners (and other creditors), because they are powerless to get the value they could have earned for those assets and hence get significantly reduced credit against their debts. (Some experienced entrepreneurs choose to buy back their assets at auction, then liquidate them in a more orderly fashion to recover greater value.)

3.2.3.4 IMPACTS OF LIFO AND FIFO INVENTORY COST ACCOUNTING METHODS The last point to note about inventory deals

[1] A Google search on September 30, 2005, yielded the following sites: www.auctionguide.com/dir/Industrial (an auction listing directory); www.dovebid.com; www.maynards.com; http://dir.yahoo.com/Business_and_Economy/Business_to_Business/Industrial_Supplies/Auctions (auction directory); www.industrialcanda.com; www.auctionnews.co.uk; and www.internetauctionlist.com.

with the cost flow assumption used to value the goods. If a business uses a LIFO method (last in, first out) to value its inventory, one might figure that it should receive a higher percentage of its carrying value than a firm using FIFO (first in, first out). After all, with inflation over the time the firm has been in business, the same items would be valued lower with LIFO than with FIFO. While that may be true, LIFO methods are viewed by some people as merely a technique to lower taxes and give a more accurate value for current costs in determining income. In accounting for LIFO inventory, one always starts with a meaningful assessment of the current cost value, then the LIFO adjustment is made. This current cost value will be approximately the same as the FIFO value.

3.2.4 *Fixed Assets*

A firm's fixed assets can be difficult to value. The approach is similar to that used to value inventory. When the assets are valued as part of an ongoing business, their replacement cost should be used as the best estimate of value. If the business would likely be totally liquidated, the value of the assets to a used equipment dealer would be more appropriate.

3.2.4.1 COMPANY CARS AND OTHER READILY MARKETABLE ASSETS Consider the value of a company car or truck. If it is going to be used as part of a new business, its retail Kelley Blue Book value should be used. It is likely to be a fair estimate of the new owner's replacement cost—assuming he wanted that model and vintage of vehicle. When the business is valued from a liquidation perspective, however, the car's wholesale Blue Book value should be used, because that is likely to be the price a dealer would pay to the liquidator. The difference between those retail and wholesale prices is one of the measures of the losses that occur when a business is sold as assets instead of as a going concern.

3.2.4.2 REAL ESTATE Many small firms have other assets with well-established markets, such as real estate: land and buildings. One can commission an appraisal of the value of such property. The appraised value represents the expected gross amount that one can expect to receive if the property is sold in an orderly fashion. The net value to the seller would be that amount minus the normal sales commission for similar property in the same area. Unlike vehicles, which can be sold almost immediately, this value must be discounted to the present for the expected time needed to sell the property. The current rate for second mortgages should be used as the best estimate of the discount rate, because that is the rate at which one could borrow against the property to obtain immediate funds. If that rate is 8% per year and the expected sales time is six months (a half-year), the current or present value of the property would be:

$$\text{Expected Selling Price} = (1 - \text{selling commission})/(1.08)^{1/2}$$

With a 6% sales commission, this would give around 90% of the expected selling price. The 10% discount represents the difference in value to the seller if the assets are sold with the business compared to their value if the business is just liquidated.

3.2.4.3 LEASING OPTIONS The owner of a business with real estate assets has another option when selling the business. The property can be used as part of the selling process. Most potential buyers of small closely held businesses are short of cash and need to preserve as much of what they have as possible for operating funds. The buyers also want to learn as much as possible about the unique aspects of this business with the lowest level of financial commitment they can manage. One way to accomplish both of these goals is to have the current owner/manager sell the business but maintain ownership of the building, leasing it to the new business owners.

This approach can be expanded to have the seller maintain ownership of all the fixed assets and lease them to the buyers of the business. In addition to preserving their cash (or reducing the debt burden), buyers may find attractive incentives in such an approach. The seller definitely has an incentive to see that the new owners are successful to ensure he obtains the rent or lease payments.

A further refinement is to give the new owners of the business an option to purchase the leased assets when their financial circumstances permit. In that kind of arrangement, however, the current owner must be careful to structure the deal so that the Internal Revenue Service does not classify the lease as an installment purchase contract. Such contracts advance the tax liabilities, and most people prefer to defer them instead.

When the alternative is having the business seller hold a note against the buyer for a portion of the purchase price, the rental arrangement offers better collateral if things do not work out as expected for the new buyers. One outcome may be that the buyer relocates the business when the lease expires, leaving the building owner with the property and fixed equipment to sell separately.

3.2.4.3.1 *Taxation Issues* Taxes should also be considered in structuring a sale where fixed assets are rented. The seller usually wants to obtain the most after-tax dollars. The sale of the business will create a long-term gain that, in 2005 in the United States, was taxed at a maximum rate of 15% (if sold as equity in the business). For sales of firms' assets with the original owners maintaining cash, receivables, and liabilities, the tax rate on the gain could go as high as 28%. That increased tax burden makes it extremely important to have the tax issues addressed before the sale. Continuing to own the property will create rental or lease income, taxable at ordinary (higher) tax rates but also an offsetting depreciation expense. This combination can probably be structured to provide cash flow with no taxable income. When the property is eventually sold, this technique could create a tax liability in which the depreciation has to be recaptured and then taxed as ordinary income. If the property is held and passes into the owner's estate, the recapture tax can be avoided.

An owner contemplating such a sale should definitely check with a competent tax advisor before choosing either the time or method of sale.

3.2.4.4 EQUIPMENT The land, buildings, and vehicles are rather easy to value with a business sale because there are readily available markets and expert appraisers for these items. The equipment component of the firm's fixed assets may be more difficult to appraise. Again, two sets of values need be obtained: what it would cost a different owner to buy it and what the current owner can get by selling it. The big difference is that those values are going to be subject to much broader spreads. The more specialized assets a business has, the more valuable those assets will be if they are sold to someone wanting to operate in that same industry, rather than just liquidating the business. Of course, potential buyers may realize the situation and try to place a discount on these assets. That situation makes it important to find as many potential buyers as possible; competitive auctions are the best way to ensure that the maximum possible amount is obtained.

In line with these broad ideas, the specific assets must be valued. The first point is to *not* start with their current book values or even their original purchase prices. Both numbers reflect history, not current markets, and good valuations are estimates of current market conditions. We must start with what the assets would cost to purchase at the time of the valuation. One fairly reliable shortcut is to base the initial estimate on the insured value of the assets. Insurance companies have good reasons to keep owners from having incentives for fires, and so will want to make sure that assets are not overinsured. The reverse logic is not necessarily true, however, so the insured value should be treated as a minimum estimate. It is wise to know how up to date the insurance assessment is and what changes have taken place in the assets since that assessment. It is also useful to see exactly which assets are covered by a policy, because some may be covered in other ways, including self-insurance.

When used equipment can be purchased easily, the appropriate valuation is the fair market price of comparable used equipment. When those prices are difficult to obtain, we need an alternative methodology. What we need to do is estimate the value of the old asset, using its remaining expected life, and the cost of a new (replacement) asset with its total expected life. Knowing the required investment return for the business and its marginal tax rate, the equivalent annual cost of operating the new asset over its life can be determined. The value of the old asset is then the present value of the equivalent annual cost for its remaining life, plus the present value of any remaining depreciation tax shield.

3.2.4.4.1 *Example, with Depreciation* Consider the following example of how to value a specific asset. The used asset is six years old and will last another four years. It is fully depreciated for tax purposes. Suppose you know that a new version, which performs similar functions, costs $10,000. To find the value of the remaining four years of expected life of the old asset, we can compare it to the replacement cost of purchasing a new version. This alternative will establish the minimum value of the old asset.

Let's assume the new (replacement) equipment would also last for ten years and, for tax purposes, is in a five-year MACRS class.[2] To show the value of its depreciation tax shield, for the sake of simplicity, we are going to depreciate the asset on a straight-line basis for five years. Assume also that the estimated required return is 12% for this business, and 31% is the expected marginal tax rate. The after-tax present value of owning that asset is its cost minus the present value of its depreciation tax shield, which is the present value of taxes saved from using the depreciation expense to lower taxable profits. As the present value of a five-year annuity at 12% is 3.505, by applying the 31% tax rate, and applying straight-line depreciation over five years, we discover that the net cost of a new piece of equipment would be $7,765.

$$\text{Net Cost} = \$10{,}000 \times (1.0 - 0.31 \times [1/5]\text{PV of annuity for five years at } 12\%)$$
$$= \$7{,}765$$

To find the equivalent annual cost of owning this asset for its estimated useful life of ten years, the $7,765 value is divided by the present value of an annuity for the asset's life, or ten years in this example. This gives $7,765/5.65 = $1,374 per year. In other words, if

- the required rate of return is 12%,
- the marginal tax rate is 31%,
- the asset is being depreciated for taxes over five years on a straight-line basis,
- and the new asset can be used for ten years,

then one would be indifferent between buying the asset with its depreciation tax shield for $10,000 or paying $1,374 after taxes at the end of each year for the next ten years.

This arithmetic is neat, but we still need to value the old asset with four years remaining on its service life. This asset is worth $1,374/year to the business, or for four years, it is $1,374 times the present value of an annuity for four years at 12%. This approach yields a value of $4,173.

$$\text{Asset's Value} = \$1{,}374 \times (\text{PV of annuity for four years at } 12\%)$$
$$= \$1{,}374 \times 3.04 = \$4{,}173.$$

In our example, the asset is fully depreciated for tax purposes. If, however, the asset still had a depreciable basis for taxes, the present value of its depreciation expense, times the estimated marginal tax rate, would be added to this value.

Now, in a real situation, MACRS depreciation would most likely be used. Straight-line depreciation was used in the example because that makes it easier to show the present value of the depreciation tax shield. The present value of the depreciation shield for all the classes of assets at various discount rates can be found in most financial management textbooks.

[2] MACRS = modified asset class recovery system, the current tax depreciation schedule under U.S. laws.

3.2.4.5 VALUING FIXED ASSETS SUBJECT TO RAPID TECHNOLOGICAL CHANGE The previous approach works fine with assets where little technological change is expected. However, technological innovation, not physical wear and tear, is the major cause of decline in the value of many capital assets. If properly maintained, many assets will last indefinitely, but most of us prefer driving our air-conditioned cars to the office rather than taking our grandparents' old carriages. Assets like computers can become obsolete before we can figure out how to use all their features. Many times we continue to use them because the time cost of training the owner and employees to upgrade cannot be justified. (How many of us have obsolete computers at which we are still typing away?!) These assets, although mechanically in good condition, are not going to be valued highly when an entire operation is sold. Since prices of old computers drop continuously as new products come to the market, an estimate of value can be obtained on the old equipment. A new business would probably like to start with up-to-date equipment, hence the best rule-of-thumb estimate of the value of the older but still fully operational machines in the previous business would be 50% the cost of the new but out-of-date computers at their current (and most likely lower) price.

The process developed to estimate the replacement cost of used assets appears quite complex. For a business with many different assets, it is probably not worth valuing all of them separately. Rather, they can be put into classes based on their similarity. Knowing the original purchase prices of the assets in a class, an average-aged asset can be selected for valuation. Its estimated remaining value can then be used to value the entire class of assets, on the assumption that all items in the class will share the same value-retention profile.

3.3 What Is Being Bought Other Than Tangible Assets?

When a closely held firm changes ownership and management, major changes will likely occur in the firm's organization and operations. Even if the name over the door stays the same, a new firm is created. This firm sells to many of the same customers, carries the original name, continues the original business relationships, employs many of the previous employees, and uses the purchased tangible assets. However, beyond using the innate tangible assets and a new corporate charter, the new firm will also form new business relationships.

3.3.1 *Maximizing the Value of Human Capital: Venture-Specific Knowledge*

A key consideration with a small closely held firm is that both ownership and management almost always change hands together. To get the "maximum value" for the business, the seller must give the maximum value for the business to the buyers. Conversely, the buyer is interested in getting the maximum value for the purchase. While the seller is giving up the name, assets, business relationships, and so on, what else would a buyer pay for?

The seller's firm-specific human capital is a valuable commodity. It includes the owner's knowledge of the people and business processes that have been developed over the years and that she has learned to operate successfully. With a quick sale, this capital (a.k.a. knowledge) is often lost. The buyer shouldn't pay for it unless it's transferred with the business, and the seller will consequently receive less than the maximum possible price. Usually, the seller wants to obtain the maximum value for the business, and the buyer wants to obtain as much of the seller's human capital as possible, because that reduces the new owner's start-up costs. To transfer this knowledge effectively usually requires a lengthy handoff process. The importance of this human capital is why transition processes often put the seller in a prolonged consulting role and why a significant part of the purchase price is deferred into that transitional period. In many cases, the ultimate price will be based on the effectiveness of the transfer of human capital.

3.3.1.1 ASPECTS OF HUMAN CAPITAL TRANSFER Before considering how to structure the sale, let us review some specific aspects of human capital. It includes such knowledge as "Who are the major customers?" Listing them is usually pretty easy, but do they have any unusual quirks that are not so obvious? The buyer will need to know as much as the seller does to retain those accounts. The seller must make the rounds to introduce the buyer to all major customers at least once (if not twice) to hand off the relationships to the new owner. Similar situations exist with suppliers, particularly when there are few sources for critical inputs.

To maximize the transfer value, the buyer and seller should go right down the list of everyone with whom the firm deals. For example, current employees must be reviewed. Possibly, the departing owner has received extremely productive work from them by providing unusual benefits. The buyer also needs to understand the firm's relationships with the community in which it operates. What licenses are required? With whom does one deal to obtain them, and so on? These are all factors that take time to learn and usually require face-to-face meetings between the seller and buyer of the firm. The importance of this knowledge transfer is one of the main reasons why many sales of small and medium-sized enterprises are structured with consulting contracts covering the first few months after the transfer.

Most buyers will want the sale structured to ensure that the seller delivers this valuable information. From the buyer's standpoint, the contract should give the seller adequate incentives to provide these introductions and consulting services. In addition to the base price for the tangible assets of the firm, bonus payments to the seller can be created to reward him for performing these functions with the specific form of payment often depending on tax considerations. One approach spreads payment for the business over several years. It can even have clauses giving greater payments if certain sales objectives are reached. This kind of deal structure gives the seller incentives to do everything possible to see that the business continues to be successful. The seller wants to be sure to collect the monies due from the business sale! On the downside, however, if the new buyers go broke anyway and file for bankruptcy, the seller will never receive all the funds due. Another approach would be to buy the business for a lower price and then put the additional value of the human capital into a lucrative consulting contract with the seller—and make the payments conditional on the effectiveness of the transfer. This method helps to assure the buyers that the seller will provide the help necessary to make the business successful for the new owners.

With either approach, both buyers and sellers run the risk of the seller dying and losing the human capital prior to the transaction being fully completed. Therefore, owner/managers of businesses must consider the succession of their businesses to ensure that maximum value is obtained. If a business is going to be willed to the children or taken over by a current employee, the terms should be formally determined well in advance of the retirement of the owner/manager. Those terms can always be changed if the situation changes. If the business is going to be sold to an outsider, the process should start while the current owner/manager is still in a position to provide the help needed for an orderly transfer. The owner/manager usually wants to sell the tangible assets, the name, and as much of his or her human capital as possible to maximize the payout. The start of a maximum value transfer must begin well before the business begins to decline in value, due to the owner/manager being unable to successfully run the operations or to teach the incoming owners how to get the most value from the business.

This succession process is the main reason we place so much emphasis on the going concern concept. When a firm is closely held by an owner/manager, a turnkey sale of an ongoing concern rarely occurs. Almost always, a new business is organized. The purchaser wants to structure the deal to obtain as much of the original firm's goodwill and organization as possible, while protecting his or her investment from unknown past liabilities. Usually, a major portion of the go-forward value is the seller's human capital in the business.

3.3.2 *Strategic Value to the Buyer*

Another consideration in valuing the business is how it is going to be integrated into the buyer's existing business operations. If it is going to be a stand-alone business, the value of the parts would be similar to what the current owners attach to the business. The new owners may change some activities and operations, but it will be basically the same business. Such transfers are referred to as straight *financial valuations*. They are relatively easy for both parties when it comes to valuing the assets and determining a contract for the seller's human capital.

Deals become more complex, however, when the buyers plan to incorporate the acquired operations into their current business. These are *strategic acquisitions* where the purchase is made to obtain specific assets that will be incorporated into the buyers' overall business. The entire firm is purchased to obtain certain items. In strategic acquisitions, the value of the acquired business is likely to be quite different from its value as a going concern. Strategic buyers usually expect substantial synergies, in which the face value of the acquired business has significantly highly multiplier effects when combined with their other operations.

In these cases, contracting with the seller is more difficult. The seller does not usually understand the buyers' total plan for the seller's assets because it is different from his or her own, and buyers are usually reluctant to divulge their strategies. Unfortunately, potential sellers rarely know how their current business assets could be restructured under someone else's management to create greater value. If they did, they might make the changes themselves to reap the gains directly rather than trying to negotiate for their value in a sale of the business. The buyers know what assets will add value to their operations, and that is the basis on which they value the business being acquired. They might be looking for a customer list, a specific geographical territory, production facilities, a brand name, or just a choice location. When someone makes an offer at a price much higher than expected, a seller can probably assume that it is a strategic offer. Still, it is difficult for a seller to perform an accurate strategic valuation without knowing a great deal about the potential buyers.

3.3.2.1 STRATEGIC VALUATION OF AN APPLIANCE BUSINESS

As an example to show this idea, some MBA business students recently brought in an evaluation of an appliance repair business they were considering buying. Their valuation came to just over $500,000. They wanted a second opinion. They presented the same data that the current owner had supplied to them. Because he was planning to sell the business, one would expect his data to be the most favorable that he could present. After analysis, it was determined that a slightly lower discount rate should be used to value this business, leading to a slightly higher $600,000 value. Then they announced that the current owner had been offered $2 million for his business, again based on the same managerial information.

There were no really unique assets in this business that might require separate consideration. Almost anyone can enter with low capital requirements. So why is someone else willing to pay so much? That bidder's strategy was to integrate this business with other similar firms the potential buyer was already operating in neighboring communities. The economies of scale allowed for central scheduling, reduced management costs, and increased advertising efficiency. Still, the question must be asked, Why buy it rather than just starting a new venture in the new location, growing it from scratch and squeezing out the existing firm? By purchasing the firm, the buyers were guaranteed immediate customers and reduced competition because a major potential competitor had been purchased. Finally, no negative reputation would be created, compared to the alternative strategies of destroying a local business or creating a price war to force the competitor to quit. This acquisition would avoid negative future recommendations from potential referrals, such as sellers of appliances. Many very large retailers, such as Wal-Mart and Home Depot, are often accused of such negative tactics in their business growth strategies.

The remaining question is why the buyer offered such a large premium over the financial value of the firm. If two different valuators came up with values of less than a third of what was offered, why not offer just $700,000? A bid that close to other valuations might trigger a revaluation, which would increase the others' initial bid, leading to a bidding war and other messy uncertainties. What about trying a trump bid at $1.2 million? It would have been twice any financial value and would still have saved the bidder $800,000. Two factors enter here.

3.3.2.2 BASES FOR STRATEGIC ACQUISITIONS AND PREMIUM PRICES There may have been other strategic bidders who could use this business, and the bidder was trying to complete the deal before they become aware of the opportunity. By offering such favorable terms, the bidder may have been trying to preempt additional inquiries. On the other side of the table, however, an owner looking for the best possible selling price for a business should carefully advertise its availability to be sure that all potential buyers are aware of the opportunity. The seller is normally best served by an auction with several bidders.

The other logical rationale for such a high offer is that the bidder is using a formula to value potential acquisitions, such as x times the previous year's sales or z times the number of customers. Such formulas discard the current owner's operations and apply the ratios achieved consistently by the acquisitor. For example, U.S. funeral homes have gone through a consolidation of ownership in recent years while maintaining many original locations and names. The buyers look at the number of burials in the previous year and pay a multiple of that number. They assume the local funeral home will be able to generate the same number of clients, but will henceforth operate as a unit of the more experienced firm. As we will discuss in the next chapter, these approaches are often used in valuing closely held firms because buyers lack confidence in the accounting data those closely held firms make available.

The second question that the owner must ask herself when facing an above-estimated value offer is: "What am I missing?" Apparently, the bidder sees ways to create value that the current owner cannot see or exploit.

If the seller is considering selling out anyway, the strategic offer represents a nice windfall and signals a good time to sell. Owners of all kinds of businesses must be aware that changes are coming to their industries in the forms of new and different competitors. Wal-Mart, Home Depot, and other Big Box merchandisers have driven many independent retailers out of business. Can they still maintain their firm's uniqueness in the market place? They might want to sell while the price is still good and the opportunity remains available.

But what if the seller is not considering selling, and the strategic offer just came out of the blue? Keeping a firm in play for possible takeovers serves as a way of assessing its position in a changing market place. Such a position must, however, always be maintained with great discretion to ensure that value doesn't erode through uncertainty transmitted to key employees, suppliers, or customers. Although one hates to get caught undervaluing one's firm, an above-estimate bid should also be a signal to reassess the way the business is being managed. Is the value evident to the bidder something the seller could capture without a sale? What would the current owners have to do differently to collect the excess returns visible to the bidder? Is it a better option to sell or to increase one's investment? If the strategic buyer's opening bid is so far above the expected value, what is the real strategic value to that bidder? To its competitors? Could the price be pushed much higher still?

3.3.3 *Which Components Are the Most Profitable/Valuable?*

Another consideration in valuing the business as a non-going concern is to break it down into parts that are as small as reasonable. Occasionally, owners will find that their profits result entirely from a monopoly position in some aspect of the business. It may be in selling a specific product, buying critical inputs, a choice location, or some other component of the business.

In the mid-1980s, one of our students wrote a business plan for a catering business. It looked like a routine student project, including the inflated profits that so many novice entrepreneurs enthusiastically project. Her projected profits were well above industry averages. When this inflated profit margin was pointed out to her, she replied that as an Iranian national, she could get beluga caviar from her family at prices substantially below the U.S. market levels. At that time, the only two sources were the Soviet Union, which closely controlled its sales, and Iran, whose producers could not legally sell in the United States. That student's near monopoly on caviar would allow her to earn greater profits than those shown in catering industry averages. The comparison she forgot (or rejected) was the possibility of smuggling caviar to established caterers with upscale clients to exploit her monopoly position for even greater profits.

3.4 Market Values for Uniform Parts

When a closely held firm that cannot be classified as a going concern is bought or sold, it is important to review what is being transferred. The value of all the assets must be considered, both tangible and intangible. The intangible assets usually do not appear on financial statements, and when they are carried, their current book or carrying value usually has little relationship to their actual current market value.

3.4.1 *Finding Market Values for Tradable Assets*

The first point in valuation is to use and trust market values for assets wherever markets for such assets exist. Many uniform assets have quoted market values. Some of these values are adjusted daily and quoted on business pages or industrial websites, similar to public stocks. Because the whole process of valuation is one of estimating market values, quoted values for similar assets should be used wherever they are available.

Suppose that you are going to become a securities trader. The price of stock exchange seats, both to purchase and to lease, is listed for the various exchanges on a daily basis. Similarly, if a taxicab business is being pursued, in major cities there is a market for taxi licenses, so their value is easily determined. These markets provide a shortcut to the evaluation process for a major part of these businesses. The other required assets, for example, capital in securities trading or vehicles in the taxicab businesses, have costs that can easily be determined in broader markets (business loans and used cars, in these cases).

One common mistake in this type of valuation is a tendency to view the market prices as wrong and to expect that one's own assets will have a higher intrinsic value. A three-bedroom bungalow in a particular neighborhood in any given year will likely sell for just about the same price as any other three-bedroom bungalow in the same neighborhood that year. There may be minor variations, but the core asset is fairly tightly determined.

The point one must remember is what value the market has placed on these intangible assets; it is based on the expected monopoly value or the capitalized monopoly profits (from operating the business) that the marginal bidder expects to make. Consider operating as a trader where the expected profit just equals your opportunity cost and the required return on the capital invested. What additional amount would you pay to buy or lease a seat? Zero! The same calculation applies to the right to drive a taxicab: if no excess returns are generated after paying all the expenses, a financially rational operator should pay nothing for the right to have a taxi. The only reason that these two assets have value is that their supply is limited. The exchange limits the number of seats, and the government controls the access to taxi medallions. With these totally interchangeable assets, the potential business owner must ask, "How can I use these assets more effectively than their market value?" If a better way to use the assets cannot be identified, then no excess returns can be made in the business.

There are many other such marketable assets. In most states, licenses to sell alcohol are closely regulated. Some states (and in New Jersey, some towns) limit the number of licenses as a function of the population. Most U.S. jurisdictions closely control the location of such businesses, as related to schools, churches, and so on. An entrepreneur starting a business that serves alcohol will need a license and must meet other criteria. Usually, the license can be purchased from another business; the right to use it usually comes along with an annual maintenance fee or tax payable to the issuing government. The other criteria, such as proximity to schools or churches, allowed hours of operations, and so on, must also be met as a condition of using the license.

From totally interchangeable assets, we move to assets where a market value can be approximated from close substitutes. Farm land prices are quoted by the acre as either upland or bottomland. In major cities, office space is quoted by its rental cost per square foot and classified as A, B, or C space for comparative purposes. These serve as benchmarks to value. One must check their quality, location, and so on prior to completing a purchase or lease. The value of land does vary in quality, and one must consider its location relative to other lands being farmed. Similarly, office space varies in the quality of the building, its location, and so on. These assets do, however, give an initial position from which to start a specific valuation, whether buying a business or valuing an existing business. Just as with our three-bedroom bungalow, the variations start from an established comparable base, then adjustments move the specific price up or down, depending on the details.

The major component in these valuations, as in all real estate valuations for that matter, is what prices occurred in recently completed transactions in similar areas with a similar asset. Real estate appraisers look at recent comparable sales. The specific values are then adjusted for different sizes and locations. The real estate valuation business has become more refined only because the actual trade data can be obtained from the Internet instead of manually from the county seat. Because the data used for such estimates are normally those of closing, that is, confirmed sale prices, the newest values are probably still several months older than the current market. Offers and acceptances may be running at different levels, and it takes some time for sales to close and values to be made real. There is always a danger when using valuation data based on anything but confirmed market prices, but there is also danger in using only closing prices. If market prices are changing quickly, old closing prices are not very accurate estimates of current market values.

Under such circumstances, good valuators will make two additional adjustments. In the first instance, they may plot trend lines on a graph, to establish the direction of changes, and so anticipate how the current market will differ from the recent past. They may also make use of less solid data, such as bid and ask prices, to estimate how the gap will close. Used carefully, those modifications can further refine the value estimate, bringing it closer to current market conditions. One must always be aware, however, of changes in trend directions. Estimating the value of dot-com company shares in 2004, based on 1997–99 data, for example, would be seriously misleading.

3.4.2 *Undervalued Assets on the Books*

Real estate is a major asset of many businesses. In many long-established businesses, it also represents a major undervalued asset, because normal accounting practice is to place real estate on the books at its original purchase price. Land is then carried at its original value, and buildings are depreciated over long periods of time. In practice, most real estate rises in market value over time. As Mark Twain once reportedly stated, "Buy land. They aren't making any more of it!" With rising populations and growing economies, real estate has been an appreciating asset in most areas—contrary to standard accounting procedures, however, under which real estate assets are likely to have a declining book value. That leaves a growing gap between book value and market value for the real estate portion of most firms' assets.

In valuing a business, one is tempted to account for this undervalued real estate twice. First, its lower value and hence lower depreciation creates a larger projected profit, compared to invested capital, when valuing the firm as a going concern. Then you might think, "Well, I have this grossly undervalued asset, which should be adjusted to its current market value." Such an additional adjustment would count the undervaluation twice, once from greater profits and again from adjusting the asset to market value. This error would produce an inflated value for the business.

When considering a going concern value, the only time such an adjustment can be undertaken is when the asset is not used in the direct operations of the business. An unused warehouse or the owner's condo in Florida, if they were still carried on the company's books, would be examples of this kind of asset.

A business might also own a prime location that allows for greater sales, greater profits, and hence a greater value. In valuing the business as a nongoing concern, one must be careful not to include this value twice. Remembering the realtors' slogan—"location, location, location!"—it is easy to think that this benefit should be accounted for in valuing the business. But the locational premium is usually addressed when the specific asset itself is valued. The same argument is true with rented property. There, the landlord is likely going to charge a higher rent to obtain what he sees as his part of the advantage of the prime location.

3.5 Valuing the Nonuniform Tangible Parts

Assets are the easiest to value accurately where established markets exist for them. Such assets, not surprisingly, are the easiest ones to borrow against because lenders can readily assess their collateral value. (If need be, they can sell the repossessed collateral, perhaps even more easily than the owners can.) Unfortunately, most assets in a business are more difficult to value, but these items should not be overlooked. Furthermore, it is important to split a firm's assets into specific parts, rather than just lump them as goodwill value (intangibles) and tangible assets. Important assets include the obvious tangible assets. They also include such intangibles as brand name, store name, customer lists, organization, and possibly business goodwill in general. These intangibles result from years of providing goods or services and promoting these items, processes that give recognition value to a firm's name. These assets are much more difficult to value.

3.5.1 *Value Estimated as Cost to Duplicate*

Although no direct market comparisons exist, the key factor in valuing these assets is still a market concept.

WHAT WOULD IT COST SOMEONE TO DUPLICATE THE ASSET? Only if the asset is truly unique does the question change to how much monopoly value or excess returns can be obtained from this asset. An owner/manager can never charge more than it would cost for the new business to obtain the assets from other sources or, in the case of intangibles, to develop them directly. A firm might be forced to charge less if traditional vendors offer additional services, such as product guarantees. When selling a business that includes these assets, it is difficult to credibly extend a guarantee, because the new owners are unlikely to accept the constraints imposed by the previous ones.

One advantage enjoyed by sellers of such assets is that it may take buyers a long time to duplicate them. Reputations, long-established credibility, durable brand names, intellectual property—these things all take time to develop. If the buyer sees an immediate need for the asset, she may pay a premium to get quick access. Without some of these assets, potential users may miss market opportunities. In such cases, buyers may be willing to pay a significant portion of the incremental profit they can obtain if they can use the specific asset. Such situations reflect the strategic value of the asset to the buyer.

The idea of market-based values is fine conceptually, but it does not produce a value to place on some specific assets. Some commonsense ideas must be remembered in considering what values to expect for the various assets of a business. These values must always be tied to a market concept because the potential buyers of a business as a non-going concern or as those looking for specific parts are presumed to make economically rational decisions. They will not pay more than they have to, and if they can get an asset cheaper elsewhere, they will.

3.6 Intangible Assets

Intangible assets include anything of value, other than fixed assets or marketable securities, that a firm has developed or purchased over its years in business. This interpretation is much broader than what is usually identified on financial statements as intangibles. It includes product image, name recognition, production processes, trade secrets, intellectual property, business processes, customers, and organization. Similar to specific tangible assets, their value is what it would cost a buyer of the business to duplicate them after starting a new business. That cost might bear little relationship to the cost the current owner incurred to develop these intangibles. Many of these items, such as customer loyalty, are specific to the individual running the business. They may have a lower value to a buyer than to the current owner, as customers realize that a new business has been created and their loyalty is diminished.

3.6.1 *What Is a Customer Worth?*

One asset sold with most businesses is the current roster of customers. For the buyer, purchase of the customer lists does not mean that future sales are guaranteed, but it does mean that the buyer should have a reasonable chance of maintaining those customers.

What is such an asset worth to the buyer of the business? The best way to begin thinking about these fundamental questions is to estimate the present value of the future contribution (sales minus direct costs) that those customers can be expected to generate for the business. Obviously, this is impossible to measure all the way into the future. Some customers will grow and purchase more. Others will go out of business. Still others will take their business elsewhere. Even so, the chance to sell once to an existing customer is worth something, compared to starting from scratch to develop sales.

In practice, two additional sales is a good estimate of what a carried-forward customer should be worth to a new owner. After two sales, we might say that the new business has developed its own relationship with that customer. Therefore, if the average customer purchases on a monthly basis, two months of net sales would be a good estimate of the value of current customers. If those customers have few choices available to them, the multiple might be higher. Conversely, if the market is intensely competitive and other firms will make a strong effort to get those customers to switch, a lower multiple may be more appropriate.

The second part of the analysis is easier. The average contribution percentage should be estimated without too much difficulty. If net sales, minus direct costs, average one-third of gross sales, and customers purchase monthly, the value of the customers would be $[(2/12) \times 1/3]$ or 5.6% of annual sales.

This approach to valuation is most prevalent in valuing small professional practices. When a doctor, dentist, or lawyer gets ready to retire and sell a practice, the only real value is the current customers. The new person gets one or two chances to prove himself before the customers (patients) will look elsewhere for services. The general rule is to value professional practices at one year's receipts (gross sales), which, with two trips to the dentist per year, works out the same as that just recommended.

3.6.2 *Alternative Costs: Building a Business from Scratch*

For a comparison, the option of building the business from scratch is considered.

3.6.2.1 GROWING VERSUS STATIC MARKETS Two factors must be considered: industry growth and size of the market. If the location in which the new owner plans to operate is a growing market or the industry is growing, there is little reason to pay a premium for someone else's customers. A new owner can easily attract new customers. If the overall market area is large, another person can move into the field without upsetting the competition. If the market is expanding rapidly, an additional supplier will not cause problems. In smaller markets, such as rural areas and small towns with normal growth, the market must be checked carefully. A market that supports three dentists quite well may leave four dentists all below their break-even points. These situations should also be remembered when selling a business. If it is priced too high, potential buyers will just build their own businesses.

LARGE, GROWING MARKET

Year 1: 8 suppliers, market value = 100; average firm has 100/8 = 12.5 customers

Year 2: 9 suppliers, market value = 110; average firm has 110/9 = 12.2 customers

Year 3: 9 suppliers, market value = 121; average firm has 121/9 = 13.4 customers

SMALL, STATIC MARKET Assume each supplier can serve 95 customers; break-even is 80.

Year 1: 3 suppliers, market = 300; average firm has 100 customers: excess demand

Year 2: 4 suppliers, market = 300; average firm has 75 customers; all firms losing $$

3.6.2.2 THE VALUE OF CUSTOMER HABITS All businesses have customers, but many, such as retail stores, do not have established or specific customers. In these situations, the value is not so much specific clients but the business name, image, and location that have value. Customers are used to shopping at this location for the product. For someone entering the business, these established habits make initial sales easier for the new business. The current owner/manager should realize this and value the name and image of the business being sold. Similar to where specific customers exist, about six months of contributions should be considered a good estimate of the value of the current name and image.

A potential buyer of the business must check on the average size of sales and the margins being generated. It is quite possible that in anticipation of selling, the departing owner/manager pursued smaller accounts or cut margins to attract sales. It may be very hard to tell these things from a simple examination of a company's books. After all, small firm accounting methods are usually quite poor. Potential buyers must carefully check the average size of sales and try to estimate the recent margin on goods sold. Falling margins and rising sales make it apparent that relatively unattractive sales were pursued to boost the gross revenues line prior to selling.

3.6.2.3 ORGANIZATION MEANS TIME SAVINGS The last type of intangible being purchased with most small firm is the organization. This asset could almost be thought of as the going concern value—except that a new firm is being started. It takes time to fully organize a new firm. Buying an existing firm greatly reduces that time. Taking on the staff and organization of the previous firm creates three types of savings. The most obvious is the opportunity cost of the owner/manager. Suppose that it is $60,00/year. If buying an existing business can save six months of organizational time, then it is worth $30,000.

We can apply a similar treatment to the capital that has to be invested prior to earning returns. With the purchase of the existing organization of the prior firm, returns will occur earlier. The new firm's capital need not all be invested at once; still, the savings might be three months' worth. If the firm must earn 12% a year on its investment of $600,000, that is, earning $72,000, then this savings is worth $18,000.

Finally, the costs of supporting and training employees until they are productive at their jobs must be considered. Assume that two months can be saved in getting workers up to speed by taking over an existing business with its workforce intact. With a projected payroll of $180,000 a year, $30,000 would be saved. (If the current workforce is rigid and inefficient, however, this item could be reversed into a net cost as the existing workers are retrained or replaced.)

Putting all three savings together, this example yields an additional value of $78,000 to the new business, arising from taking over the ongoing organization of the predecessor firm.

3.7 Liquidation Considerations

Most small, closely held businesses should be valued five ways:

- Strategic acquisition
- Going concern
- Transfer of assets to a different going concern
- Orderly liquidation
- Fire-sale liquidation

In this chapter, we've been concerned primarily with the third and fourth situations. The third model treats the existing firm as a package of assets that can be transferred to someone operating a similar business. The fourth model for valuation should be that of an orderly liquidation when the business is not worth continuing, and the assets will be sold to firms using them in substantially different businesses. Such liquidations have to be carried out in an orderly fashion to ensure that the maximum asset value is recovered. This section reviews some additional ideas to remember in the valuation of a potential liquidation.

A closely held firm should always be valued on an exit basis whenever a valuation is undertaken. This principle is particularly important when undertaking a going concern valuation to determine the value to its current owners of continuing with the business. When the firm is worth more in liquidation than as a going concern, it is time to seriously consider liquidating the business. That move would increase wealth, because it would sell the assets to other people who find them more valuable than do the current owners. In modern contingent claims analysis, this is the *put* value of the business.

Two points should be remembered when viewing this "in-the-money put option." One idea might be that the owners could sell the business to someone else at a higher price. Remember that the maximum that rational buyers will pay is what it would cost them to reproduce the business on their own. Further, they must project a positive value in the future greater than what they pay for the assets. Unless they have a different approach to bring to the business or have a much lower opportunity cost, they will see the firm as no more profitable under their ownership than it is under the current owners, and will be unwilling to pay more than a liquidation value.

The second idea is to consider the current owner's satisfaction from owning and operating this business. If it is just a job, there is a definite incentive to liquidate. On the other hand, if this business is the owner's life and provides her with such vital intangible benefits as recognition in the community, power over employees, and so on, then she might continue to run the firm even though it is worth more in liquidation. The owner's additional utility in economic terms (or satisfaction, in plain English) must be considered along with the wealth calculation. Philosophically, one should make decisions to maximize one's own happiness, which is usually a combination of many factors: wealth, business position, family, and so on. By understanding the value of the business in the different exit strategies, however, we can at least measure the cost of continuing in the business. That knowledge allows us to make better informed decisions about whether or not that cost is worth the other benefits of ownership.

3.8 Tempting Valuation Shortcuts

There are several tempting shortcuts in this valuation work, but each has its hazards.

3.8.1 *Adjustments to Book Value*

There are many factors to consider in the process of valuing a business as the sum of its assets. It is tempting to start with the firm's accounting book value and adjust the obviously undervalued assets (usually the depreciated buildings). After all, does not this represent the value put into and retained in the business? It is true, at least in a book value/accounting way; the problem is that it does not accurately represent the current value of the business. This commonly used approach—starting with book value and making a few adjustments—can give extremely inaccurate values, possibly causing one to sell a business for much less than it is worth. One could also possibly sell it for more than it is worth, but only if the buyer erroneously relies on such values—and that could lead to expensive, long-term litigation.

When addressing the accounting (book) value of a closely held firm, consider first the situation of a going concern valuation. In that case, the book value will equal the market value only when two conditions are met. First, the accounting values correctly measure the value of the assets. This principle means there has been no inflation since the assets were purchased. Furthermore, there have been no specific price changes. Finally, the depreciation booked against the purchase price of the assets actually equals the decrease in the fixed assets' market value. Second, the business earns just its required rate of return on its current operations or real investment and can expect to earn only that rate in the future and on new investments. Because it is very unlikely that either of these conditions will be met, this tempting shortcut has to be resisted.

3.8.2 *Value as the Sum of Tangible and Intangible Assets*

Now consider the approach taken in this chapter, of valuing the firm as the sum of its assets, both tangible and intangible. Usually, in this situation, a very poor estimate of value will be obtained if one just revalues grossly undervalued assets, such as real estate, to their market values. Have there been any significant price changes since the assets where purchased?

(With inflation of only 3% per year, the historical cost of assets is undervalued by 25% after ten years.) Could someone collect all the receivables? Are the goods in inventory still worth their purchase prices? Does the machinery and equipment actually have a market value similar to its carrying value? Can we approximate the goodwill from an established organization to just equal the discount of having no liquidity from this closely held business? Only when all these questions are answered affirmatively can the book value be used as a good approximation of the firm's value. Otherwise, we need to do a market-based valuation.

When an owner needs to know the value of her business, and she should always have that information available to make correct decisions to maximize wealth, it is important to take the time and incur the expenses to value the business correctly.

3.9 When Book Value Is Not Market Value

"Wow! For years, I've been reading 'book value' on my financial statements and thinking that it should tell me what the business is worth—but knowing that it didn't change when it should and did change when the value probably didn't change." Tom wore the mixed expression of a person who has just found out why something long familiar didn't make sense—without being able to figure out what to do about that.

"I know what you mean," replied Mike. "'Book value' is really only the price we paid for something—whenever we paid for it. Then we take out depreciation every year, but I've never understood why some things depreciate at one rate and other things at another rate—even when they sometimes actually went up in value. Take real estate, for example: even though we know the property has gone up in market value, it gets smaller on our books."

"Exactly. Market value and book value are quite different things." Tom was sure of this.

"So," Mike continued, "if I want to know the market value of my assets, book value is not a very good estimate."

"Right. And those intangible assets really threw me for a loop," Tom admitted. "They aren't even on the Balance Sheet at all. I wish the accounting profession would come up with a set of financial statements that really gives us owners a clear picture of what the business is worth."

"I want something that tells me if the things I'm doing are adding value!" Mike expressed a sentiment common to many business owners.

"Yeah, well, that sounds like wishful thinking," Tom shrugged. "Let's get back to this matter of valuation when the business is not a going concern. I guess we start with the things that are on the books, then add the things that don't show up on the books, then try to figure out what the market value of each one is. That would give us a baseline, a minimum value of the business as a pile of assets."

"Yeah, I think that's right," Mike agreed. "Then we can use that set of values as our bottom line for equity purposes, kind of like knowing what cash is already in the bank. It may take a while to get it out, but we can be pretty sure that we have at least that value available."

Tom saw the next step: "Then we can use those baseline values to estimate whether changes we make will increase or decrease the overall value of the business."

"You've got it!" Mike exclaimed. "After that, we can see if the other things we are doing create enough extra value to get us out of the not-a-going-concern range, turning the business into something for which someone would pay a premium, to get those intangibles all working together."

"All right, so this not-a-going-concern valuation is like a worst-case scenario," Tom declared. "We need to know what that is, so we know what the bottom-end valuation is—and so we have clues about how we can avoid that fate, how we can make our companies worth more than just their fire-sale asset values."

4

Valuation of a Going Concern

4.0 What Makes a Business a Going Concern?

One evening, as Mike's boat swung gently at anchor in a quiet bay, the friends picked up their conversation about managing the value of their businesses.

"So, Mike, I think I understand this stuff about doing both kinds of valuation—going concern and not," said Tom. "We need to know what our businesses are worth both ways, so we can make sure we are maximizing their value."

"Yup, and that depends a lot on the markets into which we'd be selling the firm—or its assets," responded Mike. "As we've been learning about this, I've also realized that I don't really know much about the different kinds of buyers who might be interested in the firm. That's something I'm going to start thinking about. It may be time for me to open one of those 'strategic ideas' files you talk about!"

Contemplating the sunset unfolding in the western sky, Tom and Mike savored their drinks and thought about the kinds of markets each might face.

"You know, I do understand that it depends on how we build the companies, on the kinds of value we build into them. But I'm still sometimes confused by the way those two factors fit together—the external markets and the internal value." Tom looked uncomfortable, despite the glorious setting for their discussion. "No matter what value we build into the firm, it'll still be just assets for sale unless we find the right market, the right buyer."

Mike thought about that for a moment before responding. "I'm not sure it's either that simple—or that depressing," he eventually replied. "Maybe we need to learn more about the "going concern" side of things, so we can see where that value is being created."

"Sounds good to me!" Tom exclaimed. "Let's call the Professor and see if he'll come out to the Club for lunch next week. He seems to have quite an appetite for Frederico's Blue Plate specials! And I have a feeling we've still got a lot to learn about this valuation stuff."

GOING CONCERN VALUATIONS Let's proceed on the assumption that our closely held firm has qualified as a going concern. Now we need to know how to value it. This chapter and the next develop the basic concepts for valuing a going concern. That process has two parts—the firm's present ability to produce financial returns, and its future ability if some things change. This chapter considers the value of the firm's ongoing operations or the value of its current ability to generate cash flows. The next chapter considers the value of its growth opportunities or the value of its inherent opportunities for growth with new investments.

Conceptually, these parts of the valuation process are the same whether the firm is a large, publicly traded firm or a small closely held one. The ideas presented in chapter 2, such as paying greater salaries to avoid double taxation or extra perks to obtain tax deductions—perks of the private owner—merely make it more difficult to get a correct estimate for the value of a closely held firm. They make a valuator work harder, but they don't change the principles of valuation.

The firm's going-concern value will be developed from two different but equivalent approaches:

- Net present value of future free cash flows
- Capitalized value of current operations

The value of a firm is the present value of future excess cash flows to the owner/managers, net of their estimated opportunity cost.

This formula is equivalent to the present value of future expected dividends from the public firm.

The value of current operations will also be shown to be the firm's current operations' capitalized value without new investments.

Before we actually start valuing a going concern, we must sort out clearly what we are going to undertake. We must determine what is meant by a *going concern valuation.* Once that is done, an estimate of the value of the firm's current operations can be developed. The key result is that the reinvestment rate has no affect on value—as long as future investments earn just the required rate of return. That is the situation for most mature firms. The firm's value is the present value of its expected excess cash, without regard to whether that cash is paid out or reinvested. We end this chapter with a discussion on how to measure "excess cash" values correctly.

The next chapter addresses the situation where a firm has future investment opportunities that earn a rate of return greater than the required rate. Those "excess return" opportunities will increase a firm's value.

4.1 Valuation Process: Cash Flows, Timing, and Risk

Conceptually, the real value of anything is how much someone is willing to pay for it. With an ongoing firm, the amount someone is willing to pay depends (in part) on the future benefits the firm is expected to produce. Investors shift their savings into new business investments because they expect those investments to perform better than their current investments. The financial value of those new investments can be estimated as a function of

- cash flows the firm is expected to generate from them,
- the timing of those cash flows, and
- the risk of not receiving the expected payoffs.

4.1.1 *Cash Flows, Not Profits*

In the case of a public firm, its cash flows will be converted into either dividends or retained earnings. Either increased dividends or increased retained earnings will raise the value of the firm, lifting its stock price and resulting in capital gains for its shareholders. With a closely held firm, *dividends* take on a broader definition. They also include excess wages, perks, and so on—that is, *value*—that the owner may draw from the business. In both cases, however, it is the cash flows, not the profits, that determine value. Only cash can be used to pay dividends or excess wages and benefits. Only retained cash can be used to undertake additional investments that are necessary to implement growth opportunities. While it is true over the long run that a high correlation exists between profits and cash flows, it is the cash flows that create the value.

4.1.2 *Timing of Cash Flows*

To value expected cash flows, we must also consider *when* they will arrive. To account for the different time periods in which the cash will be received, future flows are all discounted to the same valuation date. Because of the *time value of money*, near-term cash is preferred to more distant cash. The rate used to discount a cash flow depends on two main factors:

- the level of interest rates in the external economy and
- the risk of not receiving the cash.

4.1.3 *Perceived Risk*

Investors do not invest in risky stocks, or entrepreneurs in their own businesses, to earn just the same rate offered by a highly secure and dependable government bond. They expect greater rewards in return for putting their money at greater risk.

Given the choice, most people would prefer to receive a certain $1 million, rather than flip a fair coin with a $0 or $2 million payoff—even though most people might think that the expected value (EV) is identical.

$$\text{EV} = (\text{sum at risk}) \times (\text{probability of the return})$$
$$\text{EV1: } \$1{,}000{,}000 \times 100\% = \$1{,}000{,}000$$
$$\text{EV2} = \text{sum } [(\$0 \times 50\%) + (\$2{,}000{,}000 \times 50\%)] = \$1{,}000{,}000$$

In mathematical terms, the two options are identical, which means rational economic investors should be indifferent between them. In practice, however, most people find the certainty of the first million more valuable that the double-or-nothing option on $2 million. Investment choices involve both arithmetic and psychology.

On the New York Stock Exchange over the past seventy years, the average annual return on the Standard & Poor's (S&P) 500 has been more than 8% higher than the corresponding return on government bonds.[1] Still, in some years the stock market shows large negative returns while government bonds hold steady.[2]

The cost of taking on business risks is incorporated into the typical valuation process rate in the form of a risk discount. As risk increases, investors' required returns also increase. To accommodate that requirement for increased reward, the initial purchase price has to be reduced. This rate is called the risk adjusted discount rate, and it is the rate used to discount future cash flows to the present.

For example, if we establish a value of $100,000 free cash flow (CF) each year, and offer to buy the firm on the basis of three years' CF, then the price would be $300,000—provided there was no future risk. If, on the other hand, we foresee a 10% risk in the first year, a 25% risk against the second year's CF, and a 50% risk that the third year's CF might not materialize, we would have to adjust our valuation as follows:

$$\text{EV} = \text{sum } [(100{,}000 \times (1 - .10)) + (100{,}000 \times (1 - .25)) + (100{,}000 \times (1 - .50))]$$
$$\text{EV} = \text{sum } [90{,}000 + 75{,}000 + 50{,}000]$$
$$\text{EV} = \$215{,}000$$

Chapter 7 will look at how this rate is estimated, but we must note here that this process normally assumes that risk increases at a constant rate over time (unlike the example above, where risk more than doubled in the

[1] Based on long-run averages, 1926–94: Ibbotson Associates, *1995 Yearbook*, and discussions in subsequent Ibbotson Yearbooks. For a more recent version, see Roger Ibbotson and Peng Chen, "Stock Market Returns in the Long Run: Participating in the Real Economy," July 9, 2002, working paper posted at http://corporate.morningstar.com/ib/documents/MethodologyDocuments/IBBAssociates/StockMarketReturns.pdf (accessed December 10, 2006). See also the same-titled version that appeared in the *Financial Analysts Journal*, January/February 2003, available online at: www.allbusiness.com/personal-finance/investing-stock-investments/1032932-19.html (accessed December 10, 2006).

[2] If stocks always produced a higher return, even though they had a large variance relative to bonds, choosing them would not be risky.

second year). Thus, the risk in estimates of a cash flow two periods into the future is usually estimated as twice the risk in estimates of the first period's cash flows. This assumed relationship of risk increasing over time holds whenever a single constant risk-adjusted discount rate is used to determine the present value of future cash flows. With most businesses, it is a reasonable assumption. Once cash flows, timing, and risk are determined, the exact method of valuation can be addressed.[3]

4.2 The Value of Current Operations

Using the expected cash flows, their timing, and their riskiness, the *investment* value of a business' current operations can be derived. If a firm's future projects earn only the required rate of return, this value is unaffected by whether it has historically paid out its cash flow as dividends or reinvested them to create capital gains. Reinvestment at the required rate of return is market-neutral—an investor gets the same return inside the firm or from the outside market. There is no advantage, one way or the other. The valuation relationship follows, starting with some definitions of the factors considered in the valuation process.

C_t = Free Cash Flow expected at end of year t
V_0 = Value today
V_t = Expected value at end of year t
k = Required rate of return
g = Expected growth rate in dividends
C_1/V_0 = Expected free cash flow yield today
$(V_1 - V_0)/V_0$ = Expected capital gains yield, from year 0 to year 1

4.2.1 *Public Companies versus Closely Held Ones*

Before determining the valuation details, the specific differences in the definitions between a public and a closely held firm must be highlighted. With a public firm, the valuation process tries to forecast an appropriate market price, to help investors identify companies that appear to be over- or undervalued by the market. With a closely held firm, the valuation process estimates the firm's value as if it were being sold. This market price can be determined as either the firm's value to its present owners as they are

[3] Alternative approaches separate time and risk. The more general "certainty equivalent" approach to valuation requires a process that is either impossible to solve for a value or the assumption of total separation of risk and time. Either of those assumptions gives an unrealistic view of risk resolution over time for most businesses.

currently operating it, or to potential buyers with changes they might make in its operations.

Although owners of shares in public companies normally receive their investment returns in the form of either dividends or capital gains (or both), owners of closely held firms can choose from a much wider range of benefit types.

4.2.2 *All Financial Benefits Derive from Free Cash Flow*

Regardless of the benefit package they choose for themselves, all owners derive their financially based benefits from *free cash flow*.[4] Hence, to determine what total pot of money is available to purchase those benefits, we have to determine the free cash flow. It is not just today's benefits that are important in valuation, but the whole future stream of benefits. These *dividend substitutes* must be considered in the broad terms of pecuniary benefits being derived each year from the business. In modern finance jargon, this is referred to as the *free cash flow*, available to the owner/managers. Free cash flow is an adjusted cash flow, starting with the full profits from operations, and then deducting the cost of new investments required to maintain or enhance those profits.

What about capital gains or increased value from reinvested earnings? The only reason a rational investor will pay for a greater future value is because greater free cash flows can be expected from the larger future operations. Eventually, the firm must pay out this cash flow to its investors, either as traditional dividends or (more likely with a closely held firm) through excess wages and additional perks. In the case of owners who build their firms with the intention of making their money through the sale of those firms, the cash-out value is still going to be based on the buyer's assessment of the future cash flow potential the founders have created. Thus, even when the current owners do not withdraw their created value through excess wages, the valuation of the firm still follows this format.

The value of a firm can be expressed as the present value of these future benefits.

$$V_0 = \frac{C_1}{(1+k)} + \frac{C_2}{(1+k)^2} + \cdots + \frac{C_T}{(1+k)^T}$$

$$= \sum_{t=1}^{T} \frac{C_t}{(1+k)^t}$$

[4] Ownership can have important nonfinancial benefits, of course. This book focuses on the financial aspects so both buyers and sellers can start from a common base in valuing the financial assets. That shared financial information frees them to assess the value of any emotional or strategic premium, over and above the normal financial merits of a business.

4.2.3 *No Increase in Firm Size: The Mature Firm Base Case*

Valuation analyses always start with a *base case* that assumes the subject is a mature firm with no new investment opportunities, then introduces variations that adapt that assessment ever more closely to the real firm under consideration. This chapter follows the same format. That base case reflects a specific situation where absolutely no worthwhile new investment opportunities exist within that mature firm.

In real business, such situations can occur, and they can be the result of several factors. Many mature firms are in declining industries where not only there is no growth, but it is difficult to even maintain current earnings. In these situations, no additional investments would make sense, because they wouldn't expand the business. Only maintenance investments would be justified, to replace worn-out equipment and keep up the existing performance of the assets. Expected free cash flows in future periods look very much like those the firm is currently producing. Therefore, the value of such a firm is the present value of the current cash flow after maintenance investments—which are expected to be the same each year into the foreseeable future. In mathematical terms, we express this basic valuation equation as

$$\begin{aligned} V_0 &= \frac{C_1}{(1+k)} + \frac{C_1}{(1+k)^2} + \cdots + \frac{C_1}{(1+k)^T} \\ &= \frac{C_1}{k}. \end{aligned}$$

4.2.4 *Constant Expansion*

Now, in real businesses, few owner/managers expect to undertake no new investments and show no expansion. The first step in moving toward a more realistic valuation, therefore, is to modify our base case to reflect a firm that expands through the reinvestment of a constant portion of its earnings each year. Although a steady-state growth situation is not very realistic as a long-term model, it does give a good approximation of the way many firms plan their futures. This approach also produces a value that increases at a constant rate over time when the current dividend is expected to grow at a constant rate over time. These assumptions are reflected in the following formula:

$$\begin{aligned} V_0 &= \frac{C_1}{(1+k)} + \frac{C_2}{(1+k)^2} + \cdots + \frac{C_T}{(1+k)^T} \\ &= \sum_{t=1}^{T} \frac{C_t}{(1+k)^t}. \end{aligned}$$

The growth in future dividends results from the reinvested earnings of previous periods. This perspective shows up in the following formula:

$$C_1 = C_0(1 + g)$$
$$C_2 = C_1(1 + g)$$
$$EV(C_2) = C_0(1 + g)^2.$$

Because the g term is held constant over time in this example, the valuation relationship can be simplified. Both sides of the general valuation equation are multiplied by $(1+k)/(1+g)$. This process shows the value, V_0, as the present value of C_0, the constant growth rate, g, the discount rate, k, and time, leading to

$$\frac{(1+k)V_0}{(1+g)} = C_0 + \frac{C_0(1+g)}{(1+k)} + \cdots + \frac{C_0(1+g)^{t-1}}{(1+k)^{t-1}}.$$

Since we are valuing to perpetuity, t will be a large value. Furthermore, because firms all have finite values, the growth rate, g, must be less than the discount rate, k. (Think about it! If the value increased indefinitely at a rate greater than the rate used to discount back to the present, the value would increase to infinity. Even Amazon.com and Microsoft are valued at less than infinity—although there have been periods where the markets produced changes in the valuation of these companies during which $g > k$ for several years.) The current value of a constant reinvestment firm can thus be expressed as

$$V_0 = \frac{C_0(1+g)}{(k-g)} = \frac{C_1}{(k-g)}.$$

4.2.4.1 CONSTANT GROWTH EXAMPLE To see how value changes over time with constant growth, consider the following simple example: $g = 8\%$; $k = 12\%$; $C_0 = \$1{,}111$. Now we can calculate the current value, dividend (cash) yield, and the expected capital gain. First, the current value for the firm is

$$V_0 = C_0(1+g)/(k-g) = \$30{,}000.$$

The dividend yield that is being provided to the owner/manager can now be calculated. It is the next period's expected dividend, or excess cash flow, over the current value of the firm. (Note: When dividend yields for public firms are reported in the financial press, the stated value is the current dividend per share over the share price.)

$$\text{Dividend Yield} = \$1{,}200/\$30{,}000 = 4\%$$

The expected capital gain equals $(V_1 - V_0)/V_0$. This formula requires us to know the expected value one period from now. Because the dividends will grow at a constant rate, the value at time 1 is just the expected dividend at time 2, over the discount rate minus the growth rate or

$$V_1 = C_2/(k-g) = 1{,}200 \times (1.12)/(0.12 - 0.08) = \$32{,}400.$$

Using this \$32,400 value in the expected capital gains equation, gives

$$\text{Expected capital gain} = (32{,}400 - 30{,}000)/30{,}000 = 8\%.$$

Summing the dividend yield (4%) and the expected capital gain (8%) gives 12%, and that is the required rate of return. There are two ways that owner/managers can get their returns: dividends (or current cash) and capital gains from value growth. The expected values of these components must add up to the required rate of return. The expected value is what the owner/manager today expects will happen over the next year. Rarely, however, will the expected values and actual results be exactly equal. Investments are made on the basis of future expectations, and those are only partly conditioned by past performance.

The value relationships can be better seen through an example that considers the specific cash flows being produced in each period. In this example, after undertaking enough reinvestment to replace worn-out assets, the firm is going to retain 60% of its cash flow, which is its earnings, and pay out the remainder. The growth rate of the firm equals the retention rate times the expected rate of return that the new investments will earn or (Retention Rate × Return on Equity [ROE]) equals the growth rate. For simplicity in this example, the firm will have zero debt. This setup gives the following values:

Required return on equity, $k = 10\%$

Percentage of earnings retained = 60%

Dividend payout ratio = 40%

Value of assets at time 0 = \$1,000

Amount of debt = \$0

Return on new investments (ROE = return on assets [ROA]) = 10%

Using these relationships, table 4.1 now presents the expected profits, dividends, and asset values across time. The opening assets of \$1,000 earn 10% or \$100. Forty percent (\$40) is paid out as excess cash (C_1), and the remainder (\$60) is reinvested. The second period now has \$1,060 in assets, which earn 10% for \$106. Forty percent is again paid out, and the remainder is retained. This process is assumed to continue to perpetuity.

We see that the payouts grow at a rate of (42.2 − 40)/40 or 6% between the first and second years and (44.94 − 42.4)/42.4 also for 6% between the second and third years. We also note that earnings grow at the same 6% rate from \$100 to \$106 and then from \$106 to \$112.36. This progression results from a constant rate being earned on the reinvested cash and a

Table 4.1 No Excess Returns Example

	Year 1	Year 2	Year 3	Year 4
Earnings	\$100.00	\$106.00	\$112.36	\$119.10
Retained (60%)	60.00	63.60	67.42	71.46
Excess cash paid out (40%)	40.00	42.40	44.94	47.64
End-of-year investment	1,060.00	1,123.60	1,191.02	1,263.48

constant portion being reinvested. This growth rate is also the retention portion times the rate of return of reinvested assets ($0.60 \times 0.10 = 6\%$).

This firm can now be valued using the equation for constant growth, giving $40/(0.10 - 0.06) = \$1{,}000$ for its value. This is the same value as its initial assets. This firm has gained no value through reinvesting. If it paid out all of its earnings as dividends, giving a higher initial dividend with zero growth, its value would remain $100/0.10 or $1,000. This identical result occurs because the firm is earning just its required rate of return on the new investments.

Many small business owners find themselves in this position after several years in business. They can expand, but they earn only their required rate of return, which does not increase their firm's value. These firms will add no economic growth or value if they make new investments of this sort. Their owner/managers are equally well off whether they reinvest money in their own firms or pull the money out and have a professional invest it in the stock market for them. In valuing these firms, we do not have to know their future retention rates. All we need to know is the next period's expected free cash flow, which can usually be estimated from the results produced in the last several periods. The following equation shows how this is done:

$$P_0 = \frac{C_0(1+g)}{(k-g)} = \frac{C_1}{(k-g)} = \frac{E_1}{k}.$$

When firms earn just their required rate of return and no more, the relationships can be summarized as follows:

Required Return = ROE = Expected Dividend Yield + Expected Capital Gain.

If and only if the required rate equals ROE (and projected future ROE), then market value of the firm equals book value.[5]

There is no additional wealth-creating value produced by new investments.

The earnings/value ratio is the market capitalization rate (k).

4.2.5 *Excess Returns Earned on Past Investments*

Before we consider the situation where firms earn excess returns on their new investments, we want to consider a situation in which many closely held firms really do find themselves. They earn excess returns on their current investments, but expect to earn only the required rate of return on their future undertakings. These firms start with a unique advantage and earn excess returns from it. However, they are unable to expand the scale of the business to earn those extra returns on future investments.

[5] Note how unlikely it is that these assumptions will ever occur in the natural course of economic activity. Hence, book value will almost never equal market value. For these and many other reasons, book value is not a good starting point for an estimate of market value.

How are these firms valued? They must be treated basically the same as a firm with no excess returns. The only difference is that the value of the initial assets is going to be less than the capitalized value of the current profits. Let us reconsider our original example in table 4.1. Suppose the firm was earning 20% return on invested assets of $500 (ROE = 20%) and expected to continue to earn that rate on all current invested assets. Its new investments, however, earn only the required rate of return, which is 10% in our example. The firm still plans on reinvesting 60% of its earnings. Our initial relationships for future returns and value still hold, giving a current value estimated as follows:

$$V_0 = C_1/(k - g) = \$40/(0.10 - 0.06) = \$1{,}000.$$

Calculated the other way, it also holds that

$$V_0 = E_1/k = \$100/0.10 = \$1{,}000.$$

The value-to-earnings ratio is still 10 or $1/k$ because the firm does not have opportunities to earn excess returns on future investments.

This equivalence is extremely important. The valuator does not need to worry about future reinvestment rates but needs only get an accurate estimate of the firm's expected cash flow for the next period and the corresponding investments required to maintain that flow. With no inflation, the latter should equal the firm's depreciation expense. If this firm decides to increase its retention rate to 80% or drop to 20%, the value of the business will be unchanged, because the future investments all earn only the required return. The performance of the investment vehicle called the firm has not changed, regardless of how much or how little the current owner chooses to reinvest.

What has changed in this example is that the book value of the historical equity no longer equals the market value. An estimate of the *monopoly value* of its initial investments can be made as [E_1/k − book value]. (The terms *monopoly* or *value from excess returns* carry negative implications, so we usually see the alternative term *market value added* [MVA] to describe the same increase in value.)

Valuators who do not read this far can make huge errors. They note that, for the firm that just earns its required return on past investments and expects to earn that rate on future investments, the market value is equal to the book value. Why consider all this fancy capitalization? It is easier to just pull out the accounting books and assign a value. The problem is that firms rarely (if ever) meet those requirements. There are many situations in which a firm is in a declining industry and does not earn even its required return on past investments, let alone on new ones. In those situations, the firm's investment value is less than its equity's book value. A firm will almost never be valued in the market at the same level as its book value. Owners need to know the real value, so they should not trust the estimate represented by book value.

4.2.6 *Firms Earning Below-Par Returns*

We suspect there are many firms earning below-par returns, that is failing to earn their required return on their reinvestments. In declining industries, such as buggy whips in the late nineteenth and early twentieth centuries, reinvestment may sustain a declining level of profitability for some time, but the industry as a whole is doomed. Owners of such companies would fare better financially by pulling their capital out of such businesses and investing in (at least) average areas. Long-term growth firms do this internally—milking the cash cows in mature business units and reassigning the profits into the growing units.[6]

Family fortunes can be dissipated if the inheritors of the wealth creators fail to adapt, fail to reinvest in growth. If they leave the assets to work in areas where the rate of return falls below the required rate, the family's relative wealth will decline.

Many small business proprietors continue to keep their assets tied up in their businesses long after the returns have declined to average or below. This habit is one of the major reasons many small firms sell at such low multiples of their earnings.

4.3 Estimating Future Cash Flows

A firm's future cash flows must be estimated in order to determine its value as a going concern. Unfortunately, the only really accurate technique is to have a mythical crystal ball. It takes extraordinary insight to estimate all the future conditions that might affect sales, costs, and other conditions. This section presents three different aspects of estimating cash flows from operations. First, we discuss the problem of accurately determining the real past cash flows from reported accounting data. Second, we show a way to estimate the new investments necessary to operate the firm in the future and then forecast the effect of those investments on net cash flows in future periods. Finally, realistic estimation factors are considered. In addition, various potential problems or mistakes are discussed.

Knowledge of a firm's industry and competitive conditions must be incorporated into any estimates. These points require specific knowledge that the valuator must have or must get from the owner/managers.

4.3.1 *Converting Reported Profits to Cash Flow*

In the process of running a business, it is really easy to either not learn accounting or to forget some of the key concepts. Plus, accounting reports

[6] In one of the more popular business books of the 1990s, J. C. Collins and J. I. Porras described this concept in their book *Built to Last: Successful Habits of Visionary Companies* (New York: HarperBusiness, 1994). Several years later, R. N. Foster and S. Kaplan showed how uncommon such performance really is, and suggested an alternative set of criteria, based on performance. (See *Creative Destruction: From "Built to Last" to "Built to Perform"* [London: Financial Times/Prentice Hall, 2001]).

have changed over time. This section presents a quick review of the factors to consider when converting a reported net income into a statement of the cash flow being generated by a business' operations. One major difference is that profits (on the income statement) are determined on an accrual basis for all but the smallest businesses. On the other hand, what a valuator needs is the cash flow. It's like a running reconciliation of the firm's checkbook to see what the operations of the firm generate (inflows) and cost (outflows).

The valuator's first objective is to convert the accrual-based accounting profit into the adjusted cash flows generated from operations. The next major adjustment is to subtract the cost of required new investments. The resulting net cash flow values can be thought of as *dividend substitutes*, which represent the financial benefits being derived from the business by the owners. In modern financial jargon, this value is called the *free cash flow*, and it is our best measure of the financial rewards available to owner/managers. It is also the most important datum for potential investors (buyers), since it reflects the best estimate of their likely return on investment.

To derive the adjusted cash flow from operations, we start with the firm's net profits. Then we add back non-cash expenses, primarily depreciation expenses. Next, adjustments are made for timing differences, such as what occurs when the accrual method books an item in one period but the actual cash flow occurs in a different period. The items of interest to us are only those where differences are directly related to operations and the operating cycle.

4.3.1.1 INVENTORY, ACCOUNTS RECEIVABLE/PAYABLE For those readers remembering the cash flow statement from their old accounting classes, the adjusted cash flows from operations appear quite similar to the regular cash flows from operations. They are similar—with the major exception of the handling of inventory and the related assignment of trade credit owed or accounts payable. Investments in inventory are viewed as investment decisions and not just the by-product of ongoing operations. Owner/managers have as direct control over their inventory levels as they do over investments in plant and equipment. Firms can operate with different levels of inventory, and it is a management decision to select a target level to maximize value. As most goods are purchased on trade credit with a lag period before payment, the firm must finance the difference between an inventory coming into the firm's control and its corresponding account payable.

Revenues that have not generated cash are subtracted out, and revenues from the previous period that are finally collected are added back into the cash flow statement. Another way to look at this adjustment is that it recognizes the change in accounts receivable. When receivables decrease, more cash is generated from operations than is reported in revenues, with the difference being added to the cash flow. An increase in accounts receivable would cause the difference to be subtracted from the firm's free cash flow.

As an example of the difference, the accrual method counts some items as revenues before any cash is collected. Selling goods on credit causes revenue to be recognized, in the accrual system, when the goods are shipped, even though the cash is not received until the account is paid. There may be a gap of 30, 60, 90, or more days; some revenues booked under accrual accounting later have to be written off as bad debts when they can't be collected within a reasonable period.

Consider some specific examples. What happens if accounts receivable increase from $100K to $120K during the year? In that situation, more was sold on credit than collected, so the cash flow would be $20K less than the profits. The full amount would have been recognized as accrued profit—but $20K of it would not yet have been collected.

4.3.1.2 PREPAID EXPENSES A similar adjustment is made for other current assets, such as prepaid expenses. Prepaid items, such as rent, would be subtracted from profits when paid, and the resulting future rent expense would be added back into profits.

Changes in liabilities that result directly from operations have the opposite affect. An increase in accrued wages would be added to the reported profits because it represents an increase in wages owed to employees but not yet paid; the cash is still in the firm's possession. A similar adjustment would be required for an increase in accrued taxes. When these items decrease, the change in value owed is subtracted from the cash flows.

4.3.1.3 DEPRECIATION Suppose the business also incurs $200K of depreciation expenses on its fixed assets. These expenses lower the reported profits and taxes but do not reflect real cash outlays. They need to be added back to the profits to determine the cash flow from operations.

But won't those assets need replacement when they wear out? Yes, but that is an investment decision. Those assets are very unlikely to be replaced with identical assets. For example, this book was written on a series of computers, not a typewriter. As authors, we might have depreciated our old typewriters, but we wouldn't have bought new ones—we switched to computers. The replacement assets are not the same as the depreciated ones. (Chapter 6 deals with specific techniques for measuring the replacement of fixed assets, with particular emphasis on price changes.)

4.3.1.4 THE COST OF MANAGEMENT The valuation process to this point has been similar to determining the cash flow from operations for any firm. However, to value the closely held firm, additional adjustments must be made to determine what the business itself is worth. One must undo any adjustments the owner/managers have made to maximize their personal benefits and minimize their taxes, since those choices cannot be presumed to apply to a different owner. The wages and additional benefits paid to the current owner/managers are added back into the cash flows, as discussed in chapter 2 (refer to table 2.1), because they could be reassigned by a new owner. After that, the opportunity cost of hiring an independent professional manager is subtracted, based on comparable market costs for managers of similar firms. It is rare to find a closely held firm where these two values are even approximately equal.

4.3.1.5 CORPORATE TAXES Finally, the cash flows must be adjusted for corporate taxes. Most likely, the business will be organized as a Subchapter S corporation or as an LLP to protect the owners from personal liability exposure. Those forms of organization also minimize the owners' joint personal and business taxes. The firm's profits should have already been recalculated by adding back the owner/manager's wages and benefits, and subtracting the market-based costs of a professional manager. In the same manner, any corporate taxes paid in accordance with the current owner's statement of accounts should be added back to the pretax profit. Then, using this revised statement of profit before tax, the appropriate corporate taxes can be calculated. The cash flows for an equivalent public firm can now be calculated as the original cash flows, plus the owner/managers' known wages and benefits, plus any paid corporate taxes, minus the estimated professional manager's cost, and minus the recalculated corporate taxes.

4.3.2 *Estimating New Investment Costs*

The modified cash flow analysis represents the most recent year's cash flow. What we need, however, is the amount of excess cash that is available for the owners. From this cash flow, the net cost of planned new investments is subtracted. The net cost is the amount of the investment cost minus any debt financing that we expect to use. Suppose the firm plans on financing those investments with 30% borrowed funds. When investments are undertaken, the firm provides only 70% of the amount, and that is subtracted from the adjusted cash flows from operations.

Another way to expand is to increase inventory. Let's assume that additional inventory is purchased on 30 days credit. If the additional inventory is expected to turnover every 90 days, the firm must finance two-thirds of the increased inventory, based on the 90 days, minus the first 30 days financed by its suppliers with trade credit.

The actual net amounts required for new investments can be estimated two ways. First, the firm can estimate the actual cash flows related to debt repayment and new asset expenditures. The actual repayment schedule from existing debts is known. It starts with the adjusted cash flow from operations, subtracts those specific repayments required, and then adds back the proceeds of additional borrowing. Next, the amount of total new investments must also be subtracted.[7] This process gives the free cash flow

7 An alternative calculation method is to subtract just the portion of the investment drawn from internal sources, ignoring the principal of borrowed debt, and accounting only for the interest and fees on that debt. We think it makes more sense (and is less likely to induce errors) if the principal is taken into cash, and the principal, interest, and fees are then deducted from it.

estimate adjusted for the net new investments that equity must finance. The accounting cash flow statement is conceptually identical to the net cash flows prior to any dividend payments: cash flow from operations, plus any financing adjustments for borrowing, minus the required new investments.

The second approach is to project just the new growth in the business as the earlier examples did. The required new investments, minus current depreciation expenses, are multiplied by (1 minus the portion of debt financing) to get the net amount that retained funds must finance. This net required investment amount is then subtracted from the firm's adjusted earnings—which is the adjusted cash flow from operations as before, except the depreciation expense is not subtracted out. It implicitly assumed that the amount scheduled for repayment will be reborrowed as part of the borrowing for the new additional investments and a replacement investment level equal to the depreciation expense is necessary to maintain the current operations. With this approach, no direct adjustment is required for the scheduled debt repayments. The adjusted cash flow statement is easier to solve with this approach and, for firms maintaining a constant portion of financing with debt, it gives identical results.

The preceding discussion addresses that portion of the firm's investment activity that is required to maintain its historical levels of productivity. Optional investments, which could enhance the firm's growth potential, will be addressed in the next chapter. The methodologies are identical.

4.3.3 *Special Considerations for Estimating Actual Values*

Much of the discussion to this point has been artificially constrained to establish key principles. For example, we have worked largely with a scenario that assumes a firm has no new growth investment prospects that would produce excess returns. In this section, we remove some of those constraints to show how estimated values would actually be determined, making our scenarios more realistic.

The value of a firm now can be expressed as the present value of the future dividends it is expected to generate. Two key points must be remembered. First, when the firm is earning just the required rate of return on new investments, the value of the business is independent of the payout/retention ratio. That is the situation with many established businesses. Most businesses are started to fill voids in a market, and many earn excess returns at the beginning. Over time, however, because of market size and competition, these special opportunities peter out. When that point is reached, it makes no difference to the current value of the firm what level of future investment is undertaken.[8] If the owner reinvests at the required rate of return, the future

[8] We are ignoring, for the moment, tax avoidance that would encourage reinvestment, and portfolio diversification strategies that would encourage pulling money out of the business.

value of the firm will increase at the expense of his or her non-firm assets. The current value of the firm will, however, remain unchanged, because those reinvestments earn only the required return.

4.3.3.1 ACCOUNTING FOR GROWTH: THE PROJECTED PROFIT APPROACH TO VALUATION Second, remember that, for the closely held firm, *dividend* is a rather general term for the *net free cash flow* (NFCF) being generated after investments required to maintain the business. For prior years, this NFCF value is calculated by adding back the owner's salary and benefits, subtracting what a professional manager would be paid, and determining the after-tax value on the result. Except when no funds are being retained for increased future investments, one cannot just average the previous three to six years of known results and use that value for the projected upcoming year. The growing size of the business, based on reinvestments, should increase the expected cash inflows from future periods.

To handle the problem of a firm's changing size, we need to estimate the average rate of return that will be earned in each future period. This rate is multiplied by the level of investment at the beginning of the relevant period to get the projected profits for the period. In most situations, the best estimate is the rate that has been earned on the firm's invested capital in the most recent periods. One must be careful about overextending that history, however. When the firm is earning an excess return on its original investment, but not on recent expansion investments, the average will be biased upward. This estimating method defines the ROE as

$$\text{ROE}_t = \text{Profit}_t/\text{Equity}_{(t-1)}.$$

The ROE is the profits earned during the time period, divided by the related investments in the previous period. These values should be estimated over enough years to get a representative estimate for the firm's normal expected return. To consider both good times and bad, an extended period, such as five to six years, should be used. Other things being equal, the average value during that period might then be used to predict the next period's profits.

$$(\text{Expected Profit})_t = (\text{average ROE}) \times \text{Equity}_{t-1}$$

We know, however, that the average return over a five-year period is just that—the average return. It is not necessarily the best estimate of what future returns will be, although it is a good starting point. A better estimate would be produced by using the owner/manager's knowledge of those underlying years to explain the variations that occurred, then selecting an adjusted average return based on the most likely conditions for the coming years. If a couple of those years reflect a recession, where the coming year is not expect to be recessionary, then the ROE should be adjusted to more normal conditions. Similarly, if the ROE in one year reflects a local disaster that is not likely to recur, the ROE estimate should reduce the emphasis of that unusual circumstance. By using the intelligence available, we can produce a modified set of estimates that reflect our best assessment of the extent to which the previous five years will look like the next year.

$$(\text{Projected Profit})_t = (\text{expected ROE}) \times \text{Equity}_{t-1}$$

Using this approach, we can restate the value of the business as the next period's projected profits, divided by the required rate of return. There's no need to consider reinvestment rates or growth prospects because they have no effect on value when excess returns are not expected.

$$\text{Value} = (\text{Projected Profit})/(\text{Required Rate of Return})$$

4.3.3.1.1 *Maintenance Reinvestments and Constant Profit Assumptions* A couple of problems emerge from this estimation approach. The first is that earnings or profits—and not cash flows—are suddenly the focus. Why the change? This value for projected profit is actually the adjusted cash flow, with the depreciation expenses subtracted. A mature firm, with no growth opportunities, must still undertake some investment; its assets wear out and must be replaced. Remember: A constant future profit stream is being projected. With no replacement of worn-out assets, cash flow would decline. Although this negative growth rate with the higher initial cash payments would give the same value, it is easier and more realistic in most situations to consider the constant profit stream. And that means we have to build in the reinvestments required to maintain that profit-making capability as our base case.

With no increase in the firm's size projected, its investment in working capital should stay the same. Assuming for the moment that depreciation expense equals the replacement cost of assets, then the net cash flow from operations, after reinvestments, is the same as the profit. (Chapter 6 deals with adjustments to the reported depreciation expense to get the real level of depreciation. A 3% inflation rate can cause a big difference in value for capital-intensive firms, and chapter 6 shows how to deal with that.)

4.3.3.1.2 *Inaccuracy of Reported Equity Values* The second potential problem arises from widespread inaccuracy in the stated equity values of closely held firms. Their financial statements are rarely created using generally accepted accounting principles (GAAP). Even with GAAP-based reports, the recent Financial Accounting Standards Board (FASB) requirement to capitalize future retirement benefits,[9] for example, makes firms' reported equity values extremely small. When we divide that shrunken estimate of equity into the profits, we get a very large ROE value. That ROE figure is an estimate of the next period's profits, based on prior period equity and the additions to retained earnings. Consequently, the estimated value of the projected profit is too high.

[9] See www.fasb.org/pdf/fas36.pdf for further information.

Consider the following example, using one period of returns. Because of accounting changes, the firm's reported book equity is \$400K at the beginning of the last period and it earned \$160K in the most recent period. This gives an ROE of 40%: (\$160K/\$400K). The firm retains \$100K, so its projected profits become [(\$400K + \$100K) × 0.40] or \$200K. Now suppose the firm's reported equity should have been \$800K, giving a ROE of 20% (\$160K/\$800K). The projected profits should be [(\$800K + \$100K) × 0.20] or \$180K.

4.3.3.1.3 *Substituting Return on Assets* Whenever problems are thought to exist with the reported equity value, a good alternative is to project the next period's profits from the total assets. The average return on assets (ROA) for the same time period is calculated as the same profit value over the beginning-of-period assets. In the example, suppose total assets were \$1,600K. That situation would produce an ROA of \$160K/\$1,600K or 10%. Now, let's say the firm retains \$100K and over the year had other liabilities increase another \$100K. That scenario produces a projected profit of (\$1,600K + \$100K + \$100K) × 0.10 or \$180K.

$$\text{Expected Profit}_t = (\text{average ROA}) \times \text{Assets}_t$$

Accounting rules and leverage are going to have much less effect on this ROA approach to projecting the next period's profits. Although conceptually not as correct, for most closely held firms it may give better value estimates.

4.3.3.1.4 *Using Return on Sales* When firms rent or lease most of their assets, the ROA approach can sometimes generate problems similar to those encountered when using ROE estimates. A couple of recent good years can give extraordinarily high estimates of the ROA which, with any growth in assets, gives a large increase in the next period's projected profits. Using *return on sales* (ROS) is an alternative approach that can be reasonably accurate in such situations. To use it, the projected average gross margin over the past several years is calculated. This figure is then multiplied by the projected sales level.

$$\text{Expected Profit}_t = (\text{average Gross Margin}) \times (\text{Expected Sales})_t$$

This technique assumes that the turnover on total assets stays constant or assets increase at the same rate as the sales growth. The advantage is sales or total revenue values are usually more accurately reported numbers, compared to equity or total assets, for closely held firms.

4.4 Complications in Estimating Future ROE Values

The previous cash flow estimates are correct only in the simple valuation context. In most situations, additional adjustments must still be made to get more accurate estimates for the future ROE value. These adjustments are based on factors, known (or reasonably expected) at the time of valuation, that will affect the firm. The previous section dealt with changes occurring over the period prior to the forecast period. The present section is broken into three areas. They show how to incorporate known future real changes, consider nonrecurring items, and measure returns despite changing accounting rules.

4.4.1 *Incorporating Known Future Changes*

In using the firm's actual past returns as predictors of its future performance, the estimated financial returns must be adjusted for known changes that will affect future cash flows. One cannot just take the past estimates and then project the future values without considering the influences facing the business. These factors include changes that are known to occur and may result from specific government actions, for example, or the expiration of major contracts, leases, or other significant sustained transactions. Fortunately for business valuators, the process to enact public sector changes is public, and implementation is usually quite lengthy, so we can see them coming and adjust accordingly. No one should be surprised when they finally happen. Although not necessarily favorable to business values, their direct effects are relatively easy to quantify in the valuation process. Changes in the competitive environment and the overall demand for a firm's goods or service are more difficult to predict and usually "sneak up on you." Examination of those kinds of changes is postponed until the next chapter.

Many changes will affect almost all firms in a similar fashion. Tax changes are an obvious example since they change the portion of cash flows that the government claims. A tax increase or decrease may have real affects on future operating decisions of the firm. Consider the following football analogy. By moving the goalposts 10 yards from the goal line to the back of the end zone, football organizers changed teams' field goal strategies in a predictable way. The ball must be closer to the goal line before a team attempts a field goal, as it must be kicked 10 yards farther. Moving the ball 10 yards closer to the goal line will encourage more teams to try for the higher valued touchdown, so fewer points will be scored by field goals. In business, suppose the government changed the depreciation schedules to require a longer time to depreciate assets. That modification would be create a predictable valuation change. The cost of owning real capital would increase, and the present value of projected cash flows would be smaller for a given tax rate. If such a change had just occurred or was imminent, the past rates of return should be adjusted to reflect the new tax reality.

What is the macro-effect of such a change? The resulting higher capital costs are going to affect all businesses by increasing their costs. In the long run, with higher production costs for all firms, the prices for their products will increase. The tax increase will normally be passed on to consumers, who must pay for the higher priced goods.[10] Thus the decrease in a specific firm's value from the higher taxes, while still significant, will not be as great as initial projections would have shown. Consumers will be paying a portion of the tax through higher prices. A reduction in depreciation affects capital-intensive industries the most.[11]

Other types of changes affect only specific industries or in some cases only specific firms. Many of these examples deal with highly regulated businesses in entertainment and alcohol sales. Take, for example, a time in the late 1970s when the legal drinking age was eighteen in most of the United States. Many bars were established to attract these young people. Then the legal drinking age was changed to twenty-one. Those bars were hit hard, and many went out of business; the others had substantial restructuring costs, likewise reducing their ROEs. More recently, "adult entertainment clubs" in New York City came under attack from then-mayor Rudy Giuliani. He had new laws enacted, and old ones enforced, to regulate those clubs, causing many to close. In such cases, the value of a business is going to be greatly affected. One simply cannot use the results for years prior to the changes to accurately predict the futures of affected firms.

In these extreme cases, valuation efforts are almost like estimating the value of a new business just starting up. What will be the demand for the product? What will customers be willing to pay for it? What will be the firm's costs to produce and deliver it? The major difference is that many (if not most) costs are previously sunk into the business. When industry demand changes, those industry-specific assets are worth very little in liquidation. When using past returns to project expected future returns, one must be very careful that no predictable changes can be seen on the immediate horizon. If such changes are visible, then we have to modify our projections to account for their impact.

4.4.2 *Measuring Returns with Nonrecurring Items*

In calculating the past rates of return to predict future cash flows, no mention was made about handling extraordinary business items. These are

[10] But if customers won't pay it, then it has to be absorbed by the owners of the firm, reducing margins. At the extreme, firms (and their owners/investors) withdraw from markets made unattractive by such measures.

[11] The other factor that must be considered is the potential increased competition from those exempt from the change. In this case, imported products that are not affected by a domestic tax change will be relatively less expensive. In industries with few imports, such as the construction business or service industries, this is not a problem. In manufacturing, however, the costs increase only on domestic goods while foreign competition is not so affected. Foreign competitors can continue to produce at their previous costs. In such industries, higher taxes on domestic goods increase costs for domestic firms, hurting their potential exports and increasing import competition. The domestic firms in such industries would

expenses or revenues that are not expected to occur every period, or *nonrecurring* items. They would include such things as taking a loss for abandoning a major product line or the gain from selling a portion of the business. For purposes of valuation, however, they might also include items that could definitely change future cash flows and future cash flow estimates. Nonrecurring events cause two different types of measurement problems: including the correct items in the process, and getting the best estimate of their value from the data. Consider the following examples.

A firm has two equal-sized divisions. One earns a 20% return and the other earns only 8%. The 14% average return looks all right, but the firm is in the process of liquidating the poorly performing division. Any future projection should be based on the 20% return and the reduced asset base. But, what if the firm instead sells the good division for a gain? Now one must be careful not to extract that gain and then use the 14% rate to value the future performance of the remaining division, but rather to use the 8% return on the smaller base of the residual division. These situations represent real return problems when estimating future performance.

Without an inside position, such as being the owner/manager either doing the valuation or working closely with the valuator, it is difficult to measure the return on the continuing operations. The total return must be separated into its parts, a process that can be quite difficult. For example, overhead costs must be split between the continuing and the liquidated portions of the firm. After that and other accounting problems are addressed, the continuing operations of the firm can be valued. The key steps are to identify the continuing investment base and what returns can be expected from that base. The measurement problem is a matter of using the return on continuing assets (ROCA) to value the business.

Accountants, especially those in large public firms, seem to find many more items to classify as non-operating expenses or charges than they do as revenues or gains. Encouraged by their employers, they split out all sorts of restructuring charges and other non-operating charges from the operating performance of continuing operations.[12] Valuators, however, want to measure the performance from continuing operations. They know that the gain from a division sale is not going to be continuous, so they want an estimate of the continuing operations' profits. Realizing this, firms move as many expenses as possible into other categories to get the highest possible profit, and hence return rate, on continuing operations. Frequent "nonrecurring expenses" and "losses from discontinued operations" that always end up

---

see a permanent decrease in expected future cash flows, decreasing their value compared to firms without import competition.

[12] Similar abuse with "extraordinary items" many years ago caused the FASB to become extremely tight on the conditions required to qualify an item as "extraordinary." Accountants subsequently changed their terminology to "discontinued," "nonrecurring," and other terms to reestablish a similar split between total profit and profit from continuing operations.

greater than the "gains from the sale of a division," must be accounted for in measuring the future expected return of an investment. Thus, in valuing an ongoing business, an investor must carefully assess the likelihood that these items will be one time only. If they will recur in the future under different titles and names, ignoring them has the effect of pumping up naive estimates of ROE, and thus overestimating the value of the firm.

Similar issues arise in closely held firms. Opening a new store in a different market, closing a production line, buying a competitor—these are all unusual items for most small firms, and they will affect the apparent financial performance reflected in the financial statements. These types of problems can be present, even on a smaller or less frequent scale. When a firm loses a major customer or, even more difficult for an outside appraiser to identify, a major customer is considering other sources, accurately assessing the impacts also requires this kind of analysis.

An outsider trying to value a business must look very carefully at the financial statements provided by the current owner and ask a couple of critical questions. Do they represent the firm as it currently exists, or has the firm's structure materially changed since they where prepared? Are the underlying operations or assets likely to change in significant ways in the foreseeable future? The estimates of ROE and projected returns must be based on the firm as it exists now and as it is expected to perform in the future. Owner/managers getting ready to sell their businesses have every incentive to make their statements look as good as possible. The appraiser must be careful to see through these changes for adjustments and potential misrepresentations.[13]

4.4.3 *Adjusting for Accounting Changes*

From time to time, the FASB or another accounting body requires changes in the way firms report their financial transactions and performance. Sometimes, changes are stimulated by leading companies. In 2002, for example,

[13] This caution extends well beyond the types of deliberate misrepresentation that constitute outright fraud. Anyone reviewing the books of an unaudited company must be careful, because the books could be total fiction. As an example, a discount electronic store chain named Crazy Eddie's started up in the 1980s in New Jersey. It offered very low prices and grew quickly. Initially, while it was a closely held family corporation, the owners skimmed the books, reporting lower sales to minimize taxes. Later, when they wanted to go public, they padded the sales values to create the appearance of a larger firm, hoping to receive a larger market value. Based on that fiction, the stock was wildly received when issued. The founder, Eddie Antar, fled the country, pursued by irate investors. He eventually returned and settled the claims, as did the firms of professional advisors who had helped him organize the scheme. (See www.sirotalaw.com/press/press_01_18_93.cfm for details.) Similar manipulations of financial reports have occurred more recently, with Enron, MCI, and various other companies. When uncovered, they lead to precipitous declines in the market values of those firms.

many public firms began following the lead of Coca-Cola and reporting as expenses the stock options they grant to their executives.

Accounting changes only change the way performance is measured. They have no direct effect on the business itself; cash flows are unaffected. Whereas the previous section of this chapter looked at the problem of sorting out which values to use for the accounting numbers, the focus here is on changes in how those results are reported. The important thing to remember is that cash flows are unaffected by how the results are presented. The valuator's task is to sort through the presentation to find the underlying performance of the business. Only when the cash flows are being compared with public firms do the methods become important.

The owner/manager of a closely held firm does not care in the same way a public company executive cares about how much profit is reported. Most owner/managers have no outside shareholders to impress or to worry about when profits are low; the owner/manager is not going to be fired if profit appears to drop. What matters to these owners is how much cash is left after paying all the obligations, including taxes and new investments.

Consider the following baseball analogy. In the era of Babe Ruth and earlier, the game was the same as today with a few small exceptions. One of those exceptions was how batting averages were calculated. In those bygone days, a hitter advancing a runner with a long fly ball out was given a time at bat and no hit. Under modern rules, it is called a "sacrifice fly" and is recorded as no time at the plate, similar to a bunt sacrifice. Under the original rules, the players' reported batting averages would be lower. The same runs would have scored, however, and the same games would have been won and lost. As accountants change the reporting rules, the reported profits change, as did the reported batting averages. These changes have no effect on what really counts, however: runs scored or cash generated.

Why do we even bother with these accounting values? Well, accountants are the scorekeepers in business! What valuators must do is adjust the accountants' "scoring" to compare firms across time periods. This adjustment process becomes extremely important with closely held firms as most smaller firms never create their financial statements according to GAAP, let alone have auditors review and correct their financial statements. Instead, they have their accountants compile financial statements directly from their firms' operating data. Entrepreneurs keep score too—but they tend to do it their own ways. As a result, the financial statements they ask their accountants to prepare do not usually capitalize leases or present deferred taxes, as accelerated depreciation is used for both accounting and book purposes. The use of leasing, for example, leads to a report showing lower total assets, and the use of accelerated depreciation leads to reports that show both lower total assets and lower levels of invested equity. If the cash flow is estimated correctly, however, the rate of cash generation to equity would appear greater in the non-GAAP firm, because the denominator is smaller.

With all of those idiosyncrasies, one of the primary tasks of any valuator is to bring the current owner's data into a format that permits meaningful comparison with other investment opportunities. That isn't always easy, given the differences in entrepreneurs' financial statements, but it is essential for good valuation work.

4.5 Cash Flow Gives the Best Basis for Comparison

When a firm's value is being estimated using any comparison with small public firms, such as their required returns, the parameters for the closely held firm must be estimated using the same rules as those by which the public firms report their performances. The commonly used approach in estimating value as a multiple of profits, for example, must use the same rules to calculate the profits of the firms being compared. What is actually needed is the cash flow being generated after investments. Straight cash flow estimates offer the fewest biases or measurement errors.

When there is no ability to earn an excess return, the best estimate of a firm's value is merely the capitalized free cash flow for the next period. In the next chapter, we'll see what happens when there is a growth opportunity involving excess returns.

4.6 Watch the Cash Flow!

"The business is an investment." Mike and Tom were staring at the heading on their latest worksheet, set up for them by the Professor.

"It sounds so simple, doesn't it? But I have never thought of it like that," acknowledged Mike. "I never thought: 'Is this a *good* investment—of my money, my time, my talents?' When Dad died, we just knew someone had to take it over, and Mom wasn't in any shape to run it, so it became my job," he explained. "Over time, she gifted part of it to me, and I bought out the rest so she could give cash to my sister and brother. It became my business as well as my job. I don't think anyone in the family looked at it as an investment. We all saw it as a duty, maybe, a living for sure, maybe an asset, but never an investment. And now I realize, at age forty-eight, that it's the biggest investment I'm ever going to make . . . and I've been doing it, one way or another, all my life. I'm in shock! To be doing something so big, so important for my family, and me, and to not have a clue about that aspect of it—well, it's quite a revelation. My world has changed this week!"

"It's a little different for me," Tom mused. "I bought the business, after it became clear I wasn't very good at working for other people. We saved for it for a couple of years. My folks helped set me up, and Celia kept working so we could live on her salary if we needed to. But it wasn't the kind of investment the Professor talked about. We bought a business, thinking it was a bunch of assets, and a job with an income, but I confess we never really thought about the return on that investment in the kind of financial sense the Professor does. Now, I'm getting really curious to find some numbers and run them through his formulas and see just what kind of return we have been getting."

"Me too—although I'm afraid to see the results," Mike voiced concerns they shared. "Since we have not been thinking this way, my guess is we've not been managing the investment angle very well. If we have produced any decent returns on all those investments, it's been more luck than skill." Mike's nervous giggle revealed the mix of worry and eagerness he was feeling.

After a moment's reflection, and a long draw on his first beer of the evening, Tom said, "Then there's the second Big Question—What's the return? How's it measured? We're going to have to get help sorting out both the investment side of things, and the returns, to get measurements that make any sense."

They looked at each other, and off into space, for a long minute. "Well, the sooner we get at it, the sooner we'll stop making those kinds of mistakes."

"I feel like a teenager on a first date," noted Mike. "I'm nervous about what those analyses are going to show. I know I'm going to be embarrassed at times, yet I still want to know. Let's get our accountants to pull those data together, and compare notes as we go."

"The good news is that we've made good livings from these businesses, so we must have been doing some things right," Tom reflected. "The problem now is that I don't know which ones, so I don't know how to reduce the mistakes or increase the winners. When the Professor asks what investments we have made in our businesses the last three years—and which ones we have passed on—I don't have clear answers. It's not the way I've been managing. I just decide whether we should buy something new, take on a new line, or buy a different kind of advertising. Most of the time, I make those decisions based on what cash I have available, and a really vague idea about what difference it might make—but I know I hardly ever follow up, so I now understand that I may be making the same dumb mistakes over and over!

"When the Professor asks the key question—how are those investments doing?—I don't have a clue. It's astonishing that we've made it this far, you and I, and done this well, while being so blind about such a critical part of owning and managing a business. I'm really looking forward to seeing a different set of numbers, to seeing what I've done with blind luck."

"What are you going to ask your accountant to do first?" Mike wondered.

"It sounds like one of the critical sets of numbers, and perhaps one that shouldn't be too hard to estimate, is that free cash flow thing, so I'm going to start with that. Then, the next issue is the investments—what I have put into (or left in) the business, versus what I have taken out. Those look like the first data we need."

5

Growth Options and Valuation

5.0 The Value of Future Potential

"What's bugging you, old friend?" Mike asked. He and Tom were out in Mike's boat, and Tom's scowl had been deepening all day. It might have been the fishing, which wasn't going well, but Mike sensed his buddy was distracted. Tom seemed preoccupied with something else, something even more important than fishing.

"It's this business valuation stuff. I think I'm getting my mind wrapped around the differences between the going concerns and the assets by themselves, but there seems to be a big piece missing."

"What's that, bud?" Mike tried to keep it light but still get Tom to spill whatever it was that was ruining their usual lighthearted expedition.

"I'm not sure how the Professor would say this, but it's something about the value of future potential. For example, if two businesses are more or less equal, by the numbers, but one of them has a stable future while the other has lots of growth potential—they should have different values, shouldn't they?"

"Yeah, you gotta think so."

"Do you think it matters who the buyer might be? I mean, some people want stable, predictable futures, while others want an exciting opportunity and are prepared to work hard, maybe invest extra money, to make it happen. Which is worth more, and to whom? It seems like there are different answers all over the place, so how can we ever figure out what our businesses are worth?!" Tom looked really perplexed.

Mike thought about that while making his next cast and then working the line. "Why don't we split those issues apart for the time being, and deal with the value of potential growth first? Then we can tackle more complex things, like different market responses."

"Okay, sounds like a plan. Where do we start?" Tom still looked troubled, but his weak smile was a sign of hope that had been missing earlier.

IS GROWTH POTENTIAL IMPORTANT? A review of the financial pages showed that in early 2000, AOL Time Warner had a market value approximately three times that of General Motors—even though AOL was smaller (in terms of both sales and invested capital) and was still reporting losses. Another New Economy firm, Amazon.com, was valued at more $10 billion in early 2002 when it announced its first profitable quarter. Amazon not only had never turned a profit until then, it had accumulated an accounting book value of over $1 billion—negative! Despite that history, investors valued it quite positively.

While these examples are based on firms much larger than most closely held enterprises, they do suggest an interesting situation. Does valuation based on the present value of future cash flows (PV-CF) only work for some firms but not for all? Does PV-CF valuation have a fatal flaw that was being ignored? The answers are fortunately "no," but the whole story was not presented in chapter 4. This chapter considers the rest of the story by considering situations where valuation is significantly affected by other factors. Specifically, we will look at adjustments required to properly value businesses with great opportunities for future growth. One way to think about this is to start with the PV-CF approach as a baseline, then adjust it up (or down), depending on the extent to which we expect the future to change the firm's ability to generate those cash flows.

Most high-growth public firms operate in rapidly changing environments. Sometimes referred to as the "darlings of Wall Street," they are usually on the frontiers of innovation as they thrust into new industries. In some cases, they are creating those new industries. In others, they are merely bringing a new set of products or a new delivery method to an expanding industry. For example, Amazon.com created the Internet book sales industry. Dell Computers developed a new way of producing computers in a growing but established industry. In almost every case, firms with a high percentage of their value due to growth opportunities, that is, the opportunity to undertake new investments that will earn substantial excess returns, are in situations where demand for their products or services is growing. There is unrealized potential. As investors recognize that potential, it shows up in the firms' valuations.

Most small, closely held firms do not have or cannot create these kinds of investment options. Many, however, do have these opportunities on a more limited scale. A new location is opened in a previously unserved suburb or an inner-city neighborhood that is being revitalized. These situations offer the innovative (or sometimes just plain lucky) business owner growth opportunities to undertake new investments that will earn excess returns. The concept of "industry" or "market" must be defined in the context of the firm being valued. While innovations such as the Internet make access to global markets much easier, most markets are still quite localized.

In this chapter, we develop the valuation methods for firms with growth opportunities. We first distinguish excess returns on current investments from those associated with those future investments that are necessary to create growth. Next, we show how a firm's current value is actually the sum of the current operation's value (as shown in the last chapter) and the value of the growth opportunities (to be shown in this chapter). This revised approach is followed by a discussion on how to estimate these growth options and how to value them. A related issue is the negative affect on value of future competition, because firms earning excess returns tend to attract competitors, who then drive down the margins earned by the earlier entrants. The chapter concludes by estimating the likely effect those competitive invaders will have on the value of a firm. If the opportunities for new investments can be thought of in terms of growth options to increase value, future competition can be thought of as put options, decreasing a firm's value.

5.1 Separating Growth Opportunities from Current Excess Returns

Economists define *excess returns* as returns (on an investment) greater than the required rate of return. For example if the required rate of return is 14% and the firm earns 18%, it makes a 4% excess rate of return. Since the terms *monopoly* or *value from excess returns* carry negative implications for some people, we sometimes see the alternative term *market value added* (MVA) used to describe the same increase in value. In this book, however, we follow the convention of calling them *excess* returns. Readers should note that the term as used here is *not* a moral judgment—just a financial one. Before showing the effect on value, we must very carefully review what we mean by *excess returns* and *future investments.*

5.1.1 *Defining "Excess Returns"*

An excess return is said to exist whenever a firm makes more than its required rate of return on an investment. Suppose that the required rate is 10%, and our firm can invest $100 that will produce a free cash flow of $18 per year, starting the first year and continuing for an indefinite time into the future. Capitalizing the $18 per year at the 10% required rate gives 18/0.10 or $180. Now, subtracting the initial $100 investment gives $180 − $100 = $80. The $100 proposed investment is expected to produce a net increase in value of $80. Another way of looking at it is that this investment will earn an excess return of $8 per year, the expected dollar amount minus the required return on investment of $10 (= $100 × 0.10). This $8 is the annual economic value added or monopoly profit. (Stearns Stewart & Co. has trademarked this term as EVA.) This value is usually capitalized and is referred to as the net present value for the investment alternative. The logic of the calculations is broken out in table 5.1.

One also must be careful to make sure that the conditions are held constant in valuing these opportunities. First, does the opportunity have the

Table 5.1 Calculating the EVA

Required rate	10%
Investment	$100
Free cash flow	$18/year (beginning with the first year and continuing indefinitely)
Total annual return	$18
Required return @10%	$10
Excess return	(total return – required return)
EVA	$18 - 10 = 8$
NPV	$8/0.10 = \$80$

same riskiness as the current business or if it does not, has a different discount rate been used that properly reflects the riskiness of the new project? A common valuation error is to increase risk while still using the original discount rate. This combination falsely gives the impression of increased value. This error occurs frequently with firms in declining industries without good reinvestment opportunities. However, unless the new project still has an excess return when measured at its higher actual discount rate, no wealth or value has been created. The owner/manager has just reconfigured the firm to be a riskier business.

As we go through the process of developing methods to value these opportunities, it is important to distinguish between excess returns on existing investments and the ability to undertake future investments that may produce excess returns. Both increase the value of the business to make it worth more than its initial investment and retained earnings. However, only the future opportunities make the business worth more than the capitalized value of its current profits. These are separate characteristics and a firm can have either one without the other. The following four hypothetical examples illustrate the alternatives.

5.1.2 *A Decent Living, but No Excess Returns*

"Smith Hardware, specializing in locks," declares the sign. It is one of many hardware stores in the city. There are also many specialist locksmiths. The business earns its owner/manager a decent living but generates no excess returns. "Smith" is a well-respected name in local hardware, but so are many others. Too many similar substitutes exist for this business to either earn excess returns or have any superior growth options in either of its main product lines.

5.1.3 *An Expansion Opportunity with Excess Returns*

Delores' Delights sells outstanding cakes and other bakery products. While many of her customers have moved to the suburbs, she has attracted the new residents, and the old ones stop in when they are in the neighborhood. She is considering an expansion location in the suburbs to which her old clients have moved. She analyzes the market and realizes that she could be the only fine cake store in the growing suburbs. Most families have two wage earners, leaving little time to bake but extra money with which to buy. Her new location will earn her excess returns. Delores has a business earning no excess returns on its current operations, but she has an alternative that may earn excess returns in the new location. Her total business should be valued as greater than the present value of its current earnings.

5.1.4 *Current Excess Returns Cannot Be Expanded*

Pierre's Gourmet Deli is a local restaurant of high regard. It is always extremely busy. The owners can thank their chef, Pierre, and his image in local circles, for their great business. Truth be known, Pierre is good but not all that great. The restaurant owners are valuing an opportunity to open another location, presenting the fine food of Pierre. But wait—Pierre is still going to be cooking at the original location. Although the food at the new location might be as good as that at the original location, it won't be Pierre's. Hence, the new location will not draw the same crowds. This firm is limited because it has only one name chef. It can earn excess returns at its initial location, assuming that Pierre does not extract them all in his wages, but the business has no real growth opportunities where it will earn a premium return.

5.1.5 *Excess Returns with Expansion Potential*

Now it is possible that a chef can package his image or style of food and expand his growth opportunities well beyond a single restaurant. Consider Chef Paul Prudhomme and his blackened Cajun style from New Orleans—an excellent case. What creates the growth opportunities is the style of cooking, not the specific chef. This popular style created excess returns, at least initially, in the original restaurant. With proper packaging and promotion, it created excess returns in other locations. As we will see shortly in the developed examples, it is this ability to earn excess future returns that increases a firm's value over its current capitalized earnings. Once these options are undertaken and developed, the firm is only worth its capitalized earnings unless even more opportunities become available.

5.1.6 *Four Types of Growth (or Lack Thereof)*

We have seen four classes of firms, defined by their current returns and growth opportunities. These examples were presented to bring out the differences between the four types. In actual cases, the differences between the types will be much fuzzier. It is rare that a firm can exist for long without a chance of growth. A major part of the going concern value is usually the growth option. However, for most established firms, new investments do not represent growth opportunities as much as they do requirements to stay even with their competitors. That is why they can be valued as the present value of their current earnings—the additional investments do not result in excess returns; they just add up to no more than the maintenance of current returns.

5.2 Subtleties of Identifying and Valuing Growth Opportunities

How are those excess returns valued? Suppose one can see a positive situation for a firm. It has the opportunity to undertake a future investment that is expected to earn excess returns. For a public firm, these future investment opportunities give rise to growth and high price/earnings (P/E) multiples. For our closely held firm, they give values that are much greater than just capitalized earnings.

5.2.1 *When All Firms Share the Opportunity*

Another situation finds a firm with new investment opportunities that generate small excess returns, but the business is still valued as if no growth exists. This usually results from the type of opportunity being evaluated. Suppose the firm can either stay with its old processes or go ahead with investment in new, improved machinery. The analysis is undertaken and a positive net present value results, so the new machinery is brought in. The firm might have many of these alternatives to modernize its operations, each of which will improve efficiency and decrease costs. Should these future opportunities be capitalized into the firm's value? Does this firm have future growth opportunities?

The problem is that these opportunities are not unique to just one firm. Its competitors are making the same rational decisions and are also modernizing. As all firms start producing the goods at a lower cost, competition to get orders will drive prices down until no excess returns are being made. Hence, the firm cannot be valued as one with growth potential, because no opportunities exist to make excess returns on future business. But if the firm fails to make the modernization changes, it will most likely find that with its costs now higher than its competitors, it can no longer compete effectively and it will lose value.

Position-maintaining investments, commonly available to competitors, are required to hold value, but do not increase it. *Normal maintenance is not growth.*

5.2.2 *Separating Future Investments from Existing Ones*

A final point to remember is that these are future investment opportunities, or opportunities where investment has been started but the project is not yet producing returns. Current operations that are earning excess returns will be generating a firm's current free cash flows. Those excess profits are already capitalized into the value of the ongoing operations. This understanding was brought out in the previous chapter, where we discussed monopoly return value or its sanitized name of economic value added.

It is important not to confuse current excess returns with future alternatives to invest for possible future excess returns. Although the situation might well be that firms currently earning excess returns are likely to have more opportunities to produce even more excess returns, future excess returns are not guaranteed. What we want to show here is how the *potential* for those excess returns creates value.

5.3 An Example of the Value Created by Excess Returns

We are going to show how high-return projects create value, and we're going to demonstrate this through modifying the example presented in the previous chapter. The initial assumptions were used in chapter 4 and are presented in table 5.2.

In that example, value was shown to be \$1,000. It was calculated as either the capitalized value of the projected earnings [(\$1,000 × 0.10)/0.10] or equivalently, the capitalized growing excess cash flow [(\$1,000 × 0.10 × 0.4)/(0.10 − 0.06)]. Both methods produced the same result, because no excess returns were generated.

Now our assumptions about the future are going to change. This firm suddenly gets an opportunity to invest its retained earnings in each of the next two years for an excess return. The new investments will earn a return of 30% each year for the foreseeable future. That is, the money invested next year will earn the 30% rate forever, starting the following year. The same situation exists for the money reinvested in the following year. After

Table 5.2 Working Assumptions

Required return on equity, *k*	10%
Percentage of earnings retained	60%
Dividend payout ratio	40%
Value of assets at time 0	\$1,000
Amount of debt	\$0.00
Return on old and new investments (ROE = ROA)	10%

those two years, new investments (in years 3 and on) will again earn only the required 10% return. The reinvestment opportunities also assume that the firm maintains its current 40% payout ratio. Obviously, if it could reinvest its entire profit at the greater 30% rate, value would increase even more. This scenario gives the projected values show in table 5.3.

The profits in year 2 are a sum of the initial profits plus the return on the plowed-back profits from year 1. Since they are expected to earn a 30% return on the retained $60, this gives $18 earnings from the new investment for a $118 total. Again 40% is paid out, and the remainder is retained. The 60% retained or $70.80 is also reinvested at a 30% return. Therefore profits increase in year 3 by $21.24 (70.80 × 0.30) to give $139.24 in total profits for that year.

Since the firm only has positive reinvestment opportunities for those two years, the reinvested year 3 profits will earn only the required 10% rate. Remember that the $60 reinvested at the end of the first year and the additional $70.80 from the second year will continue to produce a 30% rate of return indefinitely. This makes year 4 profits increase only $8.35 (139.24 × 0.60 × 0.10) to give $147.59. Similarly, the firm's overall year 5 profits would increase by 6% due to reinvestment of 60% of year 4 retained profits, plowed back at a 10% rate of return on investment.

Dividends grow as follows from year 1 to year 2 and from year 2 to year 3:

$$\text{Returns in year } 2 = (47.2 - 40.0)/40.0 = 18\%$$
$$\text{Returns in year } 3 = (55.7 - 47.2)/47.2 = 18\%$$

This 18% growth rate equals the retention, or plow-back portion of 60%, times the 30% return earned on the new investments. The general formula is

$$V_0 = \sum_{t=1}^{\infty} \frac{C_t}{(1+k)^t}.$$

Table 5.3 An Example of Excess Returns

	Year 1	Year 2	Year 3	Year 4
Investment at 10%	$1,000.00	$1,000.00	$1,000.00	$1,083.54
Investment at 30%	0	$60.00	$130.80	$130.80
Earnings from 10% investments	$100.00	$100.00	$100.00	$108.35
Earnings from 30% investments	0	$18.00	$39.24	$39.24
Total earnings	$100.00	$118.00	$139.24	$147.59
Retained (60%)	$60.00	$70.80	$83.54	$88.56
Paid out (40%)	$40.00	$47.20	$55.70	$59.03
End-of-year total investment	$1,060.00	$1,130.80	$1,214.34	$1,302.86

After year 3, the increase in profits drops to 6% as the new investments are expected to earn only a 10% rate of return (0.60 plowed back × 10%). Similarly, dividends will grow at 6% as a constant portion of earnings or profits is paid out. This growth rate is expected to continue into the future, as all future investments are expected to earn just the 10% rate of return.

In these situations, the investment value of the firm can be estimated using the basic valuation equation that holds for all firms. This equation is used year by year for the first three years when the extremely large dividend growth occurs. Starting in the fourth year, the firm returns to constant dividend growth at 6% per year; therefore the value at time 3 can be determined using the constant dividend growth model. It can seem confusing, but the cash flow starting in year t always gives the value at time $t-1$. (Think of the present value model: at time 0, it always starts by discounting back the cash flows from year 1.) The present value of our modified case study can be determined from the projected value of the parts, to give the following value:

$$
\begin{aligned}
V_0 &= C_1/(1+k) + C_2/(1+k)^2 + C_3/(1+k)^3 + V_3/(1+k)^3 \\
&= 40/(1.10) + 47.2/(1.1)^2 + (55.7 + 1{,}476)/(1.1)^3 \\
&= \$1{,}226.16.
\end{aligned}
$$

5.4 Valuation in Parts: Present and Future

The value of the firm can also be expressed in parts: the value of its current operations plus the value of its future growth opportunities. In the example, the firm has increased in value from $1,000 to $1,226.16. Why is the value higher? It has increased because the firm now has *future* ability to earn excess returns. In the example, that future growth in earnings capability is represented by the reinvestment projects undertaken one and two years in the future, projects that will earn returns of 30% a year. We can separately express the value of these investments that earn excess returns, as follows:

$$
\begin{aligned}
&\text{Excess Value} = \{\text{Total Value}\} - \{\text{Value of Current Earnings}\} \\
&\text{Excess Value} = \$1{,}226.16 - \$100.00/0.10 = \$226.16.
\end{aligned}
$$

This excess value is what creates economic growth. As the valuation model accounts for the present value of these future cash flows, it is referred to as the Present Value of Growth Opportunities (PVGO).

The present value of the current operations' earning potential is often referred to as the value of the assets-in-place. It represents the value of the firm without excess return investment opportunities. As we saw earlier, the value is unchanged whether the firm pays these profits out as dividends or reinvests them at just the required return. Only when the firm has opportunities to earn excess returns on future investments will its value be greater than capitalizing its current earnings.

The value of these growth opportunities can be calculated directly and then added to the present value of the current profits to yield the total value. This technique is very useful in allowing the owner/manager to incrementally make decisions on individual investment opportunities to see if they will increase value without having to fully reconsider the entire valuation problem each time. To determine the increase in value, the *net present values* of the individual investment opportunities are calculated. These values are then discounted to the present and summed to equal the present value of the future growth opportunities.

The net present value is merely the present value of the incremental cash flows that an investment opportunity will generate minus their investment outlay. It represents the dollar increase in value from undertaking a specific project. To use this tool correctly, we need to calculate a present value of the excess returns for each project, discounted to its starting year, and then discount that whole project back to the present. For example, if a project begins two years from now, its excess returns would be first discounted back to its starting year, producing an estimate of the present value of those returns for the project. That would standardize all the project's future returns, in terms of their value in t_2. Then, that value would have to be discounted back to the present (t_0) to bring its value into terms comparable with the assets in place.

In our example, there are two investment opportunities, one in period 1 for \$60 and then one in period 2 for \$70.80. As the 30% return is being earned each year to perpetuity, its present value is just the annual amount ($0.30 \times \$60.00$) capitalized by the discount rate ($1/0.10$). This procedure gives the following values:

$$\text{NPV}_1 = -60 + (60 \times 0.30/0.10) = \$120; \text{ and}$$
$$\text{NPV}_2 = -70.8 + (70.8 \times 0.30/0.10) = \$141.6.$$

Now, because the value is being measured at today's time, also called time 0 or t_0, these future increases in value must be discounted back to the present to estimate the PVGO. Here's the formula, and the way the numbers work in our example:

$$\text{PVGO} = \text{NPV}_1/(1 + k) + \text{NPV}_2/(1 + k)^2; \text{ and}$$
$$\text{PVGO} = 120/(1.1) + 141.6/(1.1)^2 = \$226.12.$$

Adding the present value of the current earnings (\$1,000) to the PVGO gives \$1,226.12. Except for the four-cents rounding error, this is the same value we obtained from separately considering each year of dividend flows. Thus, the value of the firm is its current operations or assets in place, plus the net present value of its future investment opportunities.

From this development, we can derive several important relationships in valuation. The value of the firm that is earning only the required rate of return on past, current, and future investments can be expressed as $C_1/(k - g)$. An equivalent measure, expressed in Earnings per Share, is EPS_1/k. Furthermore, for such firms, these values will also equal their accounting book value of equity.

Now, if we have a firm that makes excess returns on its current investments but only the required return on future investments, its value can still be calculated as $C_1/(k-g)$, or its share value EPS_1/k. These values will, however, be larger than the firm's book value by the amount of excess returns being earned on its previous investments.

Only when a firm has economic growth opportunities or the ability to earn greater than its required rate of return will its value increase to more than the capitalized value of its current profits. Buyers of such firms are usually willing to pay more because they are receiving the ability to reinvest earnings at a rate of return greater than the firm's required rate of return. In such cases, $V = C_1/(k-g) + \text{PVGO}$. It is the quality of future investment options that increases the value of a business beyond the value of its current operational performance.

5.5 Estimating the Value of Growth Opportunities

Probably the most difficult task in valuing a business is putting a value on the firm's growth opportunities. An owner/manager looks at many opportunities to undertake new investments needed to stay competitive. At first glance, the firm appears to have growth opportunities. The problem is that with most established firms, a closer analysis shows nothing unique about these investments. The alternatives are really a matter of investing to stay competitive or to not investing and slowly losing the ability to compete. No excess returns exist when investments simply hold the firm's position in its industry. Most owner/managers find it difficult to accept this conclusion. Yet it is the primary reason why the majority of well-established, closely held firms have no real growth opportunities.

At the other extreme, large growth options are often seen in new venture ideas. New businesses are usually started because the owners believe they have the potential to make excess returns.[1] To be successful, start-ups must fill a void in a market or create a new market. Often, but not always, new firms are innovators, entering a new area or creating a new type of business.

To value a start-up, the approach is similar to that used with a going concern. Two major differences exist. First, *all* values, whether for the initial business or its potential growth options, are estimates. No historical data exist on what the firm has normally earned. Second, no actual investment into the business has yet been undertaken.

It is important to keep these two extremes in perspective when discussing how to value growth opportunities. With an ongoing business, it is important to know what they are and how to value them. One does not want to sell the firm based on just capitalized current cash flow and give

[1] We exclude "lifestyle" businesses, which are not generally launched with maximum economic returns foremost in the minds of their owners.

away potential growth opportunities, but a realistic seller should not expect to be paid for growth opportunities if he or she cannot identify them. (If the buyers can identify such opportunities, that may be one reason for them to offer some premium, but it is more usually an important factor in their expected profit from the purchase—bringing new resources to the business, and making it more valuable in their hands than it was to previous owners.) The following sections present three broad approaches to estimating the value of growth opportunities.

5.5.1 *Business Opportunities Approach*

The Business Opportunities approach to valuation is simple. It starts with a firm's current excess returns and projects the future investments required to earn similar excess returns. Of course, a firm cannot earn an excess return on all future investment projects forever, or we would have an infinitely valued firm! What is usually done is to have the excess returns decline over time toward the required rate of return. This approach is used extensively in valuing new growth stocks. Conceptually, it can also be used to value closely held firms with similar growth opportunities.

5.5.1.1 EXCESS RETURNS DECLINE TO THE REQUIRED RATE OF RETURN Consider the following simple valuation example. A new business has invested $1 million and expects to earn a 21% rate of return. With the estimated required rate of return for this type of business at 15%, additional value is clearly being added by the new firm. Because of competitive pressures, the new investments will earn 21% for the first year, then 19% for the second year, drop to 17% for the third year, and achieve just the required rate of return after that. Because the firm is earning excess returns, it makes sense to reinvest all its excess cash flow for the first three years. These investments are then assumed to earn their excess returns indefinitely. Hence, the net present values (NPVs) for each year are just the capitalized future earnings at the required rate of return (investment amount × rate earned/0.15), minus the investment outlay. The only tricky part is to remember that the amount of investment increases each year due to the previous year's retention being added to the base year's earnings. Thus the investment at the end of the second year will be 0.21 × $1,000,000 (initial year's return) + 0.21 × $210,000 (return of first year's reinvestment), making $254,100. Carrying out this process for the first three years of this example, with projected excess returns, gives the following calculations:

$$NPV_1 = 210{,}000 \times 0.21/0.15 - 210{,}000 = \$84{,}000;$$
$$NPV_2 = 254{,}100 \times 0.19/0.15 - 254{,}100 = \$67{,}760; \text{ and}$$
$$NPV_3 = 302{,}379 \times 0.17/0.15 - 302{,}379 = \$40{,}317.$$

The present value of the growth opportunities is just these three values discounted back to the present. That formula looks like this:

$$PVGO = NPV_1/(1.15) + NPV_2/(1.15)^2 + NPV_3/(1.15)^3 \text{ or,}$$
$$PVGO = \$84{,}000/(1.15) + \$67{,}760/(1.15)^2 + \$40{,}317/(1.15)^3 = \$150{,}789.$$

The value of this firm is the capitalized current earnings, plus the present value of the growth opportunities. For this example,

$$V_0 = \$210{,}000/0.15 + \$150{,}789 = \$1{,}550{,}789.$$

In this example the current earnings represent over 90% of the firm's current value. In the inflated market of 1999, such a firm would have been seen as showing substantially less future growth opportunity than the typical large nongrowth public firm. Only three years of excess returns were used, primarily to make this a workable example. One could get a greater value through merely having the excess returns decline at 1% per year, instead of 2%, leading to six years of excess returns instead of just three. That simple change gives a revised total value of $1,671,884, reflecting an 80% increase in the PVGO. Alternatively, one could assume that the ROE would increase even more before declining. That, too, would drive the growth portion of the total valuation higher—provided there was reason to believe it! We can quickly see how sensitive valuation can be to the choices we make for these values—and how owners and buyers might quickly disagree about their assumptions.

What estimates of future returns are actually used depends on the quality of future investment opportunities. Optimistic owner/managers view the opportunities for excess returns as occurring for many years into the future. More pessimistic appraisers need to be shown why excess returns will continue to exist on future opportunities. What is restraining competition, for example, where excess returns are being earned? When excess returns are being earned, how soon will competitors notice, then enter the business themselves, and eliminate or at least reduce the excess returns?

Even a conservative valuation can overstate the value of a closely held firm. What is to ensure that the firm can continue to earn 21% on its existing investments when the required rate of return is only 15%? Again, even without considering growth opportunities on new investments, an appraiser must be sure that the greater return is likely to continue. One must identify what capabilities this firm has that will allow it to continue to earn these excess returns. Otherwise the predicted returns must be reduced to the required rate, and the excess returns removed from the forecast value.

5.5.1.2 OWNER/MANAGERS' CHOICES ARE CONSTRAINED

Often, it is the talent, drive, and determination of the owner/manager that creates and maintains these excess returns. If a firm has grown to employ hundreds of people, its ongoing ability to generate these returns can likely survive the retirement of the original owner/manager. Many smaller closely held firms, however, rely almost entirely on their owners for the returns they generate. In these situations, an appraiser must consider the value of the business with the current owner/manager, the likely value if a professional manager were hired to run the firm after the sale, or the likely value with a different owner/manager. The differences between these three values give a measure of the unique talents being brought to the business by the current owner/manager and the likely effects of either a professional or new owner in the management role. Those values may increase if the present owner has become less than competent or decrease if the successors are less skilled or passionate about the business.

The importance of separating the value of the firm from the value added by the owner/manager was noted earlier, in chapter 2, when we discussed whether or not a separate going concern actually exists. With most relatively small going concerns, even when a separate going concern exists, the owner/manager plays a crucial role in the firm's success. Unless the business has the growth potential and the owner/manager has the foresight to expand the business with professional managers, the firm will be constrained in size. Any owner/manager has a limited amount of time to devote to the business. If new projects are undertaken, then old ongoing operations must be neglected—even when profitable. On the other hand, if attention is paid to the existing operations, there is less time for new ideas and changes, and most of those opportunities are simply skipped, regardless of their potential. Unless owners continue to at least maintain their "profit machines" at the same performance levels as their competitors, the industry will change around the business, causing the existing operations to lose their profitability over time.[2]

These limitations of managerial attention also tend to limit the growth potential of closely held firms. Furthermore, the more profitable the firms are, the more likely this situation exists. They face increased potential competition due to their excess returns and are simultaneously limited in their ability to initiate complex new projects to exploit profitable new investment opportunities. In reviewing a firm's ability to exploit growth potential arising from its existing profitable business activities, the outlook may be quite pessimistic for a closely held firm. The owner/manager, facing a severe time constraint, must continually make decisions about whether to keep old investments going or move to new, profitable ideas to preserve the firm's production of excess returns. The sum of those decisions will be critical to the performance (and hence the value) of the firm.

Dealing with this challenge is one of the reasons some closely held firms go public. Their owners take that significant step not so much to raise additional capital or to raise their personal prestige in the business community but rather to build a professional management team where stock options attract the talent needed to continue growing. More immediate and direct

[2] Our colleague Sharon Gifford, in *The Allocation of Limited Entrepreneurial Attention* (Norwell, Mass.: Kluwer Academic, 1998), developed the idea of rationed management attention as limiting a closely held firm's value. For owner/managers, management attention is a trade-off between building up existing projects versus trying to expand or develop new ideas. The specific value-maximizing approach that is best for any given business will depend on the particular industries in which the business operates and on the skills and resources of the entrepreneurs.

market feedback on the firm's decisions may also be another significant motivator in some cases.

5.5.2 *Viewing Opportunities as Options*

Another approach to valuing the growth potential of a business is to view its future opportunities as options. This method is much more optimistic for the closely held firm. All businesses have options to undertake future projects. They can be viewed as part of the value of a going concern. With that assumption, a going concern should always be worth more than its capitalized earnings. The assumption that all firms have valuable options just waiting for implementation is definitely overstated, but it is a concept that must be considered in valuing a business. Although this book will not go into a formal analysis of value options, it does discuss the concept and show the potential increases in value that might result.[3]

5.5.2.1 WHAT IS A CALL OPTION? What is an option, or more specifically a call option? On a security, a *call option* is the right to buy the underlying security at a preset fixed price during a given time period (American option) or at a specific time (European option). There are three key variables. First, the purchase price is set; second, there is a limited time period; and third and most importantly, the call option gives its owner the right—but not the obligation—to make the purchase. The call is only exercised when it increases the holder's wealth; otherwise, it expires unexercised. For example, assume one holds a call option with an exercise price (also called striking price) of $40/share. The option is at its maturity date and the stock is currently selling for $37/share. The holder can either exercise the option and buy the stock at $40/share or ignore the option and purchase it in the market at only $37/share, saving $3/share (but writing off the cost of the option). In that circumstance, the option would be allowed to expire. If instead, the stock is selling for $42/share, exercising the option to buy the stock at only $40/share would make sense. If those options had been purchased for $1/share, the expired options would reflect an investment loss, like an expired unused insurance policy. Alternatively, if the option is exercised, the total investment would be $41/share, creating a book profit of $1/share.

5.5.2.2 APPLYING OPTIONS THINKING TO BUSINESS VALUATION How does this way of thinking relate to valuing a business? A going concern has options to undertake new investments. Some of these are known and identifiable, and others are not yet known. Let's start with

[3] For a good source on using real options to value investment opportunities, see Lenos Trigeorgis, *Real Options* (Cambridge, Mass.: MIT Press, 1998).

the identifiable options. Consider the following example of a start-up business. A theme restaurant has been researched. The analysis projects an NPV of \$900,000 if very successful, \$300,000 if successful, and a loss of \$600,000 if the concept is not successful. Now if these outcomes all had equal probabilities of occurring, the NPV would be \$200,000 = [(\$900,000 + 300,000 − 600,000)/3]. The positive NPV would be one indicator that the project should be pursued.

But wait! If it is very successful, the project can be duplicated in at least three other cities. It will take at least two years to determine its result and another year to get another location set up. These are each estimated to have NPVs of \$700,000. Because of management constraints, only one can be undertaken per year. Since the uncertainty will be resolved before the additional projects are undertaken, the additional option projects will be discounted back at the time value of money. Again assuming the three outcomes are equally probable, this rollout would only be realized a third of the time. Assuming a 5% discount rate, this option nonetheless produces an increase in the NPV of the project, as follows:

$$\begin{aligned} NPV &= (\$700{,}000/1.05^3 + \$700{,}000/1.05^4 + \$700{,}000/1.05^5) \times (1/3) \\ &= \$576{,}350. \end{aligned}$$

This expansion option makes the initial project's total NPV increase from \$200,000 to \$776,350. A new business must also consider the increased investment opportunities if the project turns out to be successful.

The firm's option potential depends on many specific factors, but these can be broken into two broad areas: firm-specific and industry-specific. The previous example was a firm-specific one. The key is to look for opportunities to earn excess rates of return that can be duplicated and introduced elsewhere. The more unique the product or service, the more its replication potential increases. The key in valuation is to specifically identify these opportunities.

If the firm has not undertaken them or, even more importantly, has not even considered undertaking them, one must ask the current owner/manager why not. Possibly, the uncertainty of the outcome on the original investment has not yet been resolved. More likely, with an ongoing business, there are competitive reasons, potential price wars, and so on that have precluded these expansions. Or possibly, the owner/manager is happy with the current operations and is letting the opportunities just pass. The latter case obviously gives a situation for dual valuations, one with the business as it is currently run and then another with it run to maximize its value. These scenarios all relate to specific known alternatives that can be undertaken.

Industry-specific factors are more abstract items in the valuation process. Higher growth industries usually give above-average growth opportunities for all involved. Thus, valuators impute a large growth component to these firms. The ultimate example, in the 1998–2000 period, would have been the Internet (dot-com) firms. Investors did not have to identify specific opportunities to know that their future investment opportunities in the dot-com sector were much greater than in, say, the home appliance industry. The same could be said for a service business in the growing states of Florida or Texas versus one in more static states like New York or Pennsylvania.

A good comparison approach for industry factors is to compare the average P/E ratio for public firms within an industry versus the market average ratio. Let's say the market average is around 20 for the S&P 500 as a whole. Firms in industries where the average P/E ratio is 30 should be valued with growth opportunities; investors as a group are expecting above-average returns in that industry. At the other end of the scale, a firm in an industry with a 15 P/E ratio would have difficulty justifying any industry-specific growth value. Its growth options are likely to be only firm-specific—which is why some firms are valued above their industry averages (and some are valued below).

5.5.3 *Two-Step Valuation Approach*

A more common way to value firms with growth opportunities is a two-step approach. The known or estimated opportunities are specifically valued. These usually come in the next several years. The value after that time is valued using a constant growth model.

Reconsider the earlier example in this chapter. A business has invested \$1 million and will earn a 21% rate of return. The estimated required rate of return for this business is 15%. Originally, the new investments would earn 21% for the first year, then 19% for the second year, dropping to 17% for the third year and just the required rate of return after then.

Let's change the example slightly. Now, after the third year, the firm pays out half its earnings and reinvests the other half to get a growth rate of 8%. Since the growth rate is equal to the retention rate, times the rate being earned on the new investments ($g = \text{Retention} \times \text{ROE}$), a slight excess return of 1% ($= 0.08/0.50 - 15\%$) will still be earned. From the \$210,000 reinvested at the end of the first period, the earnings grow to the \$302,379 increment being reinvested in the third period at 17% for an additional \$51,404 in value. This amount is added to the \$302,379 earnings from the earlier investments to give a total profit of \$353,784 at the end of the fourth year. Now half of this will be paid out as cash, \$176,892 and the other half will be reinvested, causing future excess cash to grow at 8%. This formula gives this value after three years:

$$V_3 = D_4/(k - g) = \$176{,}892/(0.15 - 0.08) = \$2{,}527{,}024.$$

Remember that the excess cash starting at the end of the fourth year gives its value one period earlier, or at time 3. Since the returns from the first three periods have all been re-invested, no excess cash has been paid out. The current or time 0 value is the time 3 value, discounted back for three periods. This formula gives

$$V_0 = V_3/(1 + k)^3 = \$2{,}527{,}024/(1.15)^3 = \$1{,}661{,}560.$$

This approach is only useful for firms that can be expected to earn returns on future investments greater than their required rate of return and also continue to earn the higher rate of return on their initial investments. In this example, $1 million was initially invested at a 21% rate of return with a 15% required rate of return. These assumptions lead to a value of $1.4 million if no additional investments are ever undertaken at excess returns ($1 million × 0.21/0.15 = $1.4 million). The additional $261,560 reflects the present value of the excess return, or the extraordinary benefit, on future investments.

These values, and thus the valuation process itself, are extremely sensitive to long-run growth estimates. An unrealistically high estimate gives a totally unrealistic future value. In this example, by changing the assumption about future long-term reinvestment rates to 18% from 16%, an analyst would increase the predicted growth rate from 8% to 9% and increase the firm's value 16.7%. As a general rule, future new investments that cannot be specifically identified should be assumed to earn only 1–2% a year higher than the required return and then only when in a high-growth industry. No excess returns should be expected in average or no-growth industries, unless specifically identified.

With growth options, one should consider the portion of value that is derived in the distant future. Looking at the example, no excess cash is being obtained in the first three years. The first cash outflow is $176,892 in year 4 followed by an 8% growth for $191,043 in year 5. In present value amounts, these two cash flows are worth $196,121 or just over 12% of the firm's current value. Even the present value of the projected excess cash flows for the first ten years is just over 40% of the firm's current value. So 60% of the value is being projected to be produced more than ten years into the future when 50% is being paid out each year starting in year 4. The more distant future is a time period when values are crudely estimated at best. That uncertainty explains why widely varying estimates can be generated for the same alternative when a high-growth component exists.

5.6 What Happens When Real Growth Is Negative?

After all those rosy discussions about how to value growth opportunities, we must get back to reality. Remember that an actual sale is the only time that a closely held firm's value is actually known; all other valuations are just estimates. Professional business brokers tell us that most closely held firms sell at a lower multiple of earnings than their public counterparts. Although mistakes can be made in pricing and selling a specific firm, one cannot expect the markets to continually underprice closely held firms. This section discusses the darker side of firm valuation and what we will call the *unknown expired put option.* These common situations occur when a business is facing realistic declines in its revenues and profitability. It is the kind of experience faced by the owners of many Main Street firms when suburban malls open nearby or Big Box retailers open on the outskirts of town.

5.6.1 *The Unknown Put Option*

The call option gives its owner the right to buy something at a preset price, and the put option gives its holder the right to sell at a preset price. The put option is the minimum value for the closely held firm. If the value of the firm as a going concern is less than the firm's liquidation value, a rational, wealth-maximizing owner/manager would "put" the going concern and liquidate the business. In these situations, the specific assets are worth more to others than they are to their current organization's ability to generate future cash flows.

Working backward in the definition, an *expired put* is one where the time to exercise or undertake it has passed. As with traded options, the put option for a closely held firm has a limited time frame. When the option expires after the value has decreased, its holder loses the value of the put option. The only time that rational, wealth-maximizing holders would allow a put option to expire would be when they were not aware of holding it. Hence, we refer to this as the *unknown* portion of the unknown expired put option.

5.6.2 *The Wal-Mart Liquidator Effect*

That's the setup; now for the story. Many, particularly small, closely held firms lose track of the changing conditions around them. Their managers become insular in their views. The changes in their immediate neighborhoods are obvious, and they usually respond adequately to those changes. The problem is in the more abstract or distant changes that affect how their goods and services are delivered.

The classic example is that of small-town retailers selling nothing out of the ordinary at high (but not outrageous) prices. Sure, their owners have heard of Sam Walton's firm, but until it opens a store at the edge of their town, they don't give much thought to his business model and its implications for their wealth. Once Wal-Mart arrives, however, they fight a (probably losing) battle for survival. They cannot sell their buildings or sell their leases because no one wants to start a business on the town square when the center of gravity has suddenly shifted to the outskirts. No one wants to buy these businesses as going concerns anymore, either, because they probably aren't.

The owner/manager's put option is to sell or liquidate the business prior to the major change against which they cannot compete. If they can see the change and estimate its effect on the business, they will see that the time to exercise the put and exit the business is before the powerful competitor enters. The problem is that in the daily running of the business the owner/manager cannot see all the potential changes that can adversely affect the business. This focus on daily details creates a myopia where owners fail to see that they should get out while they can, to preserve the wealth they have accumulated in the business.

The Voice of Research: Is There any Hope for Small Retailers?

Research by Reginald Litz and Alice Stewart has focused specifically on ways independent hardware stores respond to large competitive entries by firms like Wal-Mart, Lowe's, and Home Depot. They have found that successful competitive strategies have been created for independent competitors, although the groundwork must often be laid over many years before the Big Box retailer arrives. They wrote:

> Small retailers have recently experienced the entry of several giant, scale-advantaged, category killers. One strategy recommended for these small firms is trade-name franchise membership. Trade-name franchise membership offers franchisees several competitive advantages. These advantages stem from the possibility of gaining a cost advantage through the buying power of the franchise and the brand recognition available from association with the franchise.... Results indicate that trade-name franchise membership is positively related to performance in most cases. The advantage of the trade-name franchise, though, does not appear to result from the cost-based advantages associated with purchasing. A greater advantage seems to come from the name recognition associated with the trade-name franchise. However, even this advantage may not be sustainable in highly competitive environments. In the presence of a large entrant, independent retailers in our sample seem to perform better. More specifically, in highly competitive environments, the niche-based strategies of independent retailers focusing on information-rich product and service mixes become increasingly important.[4]

5.6.3 *Negative Growth and the Effect on Valuation*

This potential sudden decline in value can be viewed as a negative growth opportunity. Earlier in this chapter, we pointed out that excess returns will draw competitors. What exists here is a situation where even average earning firms attract new competitors who produce the good or service differently. This new delivery may be accomplished at a greatly lower cost, allowing them to still make money in a market that is no longer earning positive returns for old-style operators. Wal-Mart stores versus traditional small-town retailers, or Home Depot versus the local or regional building

[4] Reginald A. Litz and Alice C. Stewart, "Franchising for Sustainable Advantage? Comparing the Performance of Independent Retailers and Trade-Name Franchisees," *Journal of Business Venturing*, 13(2), March 1998, 131–50. See also other articles by the same team, listed in appendix 3 (Annotated Bibliography).

supply stores, are examples of such competition. Internet shopping versus traditional stores is a more recent comparison.

For public firms, the market places a great value on this downside risk. With near zero inflation, the current long-term risk-free rate is around 5%. This situation prices a risk-free investment with no major positive or negative growth options, either calls or these unknown puts, at 1/0.05 or 20 times earnings. At a reasonable 12.5% discount rate for firms with risk similar to the overall market, the price drops to 1/0.125 or only eight times earnings, which is less than half of the risk-free value. Even with what appear to be nice steady earnings, public markets reflect potential changes that could occur. The increased risk could be coming from superstores, Internet competition, or another product or it might be something not yet developed or even invented. The key is that investors put a heavy emphasis on that risk of obsolescence—and charge a hefty price to insure against it.

For privately held firms, the usual market discount rates are even higher. For those firms, divestiture at five times earnings, for a 20% discount rate, would be more typical, provided all of the other comparison factors (comparables) remain equal. The privately held firm doesn't have the benefit of a publicly traded stock market to signal changes in the value of its business model. For a firm based on an established product, this lack of risk signaling causes a tremendous decrease in value because puts are more likely to go unnoticed, making closely held firms riskier. Many closely held firms have only a single location and limited managerial talent, a combination that does not give them many opportunities to shift toward new and higher valued investments. Despite the best efforts of their managers, many run a substantial risk of becoming obsolete, and that risk alone reduces their value.

5.7 Keeping Up with Growth or Not: The Manager's Challenge

This chapter started by looking at ways to value growth opportunities and ended by discussing the low values received for most closely held firms at the time of their sales. An ongoing firm operates in an ever-changing economic environment. What is a new growth idea one year becomes an established product in another year or two and obsolete several years further down the road. Finally, the much discussed "cash cows," which is what zero-growth firms actually are, must always reinvent themselves to avoid being sent to the slaughterhouse. The average closely held firm finds it hard to adjust to shifting market preferences. As a result, it is valued below those of comparable public firms.

The good news is that performance varies widely across closely held firms. Some are very effective in monitoring industry conditions and developing options for attractive new investment opportunities. Those firms will be the higher valued ones.

5.8 Walk or Run: In Which Direction?

Tom and Mike were having their weekly Monday lunch at Rosie's Diner down the street from Mike's plant. The food was good and copious, but not fancy. The two friends had been doing this most Mondays for years, serving as each other's best advisor once the post-weekend crises had been dealt with at each one's business. Each served on the other's Board of Directors, but these weren't official meetings, just friendly ones.

Once they cleared away the usual weekly agenda of business operations questions they had for each other, Mike leaned back a bit and stated, "I don't know about you, but I'm developing this love-hate relationship with the valuation stuff we are doing with the Professor. For example, I like his approach to what he calls 'excess returns.' It reminds me that our job as owner of the business is always to be looking for opportunities to find better returns than we are getting now, ways we can increase the value of the investments we make."

Tom nodded his agreement, but said, "I was kind of distressed to see the accountant's report, that my average return on investment had been only 8%, but it was a bit reassuring to see the mix of returns. Some of the things I did earned more than double that while others didn't break even. And I'm really excited to be able to see those data, to begin to understand what I'm trying to do—beat those old numbers. Now I've got a target return of nothing less than 10%, with an average of closer to 15%. After all these years as a manager, and as an owner/manager, I feel like I'm finally getting the kinds of numbers I can really work with!"

"My numbers were a bit better—but I realize that was only luck," Mike admitted. "I wasn't managing them. A couple of lucky deals made the difference for me. I'm looking forward to working these numbers, to managing the business from here on. I think his way of looking at things will help me make better choices. I hope to see much better results as I weed out more of the bad deals."

Tom cautioned: "We both have to watch out for those long-term big negatives, though. That 'Big Box' Eliminator factor is really pretty scary! I know I'm going to be paying a lot closer attention to the long-term trend data put out by my trade association in D.C. And I'm going to be reading the business pages a lot more closely. I realize now that all of this work could go up in smoke if I lose control of my ability to compete with those companies for my customers' business. That's the big risk I see out there."

"You know, Tom, it's got me wondering when it's going to be a good time to sell this business and move on. I don't want to get caught holding the bag as bigger companies take me out." Mike's concern showed in his face.

"Same here," his buddy replied, "but I think that time is still a long ways away for me. In fact, I've been wondering about the opposite strategy—is there a way I can lever my existing business into a much stronger competitor? I don't see an answer to that yet, but I'm going to keep looking."

Mike looked up in curiosity—then at his watch, and realized that particular conversation would have to wait for another day.

6

Inflation and Valuation Measurement

6.0 Real Growth or an Illusion?

In Tom's den, at the halftime of a slow Sunday afternoon football game featuring two teams neither of them cared much about, Mike turned to his friend and asked, "What do you think is really going to happen to interest rates?" Tom had taken a couple of economics courses in college; Mike always found it baffling, even though he was a successful businessman.

Although the game had been boring, Tom was startled. "Huh?! Where'd that come from? A better offense would generate a higher rate of fan interest—but I don't think that's what you had in mind."

Mike wasn't distracted by Tom's weak humor. "I keep hearing these reports about the Fed leaning one way or the other, and it seems important. I've got a couple of my company loans coming up for refinancing in the next few months, and I don't know whether to grab the current refinancing offers or wait, take a short-term loan or a long-term one. Interest rates, inflation—they both seem to affect this kind of decision—but I don't really understand how."

"All right, that's fair." Tom decided to play along. "Interest rates run pretty close to inflation. What do you think is happening to inflation?"

Mike thought for a bit. "I guess it's staying pretty low. I'm seeing some increases in costs, like taxes and health care for my staff, but decreases in other areas. Computers are really getting a lot cheaper."

"I remember that time back in the early 1980s when rates ran up over 20%. A lot of businesses got broken in that period—but a lot survived. I wonder how they stay afloat in those countries where inflation runs up into the 100% range and higher. They must have to do some pretty fancy financial management." They both shuddered at those prospects.

Mike rambled on. "You know, I hear economists saying that a small amount of inflation might be good for the economy. Yet it's clear that too much inflation can be a real wealth destroyer. I wonder what the sweet spot is."

"And I wonder what difference it makes to the value of our businesses," mused Tom. "If we ever 'see inflation coming,' would that be a good time to sell what we've got? Who's buying under those conditions? How does inflation affect the value of our equity in our own firms? You know, I never hear them talk about that!"

WHY INFLATION IS IMPORTANT IN BUSINESS VALUATION

Valuing an ongoing business on the basis of its underlying components is one of the most difficult challenges in finance. We must consider the required return, the expected return being earned, and growth options (i.e., real investment opportunities) available to the firm. To estimate growth options, we consider the excess returns currently being earned and how long we expect those returns to be available on new investments.

Inflation adds another set of problems to any valuation. This chapter shows how to deal with this issue in the context of valuation. In particular, it addresses impacts that inflation has on measurement problems when we try to forecast the future value of investments. It also shows how various assumptions about inflation can affect a firm's value due to depreciation of tax shields.

With inflation in the United States currently around 3–4% per year and expected inflation at the same levels, we tend to ignore inflation in our measurement process. After all, a value estimate that turns out to be within 3% of the actual value would normally be outstanding. Inflation-induced errors appear to be a small factor, compared to other possible sources of error. One could effectively ignore inflation in making an investment decision to buy a new computer that would be obsolete in two years and probably could ignore inflation with a decision on a new company car that would last five years. When valuing an ongoing business to perpetuity, however, even 2% annual inflation can easily lead to measurement errors of 20% in the value estimate. These errors result from two measurement problems: nominal inflation and increased nominal working capital. Adjustment processes have been developed to correct these problems, and this chapter reviews their use.

This discussion of the problems caused in valuation measurement due to inflation begins with a review of the ways inflation measurement problems can be handled. The challenge comes through trying to forecast changes in future cash flows and discount rates. By always using inflated (or nominal) values, for both future cash flows and discount rates, or using equivalent values adjusted to today's dollar and the current cost of funds in real values, good valuators get correct, equivalent value estimates. If they mix inflated and real amounts, the results are scrambled and misleading.

We next expand the discussion to consider the effect of using nominal depreciation values. Typically, in a low-growth, steady-state economy, a valuator assumes that free cash flows equal profits, plus depreciation, minus reinvestment for the growth. Such assumptions are, of course, simplified. Reality is almost always messier, but simple assumptions allow forecasters to start with a basic situation and then modify it to make their estimates more realistic.

In practice, depreciation expense is often assumed to equal the normal reinvestment required to maintain the current profit position. Later in this chapter, however, this common practice will be shown to cause large errors by significantly overestimating value. With inflation levels of only 3% per year, the required reinvestment would be underestimated by 14% for assets being depreciated over eight years. An adjustment factor should be used to correct this problematic effect that inflation has on estimates of depreciation expenses. This adjustment method is developed into a table for the average lives of various depreciable items and inflation rates. Then we show the effect of inflation as requiring an increased nominal investment in net working capital. Buyers of a business will have to provide this capital, or draw it from the ongoing firm, reducing the firm's net long-term profitability and hence its value to those buyers. An adjustment to the constant growth model is developed to handle this problem.

Last, we deal with another real problem caused by inflation: the decreased value of the depreciation expense that can be claimed against the taxes payable on future income. The depreciation expenses that can be used to shield future income against taxes are based on historical costs. If there is no inflation, those expenses are likely to be approximately the same as the actual costs business owners need to invest to maintain their productivity (i.e., income-earning potential). If inflation occurs, those replacement costs will increase, but the depreciation expenses will not keep up. Take an extreme example, where revenues per unit double, as do all cash costs. In such a case, the depreciation expense would only shelter half as much income as it would in a situation with no inflationary effects.

Why is this issue saved for last? Most businesspeople are more aware of this problem because it is better publicized. In terms of magnitude, however, it is much smaller than the potential error due to measurement problems. Remember: Our objective is to accurately estimate the investment value of ongoing businesses.

6.1 Equivalence of Real and Nominal Approaches to Valuation

The easiest way to show the inflation problem in valuation measurement is to consider a simple example. We will develop one in both "real" terms (i.e., inflation is removed with future values adjusted for inflation) and "nominal" terms (i.e., the required return is increased to account for the inflation), and show how the two different methods produce identical results—if used correctly. The most common technique for calculating the effects of inflation was developed by Irving Fisher and published in 1930

(*The Theory of Interest*). Fisher's formula for inflation, as the relationship between the required nominal return, the required real return and the expected rate of inflation, is defined as

$$(1 + \text{Nominal Return}) = (1 + \text{Expected Rate of Inflation}) \times (1 + \text{Real Return}).$$

Suppose our firm expects to sell 100 units/year, with no expectation of growth. These units sell for $1,000 each. They have variable costs of production of $600/unit and annual fixed costs of $20,000. This combination gives us a profit before tax of $100,000 − 60,000 − 20,000 or $20,000, and if taxes are 40%, the net income is (1 − 0.4) × $20,000 or $12,000. Now, suppose we require a 10% rate of return on our investment. The resulting value of the firm, assuming no future growth opportunities, is defined as the annual profit divided by the required rate of return, or $12,000/0.10 = $120,000 in this example. Remember that *growth* opportunities represent the ability to invest at a rate of return greater than the required return. Retained earnings invested at the required return do not create additional value for the current owners, although they are required to maintain the existing level of return.

Now let's introduce the effect of inflation. Assume inflation begins at 5% per year and is expected to stay at that level. Next year, we still sell 100 units, but they will be priced at $1,050/unit (nominal price). This causes our nominal profit to increase to $12,600. We also note that interest rates increase correspondingly with inflation, so our nominal required return (NRR) is adjusted to become

$$\text{NRR} = [(1 + 10\%) \times (1 + 5\%) - 1], \quad \text{or} \quad 15.5\%.$$

6.1.1 *Using Real Terms*

The firm can now be valued in two equivalent ways. If we consider *real* returns and *real* discount rates, we can see that profits in the next year, before adjusting for inflation, are $12,600. Adjusting for inflation, we divide that sum by the new size of the economy: $12,600/1.05, which equals the initial $12,000. This result should be expected as sales and expenses have stayed the same; only the dollar got cheaper. We still want to be able to buy 10% more goods from investing for one year, so our required return in real terms is still 10%. The value is thus $12,000/0.10 or $120,000. Again, since nothing has changed except inflation, this outcome should be expected.

6.1.2 *Using Nominal Terms*

We can also value the firm in *nominal* terms. To do that, we use the constant growth model that Myron Gordon presented in 1962 (*The Investment, Financing and Valuation of the Corporation*), where

$$\text{Value } (V) = \text{Free Cash Flow}/(R - G).$$

The free cash flow equals the profits in a zero growth situation (which will be $12,600 next period, with inflation included). R is the required nominal return of 15.5%. G is the growth in free cash flow. For this example, the value of G is $(12{,}600 - 12{,}000)/12{,}000 = 5\%$. The value of V can now be calculated as $12{,}600/(0.155 - 0.05)$, which still equals $120,000. The increase in the measured cash flow results only from the 5% inflation we assumed in this simple example.

Whether we use real or nominal terms, we get the same result, because nothing but inflation has changed, and we factored out the effects of that inflation. This looks simple enough, and it is—if the valuator is careful to follow the simple rule of using only real cash flows with real rates (or nominal cash flows with nominal rates) and making sure the two never get mixed.

6.1.3 *What Happens When We Mix Real and Nominal Terms?*

The real world of business requires a lot of estimating, and that can sometimes cause these incompatible terms to be intermixed. Consider the following variations, still using our simple firm. Because our business is risky, we want to earn 7% per year more than the long-term government bond rate. We look in the financial press, where we find the long-term government bond rates listed as yielding 8.5%. We add our risk premium of 7%, to get a return of 15.5%. Next we check our just-completed financial statements and find that we earned $12,000 from selling 100 units of output last year. We expect no growth in our business, so future profits are projected at $12,000/year. The value estimate, therefore, is annual profit divided by required rate of return or $12,000/0.155, giving us an estimated value for the firm of $74,419—substantially lower than our previous estimates of the value of this particular profit machine.

What went wrong? The answer lies in our having mixed real and nominal data in the same formula. We used *real* cash flows, capitalized at the higher *nominal* discount rate, thus producing the lower estimate. Bonds trade in nominal terms. Our estimate of the long-term risk-free return from government bonds *included* inflation, but our estimated profit stream of $12,000/year did not. Thus, by adding the 7% risk premium to that underlying rate we created a nominal discount rate that we then mistakenly used to discount real cash flows. Oops! This error can easily occur when people capitalize current earnings to estimate the value of assets in place. An estimate of the discount rate from market returns automatically includes an inflation component. The projected inflation estimate must be removed. The real required rate of return is

$$\text{Real RoR} = (1 + \text{nominal rate})/(1 + \text{rate of inflation}) - 1$$

or $1.155/1.05 - 1$, which equals 10%. The correct value is therefore estimated as: $12,000/0.10, or $120,000.

The opposite error can also occur, although it doesn't happen as frequently. Suppose an owner contracts an analyst to value her firm. The owner states that she expects to receive a 10% return on her investment. The financial analyst sits down to make projections. With modern spreadsheets, it is really easy to handle inflation. Sales stay at 100 units, but the selling price and costs increase 5% each year. Hence there appears to be a 5% growth rate. The value is calculated as \$12,600/(0.10 − 0.05) or \$252,000. That would be pretty exciting, but this owner's immediate retirement and cruise package will have to be postponed. Inflated nominal dollars have been discounted by a real discount rate. The correct formula should be

$$\$12{,}600/(0.155 - 0.05), \text{ which equals } \$120{,}000.$$

The discount rate must be converted to a *nominal* value, that is,

$$(1 + \text{real rate}) \times (1 + \text{inflation rate}) - 1$$

or $(1.10 \times 1.05) - 1 = 0.155$.

6.2 Accounting Measures and Valuation Difficulties

These real and nominal problems can be handled with careful thought about what is being used in the valuation. A more difficult problem to handle arises from the use of historical cost accounting data. These are not problems in valuation approaches that start with a firm's book equity and then make adjustments, a method we have already dismissed as being too error-prone for professional use. These are problems when using current and future profit projections estimated from current GAAP. In this section, we are first going to show the problem with inflation and depreciation expense and then the problem with inflation and net working capital requirements.

6.2.1 *Inflation Causes Underestimation of Depreciation Expenses*

It is well accepted and known that depreciation expenses are not great enough to cover replacement costs when inflation exists. Existing assets are always depreciated on the basis of their historical (i.e., original) costs, but replacement assets are purchased at current costs. The manager's problem becomes a matter of adjusting for the difference between the reported depreciation expense and the actual replacement cost.

Consider our earlier example. The firm had \$20,000 a year in fixed costs, using real terms, prior to inflation. Suppose that \$20,000 represented the depreciation on five machines that each cost \$20,000 when new. Each year, a new machine was purchased, and a fully depreciated machine was retired after five years of service. Now assume that inflation starts at 5% a year. All costs and prices are subject to that annual change—except for depreciation, which is based on the original cost of the individual assets.

Since only the reporting problem is being studied here, we will assume that taxes are paid at a rate of 20% on the contribution to profit or revenue, minus the variable costs. For firms other than manufacturers, the variable costs are defined as the traditional cost of goods sold. For a manufacturing business, the variable costs equal the direct costs, and the allocated depreciation expense is subtracted to show the effect of inflation. This tax method allows us to separate and postpone (for a few pages) consideration of the real tax effect of inflation on depreciable assets. The focus in this section is on asset measurement problems when inflation occurs.

Annual costs, by item and year, are shown in table 6.1 as inflation continues at a 5% rate. Year 0 is the base year, prior to inflation. In year 1, the revenues, variable costs, taxes, and cost of replacement assets all increase by 5%. Depreciation, however, stays the same, at $20,000, because it is based on the historical (i.e., original real) cost of the asset. The reported profit however increases from $12,000 to $13,600, for a 13.3% increase as a result of fixed depreciation expense. Moving to year 2, the values all increase by another 5%—except the depreciation expense and reported profits. The depreciation expense increases $200 to represent the "higher"-priced replacement machine purchased in year 1. (Four $20,000 machines and one machine at $21,000 give a depreciation expense of [4 × ($20,000/5) + $21,000/5] or $20,200.) The reported profit figure increases another 10.9% over the first year with inflation.

We continue this process for five years, at which time the last $20,000 machine is retired. With this zero-growth firm that maintains the same size in real terms, the reported profit has increased from $12,000 to $18,739 for an annual compounded growth rate of 7.9%. A naive valuation approach might consider a 7.9% growth over time in nominal terms. But that would give the wrong value. If one looks at the growth in cash flow, minus the replacement asset's cost or free cash flow, it increases from $12,000 to $12,600 or 5% for the first year. If the free cash flow growth for the entire period is considered, it increases from $12,000 to $15,315 over five years for a 5% compound growth rate. Thus, to value the firm's current earning

Table 6.1 Inflation and Firm Valuation (No Expansion of the Firm, 5% Inflation, Tax on Contribution Margin, in $K)

	Year 0	Year 1	Year 2	Year 3	Year 4	Year 5
Revenue	100	105	110.25	115.762	121.55	127.628
− Variable costs	−60	−63	−66.15	−69.458	−72.930	−76.577
− Depreciation exp.	−20	−20	−20.20	−20.610	−21.240	−22.102
− 20% margin tax	−8	−8.4	−8.82	−9.261	−9.724	−10.210
Net profit	12	13.6	15.08	16.433	17.656	18.739
+ Depreciation exp.	20	20	20.2	20.610	21.240	22.102
Oper. cash flows	32	33.6	35.28	37.043	38.896	40.841
− New asset cost	−20	−21	−22.05	−23.152	−24.310	−25.526
Free cash flow	12	12.6	13.23	13.891	14.586	15.315

potential correctly, the free cash flow growth rate should be used. These are still nominal dollars, requiring the nominal rate to be used. For this example, we get $12,600/(0.155 − 0.05) = $120,000, which is our original value.

What if we are not sure of the cost of the new, replacement machines? After all, the valuation approach is based on future profit estimates from pro forma income statements. We need to get a free cash flow estimate. Assuming straight-line depreciation, the adjustment for inflation on the nominal replacement cost can be figured directly if we know or can estimate the average depreciable life of the assets and the inflation rate. This approach assumes that inflation will remain at a constant rate, a reasonable initial assumption for valuing a firm in a steady-state position several years into the future.

Using the same approach as in table 6.1, table 6.2 shows the effects of different asset lives (N) and inflation rates. Each asset is retired after its life and replaced with an asset that is identical except for its cost being $(1+i)^N$. If inflation is zero, the replacement cost, minus reported depreciation expense, is zero. When the inflation rate is above zero, the value from the table is multiplied by the depreciation expense. That value is then subtracted from the net profits to produce the free cash flow estimate. Looking at our example, for five-year assets and 5% inflation, the 0.155 value is multiplied by the reported depreciation expense for year 5 of $22,102 to get $3,426. Subtracting this value from the reported profits of $18,739 gives $15,313, which is the profit adjusted for real depreciation. This value varies only by a rounding error from the $15,315 reported earlier as the free cash flow estimate.

With low U.S. inflation rates (around 3% in the 2000–2006 period), it is tempting to assume a zero inflation rate. That choice might be a reasonable approximation for a two- to three-year horizon. When valuing an ongoing business with that assumption, however, serious measurement errors can

Table 6.2 Additional Investment Required from Inflation with Steady-State Firm ([Replacement Cost of Assets Minus Reported Depreciation Expense] Divided by Reported Depreciation Expense, Using Straight-Line Depreciation for Reporting)

Depreciable Asset Life	3 Yrs.	4 Yrs.	5 Yrs.	6 Yrs.	7 Yrs.	8 Yrs.	9 Yrs.	10 Yrs.
1% Inflation	0.020	0.026	0.030	0.036	0.040	0.045	0.051	0.056
2%	0.040	0.050	0.061	0.071	0.082	0.092	0.102	0.113
3%	0.061	0.076	0.091	0.108	0.123	0.140	0.156	0.173
4%	0.081	0.102	0.124	0.145	0.166	0.188	0.210	0.113
5%	0.102	0.149	0.155	0.182	0.210	0.237	0.266	0.295
6%	0.122	0.154	0.187	0.220	0.254	0.289	0.323	0.359
7%	0.143	0.181	0.220	0.259	0.299	0.340	0.381	0.423
8%	0.165	0.208	0.252	0.298	0.344	0.392	0.437	0.490
9%	0.185	0.235	0.286	0.337	0.391	0.445	0.501	0.558
10%	0.207	0.264	0.319	0.378	0.438	0.499	0.563	0.627

result. Although those errors would be negligible for a firm with no depreciable assets, they are quite significant for most firms. The *Survey of Current Business* reported total U.S. corporate depreciation (in $billion) of $681B, $769B, and $824B for 2001, 2002, and 2003. For the same period, after-tax increases in retained earnings were correspondingly $200B, $233B, and $292B. Depreciation expenses averaged 3.1 times the additional retained earnings. Assuming an average depreciable life of seven years, with an approximate 3% rate of inflation, reported earnings must be adjusted downward 3.1 × 0.123 or 38.1% for the use of historical cost depreciation. Thus, the real level of retained earnings for the U.S. economy is only 61.9% of that reported—with only a 3% rate of inflation. Think what would happen if inflation rose to 5%, 7%, or even the 18% rates seen a couple of decades ago! At that time, the reported earnings of public firms were very high, but equity market indices were very low. One cannot ignore inflation and get meaningful value estimates for long-term assets of the kind embedded in most going concerns.

6.2.2 *Inflation Imposes Additional Working Capital Requirements*

The inflation effect on a firm's value, due to nominal depreciation, is only part of the inflation cost. We must also consider the increased investment in working capital necessitated by inflation. As our nominal sales increase, our accounts receivables will also increase. If we use a FIFO (First In, First Out) cost flow assumption for inventory, our investment in inventory will increase at the same rate, that is, we will add inventory at the inflated dollars and sell the oldest inventory (purchased in earlier dollars) at today's prices. Somewhat offsetting these effects, our trade payables can also be expected to increase. We want to make some reasonable estimates for these items to show the adjustments required to accurately forecast profits. If projected operating cash flows are used, these inflation-induced investments will be properly accounted.

Returning to the original example in this chapter (table 6.1), let's make some additional assumptions about trade credit, inventory, and accounts payable. The net amount of these items will represent an increased investment required each year due to inflation. Assume that receivables are collected in an average of thirty-six days. With $100,000 in sales, this lag between completion of goods and receipt of the money to pay for them means we will normally have a $10,000 investment tied up in our accounts receivable. Inventory will be assumed to have a turnover of three times per year, based on cost. If half of our variable costs are purchased supplies, our firm will have purchases of $60,000/2 or $30,000 a year and a standing inventory level of $10,000. If we pay for our purchases in thirty days, our average trade credit payables at any point in time are likely to be approximately $2,500. Ignoring other accruals and required cash balances, this combination implies a net working capital investment of $10,000 + $10,000 − $2,500 = $17,500.

6.2.2.1 FIFO INVENTORY COSTS Assuming a FIFO cost flow for inventory, this working capital investment must increase every year at the rate of inflation just to maintain the same-sized business. We continue to sell 10,000 units a year, but the price has increased, requiring us to increase the investment in accounts receivable. If inflation is 5%, as in the example, this requires an additional $875 investment for the first year, lowering our free cash flow by the same amount. The next year will require an additional $918 in working capital investment to stay at the same real size. Table 6.3 presents the analyses to incorporate the effects of inflation into forecasts of both the replacement cost of assets and the increased investment in working capital.

As happened when we used reported depreciation, the profits are overstated by the cost to inflate the working capital. The firm still can be valued correctly by capitalizing the free cash flows to investors. Remember that this is a no-growth firm. Further note that the increase in working capital each year increases at the inflation rate, 5% in this example. This is the same rate of increase as the other cash flows. We can thus use either the real or nominal value approaches to get the firm's value, considering now the increased working capital investment. Using the real/real approach, the first year's free cash flow is $12,600 − $875 for $11,725 in nominal value or $11,167 in real terms. With a 10% real discount rate, this approach gives a value of $111,670. Using the nominal/nominal approach produces an estimate of $11,725/(0.155 − 0.05) for the same $111,670 value.

As with inflation, the affect of increased working capital investment on the estimated value of a firm can be considered separately. The reduction of value for the first year is the amount of net working capital (WC_0) required, times the rate of inflation (i). With a constant level of inflation, this amount increases every year at the rate of inflation. The necessary year 2 increase in working capital is defined as $\{(1 + i) \times WC \times i\}$, whereas the year 3 increase is as $\{(1 + i)^2 \times WC \times i\}$:

$$\text{Year } N \text{ inflation-required changes in Working Capital} = \{(1 + i)^{N-1} \times WC \times i\}.$$

Table 6.3 Inflation and Firm Valuation with Working Capital Example (No Expansion of the Firm, 5% Inflation, Tax on Contribution Margin, $Ks)

	Year 0	Year 1	Year 2	Year 3	Year 4	Year 5
Revenue	$100.00	105.00	110.20	115.76	121.55	127.63
− Variable costs	−60.00	−63.00	−66.10	−69.46	−72.93	−76.58
− Depreciation exp.	−20.00	−20.00	−20.20	−20.61	−21.24	−22.10
− 20% margin tax	−8.00	−8.40	−8.82	−9.26	−9.72	−10.21
Net profit	12.00	13.60	15.08	16.43	17.66	18.74
+ Depreciation exp.	20.00	20.00	20.20	20.61	21.24	22.10
− Incr. working cap.	0.00	−0.88	−0.92	−0.96	−1.01	−1.06
Oper. cash flows	32.00	32.72	34.36	36.08	37.88	39.78
− New asset cost	−20.00	−21.00	−22.05	−23.15	−24.31	−25.53
Free cash flow	12.00	11.72	12.31	12.93	13.57	14.25

The present value (PV) of this increased working capital investment can be calculated by using the constant growth model for cash flows. The value at time 1 is $(WC \times i)$. The discount rate is the nominal discount rate (R), 15.5% in our example. And the growth rate is the inflation rate or i. This formula gives $WC \times i/(R - i)$ or, for our example, $\$17{,}500 \times 0.05/(0.155 - 0.05) = \$5{,}833$. Subtracting this investment from our initial value of \$120,000 gives the new estimated value, with inflation, of \$114,167. This approach allows us to see directly the affect of inflation on valuation. The 5% inflation rate decreased value 4.9%. Between depreciation expenses being reported on historical costs and increased investments needed for working capital, it is not surprising that P/E ratios for public firms were extremely low during the late 1970s and early 1980s when the inflation rate was so high.

Consider the same example with an inflation rate of 20%. The required rate of return will stay at 10%. Following Fisher's formula, that changes the nominal rate or required return to

$$R = (1 + 10\%) \times (1 + 20\%) - 1 = (1.1 \times 1.2) - 1 = 32\%.$$

Then, the present value of the required working capital investments would be calculated as follows:

$$PV(WC) = WC \times i/(R - i) = \$17{,}500 \times 0.2/(0.32 - 0.2)$$
$$= \$3{,}500/0.12 = \$29{,}167.$$

Based on an original estimate of \$120,000 for the firm's value, this factor alone would adjust the value of the firm downward by 24.3%, to \$90,833. We can readily see how devastating inflation can be for business owners!

6.2.2.2 LIFO INVENTORY ADVANTAGES

Our example used a FIFO cost flow assumption for inventory. Could we not lower the effect of inflation by using LIFO (Last In, First Out)? With LIFO, the recently purchased, inflated-cost, items flow through the income statement. The older, pre-inflation priced goods are invested in inventory. The firm is still undertaking the same transactions, however, regardless of its cost flow assumptions. With LIFO, the reported profits are lower, which lowers taxes. This tax saving is the only reduction in investment costs. When the marginal tax rate is (t), for a LIFO inventory base (INV), the firm saves [$t \times$ (the increased inventory value)], or $[t \times (INV \times i)]$, each year by reporting a higher value for its costs of goods sold. Thus, if we define WC' as working capital minus inventory, the inflation affect on working capital investment is $\{i \times [(WC' + INV(1 -)]\}$ for LIFO firms.

This comparison between LIFO and FIFO, and their effects on value estimates, summarizes the accounting discussion on the topic, in algebraic terms. With no inflation (i.e., $i = 0$), no problem exists. The expected profits and resulting value to a firm will be the same whether we use LIFO or FIFO assumptions. Some prices will increase will others decline, resulting in an overall zero inflation rate. Similarly, if there is no profit tax (i.e., $t = 0$), then the adjustment for inflation will be the same under either model. What this comparison does point out is the present value of tax savings due to using LIFO instead of FIFO, for any given tax rate, inflation rate, and firm discount rate. The formula for this tax savings is

$$PV\ (\text{tax savings}) = t \times INV \times i/(R - i).$$

Using a 34% tax rate for our example, with a 5% inflation rate and a 10% required real rate of return (corresponding to a 15.5% nominal rate), the advantage works out to be

$$0.34 \times INV \times 0.05/(0.155 - 0.05) = 0.162 \times INV.$$

In terms of value, a firm pays an additional tax of 16.2% of the value of its initial inventory when it uses FIFO instead of LIFO—when the inflation rate is only 5%.

6.2.3 *Inflation Lowers the Net Profits Available for Investors*

This short section will show inflation's combined effects on historical cost depreciation and the nominal increases in working capital. These are all measurement problems that inflation causes in a simple environment with known, fixed-price increases each year. While we can show how inflation affects just the investment calculation, we will totally ignore the psychological effects that high and uncertain inflation will create on the real operations of a business. By showing how the simplest static firm can adjust for inflation, we can better understand the more complex processes in the real world, with changing assets, varying price changes, and adjusting markets.

Reconsider our example. The firm had five machines, with one being replaced each year. Prior to inflation, each machine cost $20,000. Furthermore, the firm has a net real investment in working capital of $17,500. In our simplified model, inflation starts at a specific point in time, and then continues at a fixed and known rate each year. Using the values from table 6.2 to adjust for inflation, and knowing that the net working capital must increase by the rate of inflation each year, we will show what happens to free cash flow as related to reported profits. Free cash flow will be net profits, minus the adjustment factor from table 6.2, times the reported depreciation, and minus the net working capital times the rate of inflation. For our example firm with a 3% rate of inflation, this formula will mean $12,000 − (20,000 × 0.091) − (17.5 × 0.03) for $9,655, or just over 80% of reported profits. Table 6.4 shows what happens. Even with low levels of inflation, firms must retain a substantial portion of their reported earnings just to stay even with inflation.

An astute reader probably wonders why anyone would bother with all this fancy analysis with complex adjustments when using free cash flows solves the problem. There are two justifications for our approach. First, most firms' accountants and bankers think in terms of reported profits.

Table 6.4 Impacts of Inflation on Free Cash Flow and Profits

	Inflation Rate (%)				
	0	3	5	7	10
Free cash flow	$12,000	$9,655	$8,025	$6,375	$3,875
% of profits	100	80.5	66.9	53.1	32.3

Sure, these people understand that inflation creates additional problems and funds must be reinvested just to stay even, but they still think first about the bottom line according to GAAP. The second rationale is that the simple adjustments we make probably cannot be made in the real world. Our simple business, with a machine being replaced each year with an identical asset, is a bit too simplified. What happens if the business has three machines lasting five years each? Some years, the business would be making no investments in new equipment. Furthermore to show just the effect of inflation, our approach assumes that everything goes up in price by the same percentage each year. However, we can estimate the current inflation level, we know our net working capital, and we know the depreciation expense and average life of our assets. With these values, we can adjust our reported net profits downward for the inflation effect.

The really astute reader wonders what happens with the even higher rates of inflation that exist in many places in the world. Prices will increase throughout the year, unlike in the simple example where the entire increase occurs at once. The goods sold in December will be priced much closer to the expected prices for the coming January than they were to the previous January. The adjustment table above will not be very useful, which is why we stopped at 10% a year. Probably more important is the fact that accounting based on historical costs is also not very useful in high inflation environments.

6.3 Inflation Lowers the Depreciation Tax Shield

Along with increased working capital requirements, a major real effect of inflation on firm value, as opposed to the effects on measurement issues, is its devaluation effect on a firm's depreciation expenses. The depreciation expense for both taxes and reporting is determined from an asset's historical cost when purchased. With inflation, that cost today seems small compared to its time of purchase and may underestimate the cost of replacement today with a similar asset. Similarly, we have been assuming that the investment required to counteract depreciation would result in the purchase of identical machines. With advances going on all the time in engineering and other forms of knowledge, we will have to replace depreciated machines (or retiring people) with assets of higher capability—just to maintain our competitive position.

Like valuation in general, this problem can also be addressed using either a real/real approach or a nominal/nominal approach. Reported depreciation values are always nominal values, based on initial purchase cost. With the real/real approach, the depreciation values are discounted by the rate of inflation to get their current real values. With the nominal/nominal approach, all other values increase with inflation except the depreciation expense, as is done in current financial reports.

6.3.1 *Using Nominal Values*

Let's redo the example shown in table 6.1, using a 40% tax rate on profits instead of a 20% rate on the contribution margin, to see the effect of inflation on depreciation expense. Table 6.5 presents our example with these changes. The tax expense in the first year has now increased $8,800. The free cash flow, after replacing the asset, drops to $12,200 nominal dollars. Because of the historical costs used to calculate depreciation, the nominal free cash flow increases at a rate less than inflation. This annual process continues until all the pre-inflation assets are retired. After that point, the free cash flow increases at the rate of inflation.

Since the calculation of value based on an ever-changing inflation would be horribly complex, we have chosen to keep this illustration relatively simple by showing the differences that only two rates (0% and 5%) can have. Valuations are only estimates. Better estimates will have more realistic assumptions about the rate of inflation—and sensitivity analyses that show the effects of increasing or decreasing that rate within a reasonable band.

What happens to value as we make those changes? The present value of the future nominal cash flows is discounted to the present using the nominal discount rate of 15.5%. That formula gives a value of $110,400. This value is 8% less than the original value of $120,000 in a zero-inflation environment. The difference is due to the inflated tax on depreciable assets. We

Table 6.5 Inflation and Firm Valuation Example: Nominal Values (No Expansion of the Firm, 5% Inflation, 40% Tax on Reported Profits, $Ks)

	Year 1	Year 2	Year 3	Year 4	Year 5	Year 6
Revenue	$105	110.25	115.762	121.55	127.628	134.009
− Variable costs	−63	−66.15	−69.458	−72.930	−76.577	−80.406
− Depreciation exp.	−20	−20.20	−20.610	−21.240	−22.102	−23.207
− 40% profit tax	−8.8	−9.56	−10.278	−10.952	−11.580	−12.159
Net profit	13.2	14.34	15.416	16.428	17.369	18.237
+ Depreciation exp.	20.0	20.2	20.610	21.240	22.102	23.207
Oper. cash flows	33.2	34.54	36.026	37.668	39.471	41.444
− New asset cost	−21.0	−22.05	−23.152	−24.310	−25.526	−26.802
Free cash flow	$12.2	12.49	12.874	13.358	13.945	14.642

must also subtract from our estimated value of the firm the inflation-created additional investment required in working capital. It was shown to equal the inflation rate, times the net working capital with FIFO inventory, and the net working capital without inventory for LIFO firms. The additional investment in working capital increases each year at the inflation rate. In our example, it caused an additional investment requirement of $875 in year 1, another $919 in year 2, and so on. The net affect was a decreased value of $8,333, or another 7%. The 5% per year rate of inflation has thus caused a combined decrease of 15% in our estimated value of the firm.

6.3.2 *Using Real Prices*

The valuation can also be done using real cash flows and the real discount rate as shown in table 6.6. With this approach, all the values stay the same—sales, variable costs, replacement costs—except for depreciation and the resulting taxes. The "real" depreciation values decrease with inflation because these nominal values are constant. They only decrease by 5% the first year. In future years, real depreciation decreases at a rate slightly less than the rate of inflation because the replacement assets cost more. In our example, between years 1 and 2, the real amount of the depreciation expenses decreases by 3.8%, from $19,048 to $18,322. By year 5, when the last prior-to-inflation asset is retired, the real depreciation expense levels off at $17,317. The depreciation tax shield is worth 13.4% less for five-year assets with a 5% rate of inflation.

An accelerated depreciation method, such as the current MACRS (modified accelerated class recovery system, a result of the 1986 Tax Reform Act) in the United States, will lower (but not eliminate) the effect of inflation on depreciation. If we take the present value of real cash flows at the required 10% real opportunity cost, we again produce a value estimate of $110,400.

Table 6.6 Inflation and Firm Valuation Example: Real Values (No Expansion of the Firm, 5% Inflation, 40% Tax on Reported Profits, $Ks)

	Year 1	Year 2	Year 3	Year 4	Year 5	Year 6
Revenue	$100	100	100	100	100	100
− Variable costs	−60	−60	−60	−60	−60	−60
− Depreciation exp.	−19.048	−18.322	−17.804	−17.474	−17.317	−17.317
− 40% profit tax	−8.381	−8.671	−8.878	−9.010	−9.073	−9.073
Net profit	12.571	13.007	13.318	13.456	13.610	13.610
+ Depreciation exp.	19.048	18.322	17.804	17.474	17.317	17.317
Oper. cash flows	31.619	31.329	31.122	30.930	30.927	30.927
− New asset cost	−20	−20	−20	−20	−20	−20
Free cash flow	11.6	11.329	11.122	10.930	10.927	10.927

6.4 Conclusions about Inflation and Valuation Measurement

Inflation, even at low levels, can cause problems in estimating the value of going concerns. One must always remember to use real cash flow estimates and discount them with real rates, or nominal cash flow estimates discounted with nominal rates. Almost everyone is aware that depreciation is calculated on the basis of historical costs, but it is tempting to ignore the long-term distortions resulting from even low levels of inflation. As shown in table 6.6, these effects can be quite significant, even with rates as low as 3%. Inflation is also going to require owners to inject more working capital—just to stay even. Those additional investments can be significant even at low levels of inflation, and they, too, result from the accounting rules. Both of these problems can be eliminated in valuations by basing valuation estimates on the free cash flows from operations (net profits + depreciation expense − incremental investments in working capital − investments in fixed assets), instead of the reported profits. Especially for valuation of private firms, free cash flows should be used more often than they have been.

Although measurement problems are caused by inappropriate treatment of inflation, there are also real valuation decreases. Firms must continually increase their investments in working capital just to stay even with inflation. Except for LIFO inventory, this working capital investment uses after-tax profits. Depreciation expenses for both reporting and taxes are determined from historical costs. With inflation, the value of depreciation to lower future taxes is worth less. Accelerated depreciation lowers, but does not eliminate, the wealth lost due to inflation.

6.5 Real Value—or Inflated Mirage?

"Mike, how did your dad deal with things back in the seventies and eighties when they had all those inflation problems? We've been blessed with low inflation during most of our ownership times, but I can see how 18% interest rates must have thrown all kinds of problems at their business plans back then!"

"I don't know, Tom. He didn't talk about it much, just showed the stress. It sounded like things were really dicey for quite a while, but we were kids. You know, so long as the water's in the pool, and there's gas in the car, we're doing okay. Looking back now, I can see how he aged, how he seemed to withdraw from the good times we had, spending more late hours at the shop. I've wondered if that stress contributed to his early heart attack."

Giving himself a shake, and steering their conversation deliberately in a different direction, Tom asked, "What did you find out about your real growth rate, your real return on investment?"

Mike pulled himself back from gloomy memories. "It looks like a real growth rate of about 6.5% over the last ten years, once I got the business running properly."

"Hmm. Mine came in at 5.4%." Tom laid his on the table. "What inflation discount did you accountant use?"

"She used 3.5%"

"So did mine," Tom agreed. "Then I looked up the historical figures and saw that it was a fair bit higher in the eighties, and lower recently. We did a second run with the annual rates for those years, and the results were a bit different. Recent years looked better. Same trend, though."

"Sure knocked the stuffing out of my earlier numbers!" Mike looked a bit sheepish. "For a while when we started this exercise, I thought I had double-digit growth. I still do—but now know that a big part of it hasn't been real, just inflation."

7

Calculating the Discount Rate for Closely Held Firms

7.0 Wrestling with Discount Rates

After lunch with their peers at the monthly Chamber of Commerce meeting, a troubled Tom pulled Mike aside. "The more that university economist talked, the more it seemed like 'the discount rate' is pretty important to savvy decisions about investment—and that probably applies to what we do with our businesses, too. But what discount rate was she talking about? It didn't sound like it was the kind of discount we give our customers—or the kind we get from our suppliers. And it didn't sound like the same thing as inflation. Do you understand this?"

Mike was relieved that his longtime friend shared his discomfort. "You know, I wondered the same thing at first, but she kept talking about *the* discount rate, like there's only one. You and I both deal with lots of different discount rates in our businesses, so that would have been a plural. I know they sometimes get detached from real business up there on the campus, but I don't think that's the problem here."

Tom picked up. "My next guess was that it might be the same thing as the interest rate we pay to the bank on loans, but that couldn't be the case either, because loan rates vary a lot. She seemed to be talking about a single rate that applies to all parts of a company at the same time."

"Yeah," replied Mike, "I wondered if she might be talking about that Federal Reserve Bank rate the business analysts on TV seem to think is so important. But that doesn't seem to be it either. That rate can be changed any time the Federal Reserve Board meets, and she suggested that 'the discount rate' was more stable than that. In the end, I'm still stumped."

"Glad to know it's not just me," Tom exhaled. "Guess it's time for another session with the Professor. We have something more to learn."

WHAT IS THE DISCOUNT RATE? Up to this point, we have been postponing an item of obvious importance when forecasting the future value of economic assets: what is the discount rate? Those projected future cash flows must be brought back to the present (i.e., discounted) to obtain a standardized value that can be used to compare alternatives. The appropriate discount rate will depend on several factors, including the

- risk-free required rate of return,
- systematic risk for public firms in the same or similar industries,
- market price of risk for public firms,
- size of the firm, and
- additional costs of illiquidity.

The major problem that we face is that no basis exists to directly estimate this rate unless one assumes that the owner/manager holds only a small portion of his or her wealth in the firm. In chapter 2, we discussed the importance of separating the interests of the owner/manager from those of the firm, even while recognizing that such separation is often difficult. This matter of the discount rate is the only material for valuation of a small private firm that is conceptually different from that of valuing a large public firm.

To show how we estimate the required return for a closely held firm, we first review the required return for a public firm. Then we focus on additional adjustments required to adapt the method for use on a closely held firm. This approach deals specifically with the lack of liquidity and diversification of the owner and the lack of market information for small firms. Finally, we will show how the discount rate should be estimated for a closely held firm.

7.1 Required Rate of Return for a Public Firm

Determining the required return for a risky firm is a lengthy process with multiple parts. Current understanding of this process began in 1930 when Irving Fisher pointed out that people must be compensated for postponing consumption.[1] This need can be observed when "risk-free" government bonds have to pay a positive interest rate to attract investors.

Other thinkers followed Fisher, identifying additional costs or required returns to investors for projects with risky outcomes.[2] Still other researchers have examined the trade-offs associated with holding illiquid investments (i.e., those that cannot be easily sold). John Maynard Keynes noted that individuals hold liquid assets, such as cash, to be able to promptly seize good opportunities as they arise.[3] Investors pay a premium to be able to convert

[1] See Irving Fisher, *The Theory of Interest* (New York: Macmillan, 1930).

[2] A thorough discussion on risk aversion is found in John Pratt, "Risk Aversion in the Small and in the Large," *Econometrica* 32 (January–April 1964): 122–36.

[3] John Maynard Keynes, *The General Theory of Employment, Interest and Money* (London: Macmillan, 1936).

investments into cash quickly and at a low cost. These can be risky investments, such as equity positions in large public firms, but they are liquid investments, as opposed to, say, owning one's own house.

Most investors are unwilling to undertake fair bets when the stakes are high. As a current example, consider the *Who Wants to Be a Millionaire?* television game show. Imagine a contestant going for $250,000; he is stumped by the question and takes the 50/50 lifeline, ruling out two of the answers. Still befuddled, this contestant can walk away with $125,000 or guess for $250,000—with a $32,000 consolation price if he's wrong. Having no idea which answer is correct, the contestant has a 50% chance of guessing correctly for the $250,000 and a 50% chance of missing for the $32,000. The expected payoff is $\$250{,}000 \times 0.50 + \$32{,}000 \times 0.50 = \$141{,}000$, which is obviously larger than $125,000. So a "rational" investor should take the chance, flip the coin, and live with the results. Despite the greater expected value of that approach, many contestants have walked away with the certain $125,000, rather than make a guess. Simply selecting the largest expected payoff is clearly not the only basis on which humans make decisions!

In analyzing risk in equity investments, Markowitz showed in the early 1950s that diversified portfolios gave better risk-return performance for investors than did concentrated holdings.[4] This led to the Sharpe-Lintner-Treynor Capital Asset Pricing Model, where systematic risk is priced in the market place and other, unsystematic risk is eliminated through a well-diversified portfolio.[5] This method produced a specific risk premium, defined in terms of an additional required return to cover a public firm's systematic risk. Thus, for large public firms where one can assume that there is a diversified ownership, the required rate of return can be defined. It is the risk-free rate for the straight time value of money and a risk premium that is the product of the firm's relative systematic risk times the market price of risk.

Finally, empirical research by Fama and French found that a greater rate of return was required for investors, including owners, of smaller firms.[6]

[4] Harry Markowitz, who was later awarded the Nobel Prize in Economics, published this in "Portfolio Selection," *Journal of Finance* 7 (March 1952) 77–91.

[5] This idea was developed independently by several scholars. William Sharpe published "Capital Asset Prices: A Theory of Market Equilibrium under Conditions of Risk," *Journal of Finance* 19 (September 1964): 425–42. Shortly thereafter, John Lintner published "The Valuation of Risk Assets and the Selection of Risky Investments in Stock Portfolios and Capital Budgets," *Review of Economics and Statistics* 47 (February 1965) 13–37. Jack L. Treynor's classic working paper is dated 1961 and widely referenced in the literature, but was not published until 1999: J. L. Treynor, "Market Value, Time and Risk," in *Asset Pricing and Portfolio Performance: Models, Strategy, and Performance Metrics*, edited by R. A. Korajczyk (London: Risk Books, 1999).

[6] Their three-factor model finds returns a positive function of systematic risk (betas), earnings/price ratio, and size. Eugene Fama and Kenneth French, "The Cross Section of Excepted Returns," *Journal of Finance* 47 (June 1992) 427–65.

Their work considered portfolios of firms by size, systematic risk, and price/earnings (P/E) ratios. They found smaller firms, higher systematic risk firms, and lower P/E firms earned greater future returns. Except for systematic risk, there is no theoretical justification for the greater rates of returns for smaller firms or lower P/E firms.

These various factors must be incorporated into the required rate of return for the valuation of a closely held firm. But how? The closely held firm's owner/manager is most likely less risk averse than the market average, holds a nondiversified portfolio, has a closely held illiquid business, and has a firm much smaller than even small public firms in the same industry. In adapting the valuation models developed for public companies for use in closely held firms, only the risk-free required return causes no problem. All of the other criteria need to be adjusted. The next section considers how to incorporate these concerns.

7.2 Required Rate of Return for a Closely Held Firm

The model described for a public firm is fairly close to the actual process for estimating its required return. Although there are measurement problems, they are minor compared to what is faced when estimating the required rate of return for a closely held firm.

In estimating the value of the future benefits a firm may provide to its owner/manager, it is practically impossible to define an exact single discount rate to use. The only readily available approach is to find the owner's point of indifference between owning the business versus a diversified portfolio of marketable securities. An analyst using the indifference approach questions the owner/manager about the portfolio value at which he or she would be indifferent between owning the business and taking the portfolio. This approach gives a totally subjective value about what the business is worth to the owner/manager. This value is very useful in helping an owner decide whether or not to accept a takeover bid, provided the value is well-determined and remains stable in the face of the opportunity. Bids greater than the indifference value should be considered, and those below it should be rejected.

This is not a satisfactory way, however, to get an objective estimate of business value from a market investment perspective. Suppose that the business is objectively worth \$3 million. (Okay, suppose we have a crystal ball!) One owner/manager might be tired of the hassle and daily grind of responsibilities and be willing to take \$2 million to get out cleanly. Another might enjoy running the business and being independent. Her indifference value might be \$4 million. This approach, unfortunately, does not separate the manager's perception of risk and the required rate of return from the personal benefits (or pain) that she gets from running her own business.

What one really wants with a valuation is an accurate estimate of the firm's market value. What is the business worth, as it is currently being run, to others who might buy it? This goal requires using a comparable discount rate that considers the time value of money, the firm's systematic risk and the market price for risk, plus additional adjustments for small firm status and for the lack of liquidity.

This analysis ignores the unsystematic risk that the owner/manager faces while operating his or her own business. That risk could be diversified away by holding a broad portfolio of firms. When the owner/manager of a closely held firm is not as risk-averse as the average stock-market investor (or views risk as lower when he or she has inside knowledge or control), then one could also concede that he or she might be psychologically willing to absorb the unsystematic risk associated with concentrating assets in an undiversified holding, that is, the core business.[7] For owner/managers who are as risk-averse as the general investor population, however, or even more cautious, an additional discount should be added to compensate for the additional risks inherent in small business ownership. Such individuals, however, are unlikely to be career small business owners because, except for firms launched to commercialize rare new innovations, market competition would not support superior returns.

The required return for the closely held firm is driven by the sum of the

- time value of money;
- market-priced systematic risk;
- relative size effect; and
- lack of liquidity.

We will now show how these estimates should be developed.

7.3 Methods Used to Estimate the Required Return

7.3.1 *Time Value of Money*

The time value of money is the *risk-free* borrowing rate. At what rate must people be compensated for postponing consumption when no risk is present? The U.S. federal government borrowing rate represents the best estimate of the risk-free rate, based on an almost universal confidence in the ability of Uncle Sam to meet its financial commitments. Similarly, a Canadian business would use the Canadian bond yield; a European firm would use the Euro rate; and so on.

The rate varies with maturity. On December 1, 2006, for example, the 30-day rate was 5.21%; the 1-year rate was 4.87%; the 2-year rate was 4.52%; the 10-year rate was 4.43%; and the 20-year rate was 4.64%. The relationship between no-default government bond yields, where only the time to maturity varies, is referred to as the *yield curve*. Almost always,

7 This concept has been developed in a recent working paper, Xiaoli Wang, "Entrepreneurial Spirit and Asset Allocation from a Risk Perspective," Department of Finance, Rutgers Business School, Newark, N.J., 2005.

bonds with longer times to maturity require a greater rate of return to attract investors away from short-term (i.e., more certain) instruments because they face a greater price decrease if rates rise. Which rate should be used in business valuations? Because an ongoing firm is valued to perpetuity, the yield of the longest maturity bond represents the most reasonable choice. On December 1, 2006, for example, a 4.64% rate should have been used, based on the quoted 20-year rate.

All these government bond yields represent nominal rates, as discussed in chapter 6. They include *expected* inflation. The longest maturity bonds reflect the expected inflation rates on the long horizon.

7.3.2 *Systematic or Market Risk*

Investors must be rewarded for accepting greater risk, or they will keep their money in the most secure investments. What we need to know for valuation work is:

- How much of a reward is required to attract investments, given various risk levels?
- What does a business owner have to pay to attract the investors needed to support the business?
- In a more personal sense, what is the minimum reward that would encourage an owner to stay invested in his or her own business—instead of cashing out and buying U.S. Treasury Notes, for example?

The cost a business has to pay to attract capital is a function of the kinds and magnitudes of risk the business incurs. This section measures the cost of that basic business risk. The cost is defined and calculated as the product of the price of risk times the industry-specific risk estimated for the firm being valued. Assuming they are rational wealth-maximizers, investors will hold well-diversified portfolios to obtain the best risk-return trade-off. The risk that cannot be diversified away through a broad portfolio is referred to as *systematic risk*. It is measured relative to the overall market risk of the market portfolio and is referred to as *beta*. The average beta of all risky securities, by definition, is 1.00. Those opportunities with beta values greater than 1.00 face increased market risk and require a greater rate of return to attract investors, while the opposite occurs with those having betas lower than 1.00. Many sources, such as Standard & Poor's and Value Line, publish beta values for most of the larger public firms. There is no reason to recalculate beta values for large public firms.

Wait a minute! Aren't we talking about valuing a closely held firm? No market reports exist to help us establish the variation in share price over time for private firms, so it is impossible to calculate their beta values. This difficulty in valuing closely held firms brings out another problem—estimating systematic risk. The best approximation available to us is an average of the beta values of public firms that produce similar products. Do not worry that they are from substantially larger firms. Additional adjustments will be made later for small firm effects. This part of the work estimates just the volatility effects in the larger market for firms in any particular line of business.

7.3.3 *Reward for Accepting Risk*

Now that an estimate has been made of the systematic risk level, we need to know how much extra return is required to justify accepting this risk. In other words, what value should be added to the risk-free discount rate? Over the seventy years from 1926 through 1995, the stocks of small public companies earned an average annual rate of return of 17.7%.[8] Long-term government bonds earned an annual average return of 5.5% over the same period. Therefore, the risk premium for small public firms should be the estimated beta value, times the average difference earned by the small public firms over government bonds, or $1.00 \times (17.7\% - 5.5\%)$ which is 12.2%.

Closely held firms are usually quite a bit smaller than the small public firms for which we have data. We need to find a way to adjust those values from the market of known (public) firms, to the market of private firms. As a comparison on the other side, large public firms, as represented by the S&P 500, earned an average return of 12.5% per year over the same period—5.2% less per year than the smaller firms. These firms are in magnitude 50–200 times larger on average than small public firms. Therefore, when it is remembered that the small public firms are valued between $25–250 million, a closely held firm with a value over $30 million would require no additional adjustment on this dimension. One in the $20 million range requires an additional 1% return. Those private firms in the $10 million range require an additional 2% return, and smaller firms an additional 3%. The discussion that follows will explain the justification for these additional risk premiums.

7.4 Special Considerations for Closely Held Firms

What justifies this 12% to 15% risk premium for a small closely held firm, compared to the 7% risk premium for large public firms, when both have the same average systematic risk? Can it be just the size difference? By itself, that makes little sense. After reviewing the valuation literature and thinking about this issue, we have broken it down into three different, though not entirely independent, factors:

- Increased probability of bankruptcy
- Lack of liquidity

[8] These market return values are all from *Stocks, Bonds, Bills and Inflation: 1996 Yearbook* (Chicago: Ibbotson Associates, 1996), the classic in the field. See more recent Yearbooks for updates, and especially R. Ibbotson and P. Chen, "Long-Run Stock Returns: Participating in the Real Economy," *Financial Analysts Journal*, January/February 2003, available online at www.allbusiness.com/personal-finance/investing-stock-investments/1032932-1.html. The latter article includes a synopsis of Ibbotson's work in this field over several decades.

- Lack of public information (independent, verifiable, credible) about the business

Here's how each of these factors contributes to the risk premium for closely held firms.

7.4.1 *Increased Bankruptcy Risk*

The excess return required for smaller firms could be derived from additional bankruptcy risk, often called, in honor of the premier recent destroyer of small-town retailers, the "Wal-Mart Liquidator." In a typical valuation, one views past profits, current and expected economic conditions, and makes predictions about future profits. No real thought is given to a total change in the economic environment. New competitors, however, such as Wal-Mart or Home Depot, can enter a local marketplace, and change forever the future value of local firms. Although such large competitors affect firms of all size, smaller firms, particularly closely held ones, are more vulnerable. Therefore, increasing the required rate of return approximates this affect, reflecting the increased risk associated with potential future competitors. (See also the more extended discussion of this set of issues in chapter 5.)

A major portion of this required return results from a higher percentage of small public firms being delisted from trading. One study found that over 35% of the smallest 5% of NASDAQ firms are delisted each year. The next smallest 5% group saw the delisting rate drop to 19%. The third smallest group had an even smaller 13.8%, while only 0.6% of the largest NASDAQ firms stopped trading each year.[9] Further analysis showed that almost no value was salvaged by the shareholders of the delisted firms. In extending those data, it was found that the realized return for small firms is almost identical to the large ones. Only the smallest 15% of these NASDAQ firms show average returns, adjusted for delistings, greater than the average returns of the largest 5% group.[10]

Since one does not know a priori when or where Wal-Mart (or other powerful competitors of closely held firms) will open next, and hence which businesses will be forced out, we can acknowledge their increased competitive risk by increasing the required rate of return for small firms. What this means is that investors (including rational owners and potential buyers) would require at least that additional premium to continue to invest in such firms.

9 Tyler Shumway and Vincent A. Warther, "The Delisting Bias in CRSP's NASDAQ Data and Its Implications for the Size Effect," *Journal of Finance* 54 (December 1999) 2361–79.

10 These adjusted average returns are from Michael S. Long, Xiaoli Wang, and J. Zhang, "Growth Options, Unwritten Call Discounts, and the Valuation of the Small Firm," working paper, Department of Finance, Rutgers Business School, Newark, N.J., 2006.

Note, however, that some small firms are more vulnerable, and others are less vulnerable. As one values a specific firm, this is one of the factors that should be adjusted on the basis of the nature of the specific threats and defenses posed to the firm's future value. In some cases, the adjustments may be substantial. If a major Big Box shopping center has just been announced for the suburbs a mile away, this risk factor has suddenly increased a lot. Conversely, if a business is supported by a very loyal clientele with a broad demographic range, has a strong local brand identity, and has already survived the arrival of big corporate competitors, the appropriate risk factor might be lower than average.

7.4.2 *Lack of Liquidity in Closely Held Firms*

The next special consideration in determining the required return for a closely held firm deals with its liquidity—or rather, its lack of liquidity. Liquidity refers to the ability to convert assets into cash both quickly and inexpensively. An easy example of a liquid asset is shares of stock in large publicly traded firms such as ExxonMobil, General Motors, or Microsoft. To convert such shares to cash, one merely calls a stockbroker and places a "sell" order. Within minutes, it is sold and a check arrives at the end of the clearing period. Unlike that situation, the owners of closely held firms cannot sell a few shares or margin their stockholding accounts quickly to obtain cash. After looking at liquidity in its traditional sense, we will also discuss its relationships to information and risk. These factors of liquidity are what really cause illiquid assets or businesses to sell at large discounts to their economic value.

We measure liquidity costs against an ideal situation where no time elapses and no discounts apply, that is, cash is immediately available for the full value of the asset, and where there is zero cost to complete the sale. The degree to which reality deviates from that ideal defines the liquidity cost or, more properly, the costs of illiquidity. Remember, liquidity cost consists of two parts: the speed with which assets can be converted to cash, and the cost of the conversion. Liquidity cost is defined as the sum of the

- alternative income that could be earned while assets are tied up during the selling process and
- transaction fees.

A good example of an illiquid asset similar to a closely held business is homeownership. When a home is put on the market, its sale will usually take an amount of time that cannot be fully determined in advance, and its owners will incur a substantial transaction cost. Depending on the market, completion of a sale can take from several weeks to more than a year. The real estate commission in most cities is 6% of the selling price; in rural areas it can easily be over 10%. In addition, the costs of surveys, title verification, and so on are all deducted from the final realized value of the property. Put together, those items are the transaction costs, the second cost of illiquidity.

The illiquidity cost says nothing directly about the risk of the asset. Home equity in most markets, most of the time, has much less risk of significant depreciation than an investment in corporate equity. This distinction is an important factor to remember when considering the cost of illiquidity with a closely held firm. The closely held firm might also have greater risk, but that is treated separately.

7.4.3 *Liquidity and Value*

How important is the effect of illiquidity on value? The importance of liquidity (or lack of it) for estimates of value must be understood as the equity in closely held firms is generally quite illiquid. According to academic studies of valuation, the effect is quite large. A review of the differences between investments in public and closely held firms showed that more than liquidity changes. For example, the price of restricted stock, which cannot be easily sold, versus registered stock in the same firms, which is readily marketable, appears to be discounted 30% to 35%.[11] Thus, 100 shares of restricted stock in a public firm would be worth the same as 65–70 shares of the same stock without restrictions. One must be careful in drawing these conclusions, however. A major portion of that discount appears to result from ownership by minority shareholders or attached forfeiture clauses, and not strictly from the stock's illiquidity.

Liquidity costs result from the time and cost of converting an asset into cash. Although it is still not a direct measure of these costs, an approximation can be found from viewing the costs incurred in selling a closely held firm. This frame of reference is based on selling the entire business and not merely cashing out a portion of the investment. A broker of closely held firms supplied us with a range of commissions for business sales, shown in table 7.1.[12] In addition, extra legal costs would be incurred, which he estimated at around $50,000 for a $2 million sale. These would increase to $75,000 for a $10 million transaction. Therefore, for a $2 million business, total transaction costs are likely to be approximately 7% selling costs, plus 2.5% for legal costs—9.5% on a $2 million transaction—substantially less than the overall 30–35% discount that the finance literature reports.

In assessing liquidity costs for a closely held firm, however, two other factors must be considered for a proper estimate. First, if our relatively small closely held firm were public, what kind of transaction costs would

[11] This summary of empirical studies was reported in Aswath Damodaran, *Investment Valuation* (New York: Wiley, 1996), 496.

[12] Alan Scharfstein, president of DAK Investments, provided these data. His Paramus, New Jersey, firm is a major broker/investment banker, advising owners on the sale of closely held firms.

Table 7.1 Approximate Selling Costs for Closely Held Firms

Value of Firm	Legal Costs	% Legal	Selling Costs	% Selling	Total Costs	% Total
$2M	$50,000	2.5	$140,000	7.0	$190,000	9.5
$10M	75,000	0.75	250,000	2.5	325,000	3.25

we face in selling its stock in the secondary market? Remember that an illiquidity cost of 30–35% of the value was implicitly compared with zero transaction costs. This approximation is probably fine when comparing it with large public firms, such as ExxonMobil, General Motors, or Microsoft. Here, however, the comparison is between a closely held firm and a similarly sized small public firm. The costs of buying and selling shares in small public firms are much higher than the costs associated with large public firms, so the real comparable cost associated with a private holding won't be the full 30–35%.

The cost of selling shares in small public firms is not so much the direct broker's fee as it is the market maker's spread. (This principle underlies the reason that discount brokers can advertise such low transaction costs and still make money.) What is the difference between what a buyer pays for 100 shares and what the seller receives for 100 shares? This logic is the same type of comparison as the cost of selling the firm, with the difference being the comparable fee packages. For public exchanges of equity, it is the percentage spread between prices bid and asked. A recent study found these spreads to be extremely high for small NASD securities. For small public firms (those with a market value of under $10 million), the average spread is about 10%. The cost of the bid/ask spread is about the same as the cost of selling the entire business.

A small equity position in a small public company, however, can still be sold relatively quickly. Selling an entire closely held firm can easily take two years or more, a time span that many owners of closely held firms ignore until it is time to sell. This matter presents a second consideration: time. With a closely held firm, sale of an owner's equity position often requires selling the entire business.

With a temporary need for liquidity, comparison to a homeowner is again relevant. One can get a second mortgage or home equity credit line using the property as collateral. With a closely held firm, an asset-backed loan can be obtained using the firm's real assets (usually trade receivables or inventory) as collateral. The equity line of credit requires an appraisal of the property. An asset-backed loan requires the same initial valuation of collateral assets, although these assets are more unique than most homes and hence more difficult to value. Although getting cash with these two alternatives will take a similar amount of time, the cost is likely to be higher for the business, because it is not a routine appraisal.

Let's say the premium might be 5%. That means that we have now identified discounts equal to 10% for the transaction costs, 4% for the systematic risk, and 5% for the collateral risk, for a total of nearly 20%. Still, the difference in costs should not justify a 30–35% discount in the value of the business. This rest of the discount, if it really exists, must result from other considerations.

7.4.4 *Liquidity or Information Costs?*

The cost of what is usually referred to as *illiquidity* results in only a small portion of the cost of quickly converting closely held business assets into cash. The major cost of illiquidity can really be shown to be an information cost. This is our final point on small firms having greater required rates of return. Much less information is publicly available on these closely held assets, compared to those of large public firms. Many experts believe that market information from stock price movements, not available to the managers of private firms, outweighs the advantage of having inside or private information about the business. As a result, the market information benefits appear to more than compensate for the costs of being public. Some people may confuse the issue of liquidity costs with what is actually an information cost. This cost occurs, however, only in illiquid firms because little information is available due to the absence of disclosure and market-based pricing of the equity value.

Consider the key points made in two important and parallel speeches. Maureen O'Hara, a leading scholar on the microstructure of financial markets, noted that low liquidity gives rise to higher risk.[13] This risk and its associated valuation discount result from there being less market information available when analysts and investors attempt to value the securities of relatively illiquid firms—because there are fewer transactions with their inherent information about value. Where markets are operational, otherwise unknowable information is provided to the firm's managers. Almost by definition, a lack of liquidity means less market interest in a firm and fewer (if any) analysts and investors trying to determine what the business is actually worth. This lack of coverage results in information asymmetry, with insiders knowing much more about the business than outsiders. This asymmetry means that outside investors are at a significant disadvantage, raising their risks. The greater risk to outside investors lowers the value of the business because fewer people will be inclined to invest—and those who do will want a higher reward. That reward, given the fixed capability of the firm to generate profits, will have to come in the form of a discounted price on the purchase of equity shares.

[13] O'Hara is a professor at Cornell University and chairperson of the NASDAQ Economic Advisory Board. She is also the author of *Market Microstructure Theory* (Malden, Mass.: Blackwell, 1995). This information was drawn from her 1998 Keynote Address at the Financial Management Association's Annual Meeting.

Sam Zell, a major real estate investor, emphasized this point as well.[14] He noted in early September 1998 that the prices of real estate investment trusts (REITs) had dropped suddenly. Further liquidity became tight as bank stocks dropped in value, limiting the banking industry's ability to make loans. (REITs own equity positions in real estate that, like most real estate, is highly levered, making access to debt capital very important.) What were the markets telling this industry? Those signals from investors told real estate executives that they were in the process of overexpanding, even though rents were up, occupancy rates were near record highs, and mortgage rates were down—all factors that point to high profits in the real estate business. As a result, real estate companies pulled back on the size of future projects and postponed those they had planned. The massive increase in the amount of publicly held real estate since 1991 allowed this adjustment to occur in the industry. During past downturns, such as the one in the late 1980s, the mostly private industry had record defaults because no market information was available to signal its managers what was about to happen. Zell concluded that "liquidity = value." It was apparent from his story that really "information = value"—and information results from liquidity.

7.5 Leverage Differences

We have approximated away the market risk, but have not considered different firms using different portions of debt and equity to finance their assets. This balance is usually referred to in North America as *leverage*, although our English friends will recognize it as *gearing*. How can we compare firms that use large amounts of debt with those that use almost no debt? In the models developed in chapters 4 and 5, we capitalized free cash flow to shareholders, making the assumption that debt holders had been paid first. The required return to the owner/managers is by definition the required return on equity as they receive the residual. Fortunately, traditional finance theory can handle these leverage differences.[15]

The equivalent beta value for a debt-free firm can be calculated for public firms with taxes, and assuming 0 systematic bond risk, as

$$Bu = Bl \times E/[E + (1 - tc)D],$$

where the beta for an equivalent debt-free firm, Bu, equals the reported beta of the levered firm, Bl, times the amount of equity financing, E, and divided

[14] Samuel Zell, chairman of Equity Group Investments, presented these points in his speech accepting the 1998 FMA Outstanding Financial Executive Award on October 16, 1998, in Chicago.

[15] The method presented here was developed by Robert Hamada and is presented in Hamada, "The Effects of the Firm's Capital Structure on the Systematic Risk of Common Stock," *Journal of Finance* 27 (May 1972) 435–52.

by the value of the equivalent debt-free firm. This approach removes the advantage of the tax deductibility from debt. The value of the equivalent debt-free firm equals the equity (E), plus the value of debt (D), times 1 minus the corporate tax rate (tc), which is currently 35% for large corporations and 34% for smaller ones in the United States. The average Bu value from the public firms is used for the privately held firm's equivalent debt-free beta value. The levered beta is

$$Bl = Bu \times [E + (1 - tc)D]/E,$$

where the E represents the equity in the closely held firm, D represents its borrowed capital, and tc represents the marginal tax rate on this business. Conceptually, market values should be used instead of book values, however, we are solving the formula to estimate the market value of the firm. Therefore, we approximate the value by using the book or accounting value weights for both the public firm and the closely held firm.

7.6 An Estimate of the Required Rate of Return

T-M Drugs is an ethical drug firm with several patented products.[16] It is quite small and has been able to establish itself with products that have only a limited market. These are often referred to as *orphan* drugs. A valuation is necessary to see what value the owners might expect in a takeover offer. They would be happy to sell T-M to a large firm to diversify their wealth. It is always difficult to predict when the next breakthrough from their research will improve their returns—or when one from their competitors might introduce a product that reduces T-M's returns and possibly even destroys the firm.

T-M Drugs currently has reported a book value for equity of $8.5 million and total debts, on which it pays annual interest expenses, of $4.5 million. (Remember that accounts payable and other accruals on which interest is not paid are not included as debts for these purposes.) As a smaller U.S. business, its marginal tax rate is only 34%. To obtain a value estimate, what is needed is an estimate of its required rate of return on equity.

The following firms, although many magnitudes larger, represent similar risks: Eli Lilly, Pfizer, Merck, and Schering-Plough. In the *Value Line Investment Survey* for the end of 2001 we find the data presented in the first three columns of table 7.2. We then calculate the value of each firm's equivalent unlevered beta, using the relationship presented in the previous section ($Bu = Bl \times E/[E + (1 - tc)D]$). We'll use 35% as their tax rates, because they are all large, profitable firms. The unlevered beta values are reported in the fourth column.

[16] T-M Drugs is a realistic fiction. There is no such company. Instead we have created a composite picture that realistically reflects the characteristics of many firms. The same is true for Huge Drugs.

Table 7.2 Calculating the Equivalent Unlevered Beta

Representative Firms	Equity Beta	Equity ($M)	Debt ($M)	Unlevered Beta
Lilly & Co.	0.70	10,920	4,492	0.55
Pfizer	0.80	68,278	7,279	0.75
Merck	0.80	17,288	4,691	0.68
Schering-Plough	0.90	7,555	2,392	0.75
Average unlevered beta				0.68

We now use the average unlevered beta value of 0.68 to estimate T-M's beta value. Using the relationship from the previous section to determine the levered firm's equity beta, $Bl = Bu \times [E + (1 - tc)D]/E$, we get a beta estimate for T-M Drugs of 0.92. This is approximately equal to Schering-Plough's—an unlikely situation—but the smaller firm will also face an illiquidity risk, probably raising its required rate of return about 7% above Schering-Plough's.

Use of the average (or *mean*) beta removes much information from the estimate, but it does provide us with a useful starting point. Alternative methods, using more of the available information, and thus probably more accurate, would recognize differences between the comparison firms, leading to their different betas, then assess the applicability of those factors to T-M. The best match will probably be the company whose products and capital structure are most similar.

The required rate of return for T-M Drugs can now be estimated after finding the current long-term risk-free rate (long-term government bond yield) and adding to it the risk premium (beta value, times the risk premium). The risk-free rate, as derived in section 7.3.1, is 4.4%. The market risk premium for small public firms was 12.2%, to which we add an additional 2% for an even smaller firm to get 14.2%. This higher market risk premium compensates for the higher bankruptcy risk, lack of liquidity, and absence of information about these firms. This method gives, as our estimate for T-M Drugs,

$$\text{Required Rate of Return} = 4.4\% + [(12.2\% + 2\%) \times 0.92] = 17.5\%.$$

In other words, the required rate of return, to capitalize returns to equity for this company, would be 17.5%.

7.7 Applying the Discount Rate

We will now show how the value of T-M Drugs has a 30–35% discount compared to a large firm with a similar systematic risk and the same capital structure. We assume zero growth options for this example. T-M Drugs produces cash of $1 million a year for its suppliers of capital—its owners' $8.5 million in equity and the borrowed $4.5 million, for a total of $13 million in capital. It pays 8% interest on its borrowings and is in the 34% marginal tax bracket. This situation puts its weighted average cost of capital (WACC) at

$$WACC_{T\text{-}M} = 17.5\% \times (8.5/13.0) + 8\% \times (1.0 - 0.34) \times (4.5/13) = 13.3\%.$$

By capitalizing its $1 million in cash flow at this rate, we generate an estimated market value of

$$Value_{T\text{-}M} = \$1/0.133 = \$7.52 \text{ million}.$$

There's one estimate of the investment value of T-M Drugs.

T-M Drugs will next be compared with Huge Drugs (a representative firm, not a real one), which earns a net profit of $1 billion a year. Let's assume that Huge has the same capital structure and the same borrowing costs as T-M. However, its tax rate is 35%, 1% higher than T-M's. The real valuation difference deals with the difference in cost of equity capital. Using the average risk premium of large firms (7%), Huge has an equity cost of $4.4\% + (7\% \times 0.92) = 10.84\%$. Accordingly, Huge has a weighted average cost of capital that can be calculated as follows:

$$WACC_{Huge} = 10.84\% \times (8.5/13.0) + 8\% \times (1.0 - 0.35) \times (4.5/13) = 8.9\%.$$

By capitalizing its $1 billion in cash flow at this rate, we generate an estimated market value of

$$Value_{Huge} = \$1/0.089 = \$11.24 \text{ billion}.$$

By comparing the relative values, $(11.24 - 7.52)/11.24$, we can see that the market value of T-M Drugs value is 33.1% below that of Huge Drugs, relative to their free cash flows.

This analysis provides one example of the discounted value faced by owners of equity in closely held firms. We may not like it, and we may want to change things so that different answers emerge in the future, but it helps to explain why closely held firms appear to sell at that persistent 30–35% discount relative to the ratios applied to their publicly held large brethren.

7.8 Discounts Redux

"Mike, I'm not sure I'm ever going to understand this discount rate stuff," Tom complained a couple of days later as they teed off their weekly round at the golf club. "For example, is there really any such thing as 'risk-free' capital?"

"Well, I'm not sure I understand it all yet either, but that 'risk-free' part I think I do get," Mike responded. "U.S. Government bonds are about as risk-free as you can get, so that's a pretty good estimate. From there, though, I'm not sure I could really figure out the right rate for my company, but I expect it would be different from yours. One of the standard references is what public companies in similar lines of business have to pay. Since your industry is very different from mine, I expect those numbers to be different."

"Even if I can find out that rate for half a dozen of the public companies in my sector, what does that tell me?" Tom couldn't see any light at the end of this proverbial tunnel. "My company is not like those ones, so those rates don't apply to me. If I go in to see my friendly neighborhood banker, she's not going to compare my data to those of companies a thousand times larger! She's going to compare me to similar stores in our trading area. They are my standard of comparison, not those giant multinationals. We all get thrown into a Prime-plus basket, and she can make little adjustments, based on how good each firm is relative to the group, our credit histories with that bank, and so on. I've been with this bank almost since the beginning, and I'm taking pretty good care of them, so I get Prime plus 1% while the rest of these shops probably get Prime plus 2%. They're not going to compare me to Wal-Mart."

Mike stepped into Tom's rant. "OK, let's assume that's all true, that your bank rate is Prime plus 1%. Remember what the Professor said at the end of our last session, when we asked for a simple rule of thumb that might get us a good approximation? He suggested that we should expect to pay about 300–400 basis points more, in return for the risks we face running a small business. That would make your discount rate about 3% above Prime plus 1, since your business is well-established and you know how to run it pretty well. So, if Prime is at 6.5%, then your discount rate is 6.5 + 1.0 + 3.0 = 10.5%. Mine's about half a point higher, given the challenges all manufacturers face at this time."

Tom's expression was shocked, bemused, angry: "Well, that's pretty simple! Why didn't someone say so before this?"

"What," teased Mike, "and save you all those worry lines? Actually, I think it's because we asked the question seriously, like we really wanted to know the details, the 'right' way to figure this out. What the Professor gave us was the way he would try to find the most appropriate rate, what he would go through as an expert witness in a court case. I wonder if any judge or jury could follow him through those calculations! Anyway, what he eventually broke down and gave us, that jiffy version, probably wouldn't hold up in court, but it's good enough for me at this stage. I can tell that the right rate for me is not 5%, and it's not 15% or 20% either. But, back when prime rates were 20%, like in 1979–80, it might have been as high as 30% for my dad. You don't see many opportunities that return 30% or better. That might explain why your business was available when you went looking for something to buy—and why Dad was so stressed about my college choices!"

"OK, OK, some things are finally becoming clear. Do you think that 3% risk premium would be higher if I was thinking about investing in another business? Yeah, probably, eh?" Tom answered his own question. "Because I know my current business better, and would therefore have a lower risk factor if I were reinvesting in it, compared to putting the money into some other venture."

"Right," agreed Mike. "My business is my lowest risk investment, even if other people don't see it that way, because I know it really well. If I were to pull my money out and put the cash into something else, I'd want to see the potential for a significantly higher return, to compensate for the added risk. Depending on what the venture was, I might want to put a 10% risk factor on it, making my target ROI about 18%."

"So," Tom mulled this over, "the calculation would be: Can you make 11% by reinvesting in your own business, versus at least 18% by transferring the money to something else that is higher risk because you don't know it as well?"

"That's the way I read it," Mike confirmed. They both leaned back to think about that as they watched Tom's drive sail into the rough.

8

Planning to Buy?

Considerations from the Other Side of the Sale

8.0 Should Tom Sell to Tracey or Mike?

"Tom, it sounded like you had something specific on your mind a couple of weeks ago when you asked me to bring the family out here for the weekend. It's great to be back at the lake on such a nice summer day. What's on your mind?" Mike's coffee cup was steaming, as the friends sat on the veranda, overlooking the lake. Tom's parents had built the cottage years before, and it seemed to have always been in the family. Now, after his mom's passing a couple of years ago, it belonged to Tom and Celia.

The kids were down at the dock, hooking up the speedboat for water-skiing and wakeboarding. Tom's oldest, Tracey, was taking charge of the younger ones. The wives were back inside, working on one of their projects. Breakfast had been leisurely and was now cleared away. They had a couple of hours before anyone needed them to do anything.

Tom paused before answering, sucking back more of his special java brew. "Tracey and I and Celia have been talking about things since Thanksgiving last year, trying to sort out what kind of career Trace is going to pursue now that she's graduating. As you know, she's working with me in the company this summer, while she gets ready to start her MBA program in the fall. She's been around the business all her life, it seems, and we've carved out little projects in it that allow her to test her mettle. A couple of months ago, she pulled me aside after dinner, and asked what I'd think about her preparing herself to take over one day." Tom was talking slowly, and Mike sensed he was wrestling with some important concerns. He sipped his coffee and waited.

"Y'know, it's something you and I have chatted about over the years—whether the kids would come into the business, how we would ever retire, how we'd make out financially for all the work we've put into building our companies. But we've never really addressed those issues. When Tracey asked that question, I was floored. So many questions flooded through my head and heart, I couldn't say a thing. I didn't know what to tell her! I'm so humbled that she thinks my work is worth something as important as her career. But I'm in my prime; I'm not ready to face retirement for a long time. And I don't think there's room in this small business for both us to make a good living. I wouldn't know where to begin to make her a fair deal, or even how to groom her to succeed me." Mike could sense Tom fighting a flood of emotions and kept his eyes focused on the lake. "Mike, I really need your help. This is as important as anything I've ever done, and I don't know where to start."

Mike's mind flashed back to a time twenty-five years earlier, when he served as best man at Tom and Celia's wedding. Tom had been an emotional basket case the week before the big event, and Mike had had to carry him through all the final stages. Tom got through it and had flourished by the end of their honeymoon week in Bermuda—or so Celia claimed. "I don't think she's making you an offer this weekend, my friend, so we have plenty of time to think this through."

"Yeah, you're right. She's talking about a transition ten to twenty years from now. But she is asking whether it's a good possibility—a kind of agreement in principle—so she can plan her MBA program accordingly. She's ready to make a commitment to preparing herself to take over the business, if I'm willing to agree. If I'm not, if I have a different plan for the business, like selling to some other firm, then she'll choose a different path. I owe her an honest answer, and soon. Trouble is, that answer is dependent on a whole host of questions that I haven't even begun to address."

Mike nodded slowly. He did understand. He'd thought about the same thing himself, seeing his nineteen-year-old son Billy taking the occasional part-time job in his own firm. Daughter Michelle had started asking a lot of questions about the firm and his work, too, and she was only sixteen. Good answers were not going to be fast answers. "OK, buddy, I do understand. I'm starting to think about the same things myself. I guess it's time we started thinking harder about our 'Bigger Pictures,' about taking a new look at the larger meaning for ourselves and our families of all this business stuff we've been doing for the last fifteen years. There are many questions we're going to have to answer. You're further into this than I am; what's your sense of the more important ones?"

Tom relaxed a bit; it was good to know he wasn't alone with this complicated set of problems. Still, he knew they weren't solved, just shared. "I think I can see how to prepare Tracey and the firm for a transition. Preparing me might be the hardest part! But, I keep coming back to one of her implied questions: 'What's a fair price?' How could she pay it? Would we all be better off selling out to a big company and splitting the cash? Where will we get the best deal? Those are probably premature questions, but it feels like we have to deal with them now.

"You know, many years ago you and I took that sales management course," Tom continued, "and every once in a while I come back to the key principle—get inside the head of the buyer. What buyers are there for a business like mine? What value do they see? If we're heading toward a process that puts a fair price on the business, then we have to know about the other possible buyers. Which ones would value it most?"

"Yeah," Mike vibrated with the litany of questions—or maybe it was the coffee. "We have to know the potential buyers for any product, to know which ones will pay the highest prices. But, apart from guys like you and me, who buys used businesses? We bought ours cheap and small. Who buys $5 million companies? We bought tangible assets, but we both know there's a lot more than that to our companies now. How do premium buyers value those things? Sounds like we've got quite a lot to learn, my friend!"

Tom almost growled in frustration. "I never thought there'd be this much to learn about business ownership. It all looked pretty simple when we were in our twenties, didn't it?"

"Yup, but that's why we pay ourselves the big bucks!" exclaimed Mike with a chuckle. "Let's reload these coffee mugs, pull out some pads of paper, and see how much we already know. Why don't we start by seeing what we'd want to know if we were thinking of buying each other's businesses? By trying to think like buyers, we might get a first good cut at this thing."

Tom looked both concerned and relieved as they hauled themselves out of the deck chairs and headed indoors. The second step was under way.

TO SELL WELL, KNOW THE BUYERS! To sell a business well, one should understand how it will be bought. By knowing the other side of the transaction, a seller can identify good buyers, anticipate their needs and negotiating strategies, and prepare accordingly, en route to a successful sale. In this chapter, we'll cover special valuation considerations for buyers of closely held businesses. Purchasers must consider taxes, incentives, and available capital. They must do their homework, so to speak, before buying an existing business (or starting a new one), if they expect to make good decisions and receive above-average returns on their investments. Among the most important outcomes of such analyses should be a determination of a reasonable maximum price to pay and how to make the payment.

Although this chapter focuses mainly on the process of buying an existing firm, many of the basic concepts also hold for the creation of a new business. Consider the following comparisons. With an existing business, a major uncertainty factor is the degree of trust a prospective buyer can be put into the data supplied by the seller. Financial reports prepared by the current owner may have lots of personal idiosyncrasies, errors, or non-GAAP procedures embedded in them. There are many good reasons why we cautioned at the beginning of this book that the financial statements of closely held firms must not be treated as reliable. (Indeed, there are reasons why the financial statements of regulated, disclosed, public companies should also be treated with caution, as Enron and other recent scandals have reminded us!) By learning the history of the book-value numbers, however, an assessor may learn important clues about the relationship between current values and book values.

With a new business, there are no hard data at all, no track record to assess, just estimates of potential. By knowing the care and expertise that went into producing those estimates, an assessor may be able to improve his or her judgment about their reliability.

In both cases, decisions must be made without the benefit of complete or accurate information; estimates and approximations are required. With an existing business, one deals with the seller and takes over that person's organization and then modifies it to suit the new owner; with a startup, one creates the organization from scratch. In planning to buy an existing business, a potential buyer estimates its value under the current owners to determine the minimum price they will accept. That potential buyer also estimates the value of the business, under the new owner/manager, to establish the maximum price to pay. When starting a new business, the would-be entrepreneur estimates the potential that it can produce and whether it is worth his or her opportunity costs in forgone salary to launch it, instead of taking a job elsewhere. Each alternative requires a mixture of judgment and quantitative analysis.

We must always remember that, when a business is for sale, the seller is trying to get the highest possible price with the fewest conditions, while the buyer is trying to get the lowest price, with sufficient conditions to warrant that the purchased firm will perform as expected. The lower the price the buyer has to pay, the higher the return on that investment. To the extent that a buyer is concerned that hidden problems remain, he or she will further reduce the offering price to hedge against those possible costs. A wise seller, therefore, will organize the business and its books so that it is a WYSIWYG (what-you-see-is-what-you-get) opportunity.[1] The development of mutual confidence or trust makes a big difference in the value of a private sale. Its absence causes substantial discounts, as buyers insure themselves at the seller's expense.

8.1 Why Is the Firm for Sale?

The first critical question for a buyer is: "Why is this firm for sale?" The second is like unto it: "Who is selling?" The answers to those questions may significantly affect the value a buyer would have to pay, and the negotiating strategy most likely to be effective.

[1] Our Australian colleague Tom McKaskill calls this "avoidable risks that reduce the price." He devotes a whole chapter to them in his book *Selling Your Business for a Premium* (Ashburn, Va.: Gazelles Publishing, 2005).

8.1.1 *Estate Sales*

In an estate sale, for example, when the owner/manager has died and no one from the family is taking over, trustees will liquidate the estate's assets. In many cases, the trustees will not be industry-knowledgeable. That means they may be little help in providing useful information about industry trends, historical meanings of financial records, hidden assets, and so on. Due diligence will need to be more exhaustive, rely more on employees, and be more exposed to competitors. In other words, the risks will go up, and hence the value is likely to go down along with the price. It is also possible that the trustees will be willing to accept a lower price to have a clean, all-cash transaction that allows them to close the books on the estate and distribute the funds to the beneficiaries.

Conversely, some trustees or inheritors are emotionally wedded to their family's firm, without having the business acumen to understand its value to the buyers—or the expertise to run it competently themselves. They may sell for less than it is really worth, or hold out for more than buyers will pay, eventually damaging the firm's value that way as well. In both cases, a buyer faces the prospect of having to educate the seller, and that education is likely to have a price as well—if the buyer is even willing to supply it.

8.1.2 *Retirement Sales*

When the owner is retiring in good health, however, the circumstances change. He or she may be available to help with a transition, may even need the emotional progression associated with a gradual change in status. He is likely also to have valuable expertise about the inventory, other assets, employees, suppliers, and customers. If those values can be incorporated in the sale, new owners are likely to pay a higher price, because they would be receiving a more valuable, less risky package. Transition roles, staged payments, performance guarantees, expert consulting, training contracts, and other features may come into play as part of the transfer process. They are likely to affect both price and terms. They do provide many additional ways for the parties to transfer (or withhold) value.

8.1.3 *Serial Entrepreneurs, Moving On*

In a transaction in which one of us was involved, the seller was a highly motivated, albeit relatively inexperienced, serial entrepreneur who wanted a quick cash sale. His wife had been bugging him to get the money out of the business so they could change locations. They had found a new home, and he had even made an offer to purchase a new business two thousand miles away. He needed out quickly, and he needed cash to meet his new obligations. He was not prepared to even consider staged payments, consulting services to transfer knowledge, or future performance guarantees.

As a result, he significantly reduced the value he could extract from the business he had built—and reduced its value for prospective buyers. He took value off both tables.

In that particular case, a premium buyer walked away because he just didn't have enough industry-specific knowledge to be comfortable taking over the firm without a staged transition. For that buyer, the risks of losing his entire investment were too great. That seller needed a buyer who could make full use of the assets right away—in other words, an industry insider with enough cash available to complete a clean transaction quickly. Instead, this seller sacrificed the value of his expertise and the future value of the assets, because he was not transferring those values to the buyer.

These differences are among the reasons to carefully consider what kind of buyer is the best fit for the business being sold and vice versa. Bad fits will cost both parties money, and often lead to "walk-aways" instead of successful deals. A well-prepared buyer has to know what she has to offer, and what she needs, or what it will cost to buy those additional resources. Then we can begin a useful search and head into negotiations with a workable plan.

Conversely, a smart seller has to target the sale for a market where several possible buyers exist, so some form of auction can be started and the business will be sold to the buyer willing to pay the most. When a sale is targeted for a market of one, the buyer has all the negotiating power. Worse, when the sale is targeted for a market with *no* likely buyers, not only will a sale not happen, but the value of the business will likely be damaged by a selling period with no takers, and the eventual sale price will be further reduced as perceptions of a damaged property accumulate.

In the case cited above, the fact that both buyer and seller were relatively inexperienced led to an additional problem. In most markets, there are sources of capital available for a kind of intermediary financing. A third party could have been found to provide the cash the seller needed to exit the deal, in return for the repayment of that investment by the cash-strapped buyer. Neither party had the financial acumen or networks to find such an intermediary. Hardly anyone would think of buying a house this way. We almost always use mortgage financing to allow us to buy a much more valuable house than we could afford in an all-cash deal. The seller of the house gets cash, and the buyer pays down the mortgage over time. Without mortgages and professional real estate brokers, the housing market would be severely constrained. Similar facilities exist in business markets.

8.2 Know What You Are Getting

The first and foremost principle in buying any business is to know what is actually being bought, including both tangible and intangible assets. In addition to the positive assets, the transaction must also address present liabilities that would be assumed and possible future ones inherent in the deal. Both assets and liabilities should be valued in terms of what it would cost the proposed buyer to replace them. In doing that, one must be careful not to use their book or historical cost accounting values—particularly for real estate—although the history of those book values may be very useful in discovering hidden assets. The firm's specific assets should be examined and assessed, even if the firm will be valued as a going concern, to be sure these things are as they appear, or at least so the buyer does understand what they represent.

8.2.1 *Valuing Assets and Liabilities*

In valuing specific assets, we will start with the tangible assets and then consider the intangible ones. Not all of the items discussed will be present in every potential purchase, but all these assets should be researched. The tangible assets include:

- Cash
- Trade receivables
- Inventories
- Investments in other firms
- Fixed plant
- Equipment
- Real estate

Unless the transaction is classified as a merger rather than as a purchase, the seller rarely transfers any cash, or any investments the firm may hold in the debt or equity of other firms. Those assets normally remain with the selling owner. The buyer is expected to provide all of his or her own working capital. The seller usually keeps responsibilities for the trade credits, both receivables due and payables owed. (The advantages and disadvantages of keeping the trade credits were discussed in detail in chapter 3.) Thus, the available tangible assets are usually limited to inventories and fixed assets, with real estate treated as a separate issue.

8.2.1.1 VALUING INVENTORIES The key issue with inventory valuation is to know what one is getting. Industry-specific knowledge is very important in this part of the valuation, because the real market value of inventory often has a lot to do with the marketability of specific brands and models of goods. A two-year-old car, for example, is likely to be considerably less valuable than its original sticker price, whereas the value of an airplane may be higher. Doing one's homework to value the inventory accurately is extremely important.

8.2.1.1.1 *Liquidation of Stale Inventories* *Caution:* A seller planning ahead might quickly liquidate obsolete inventories at reduced prices if he thinks that they could not be sold as part of the business. That way he would at least get whatever cash those sales would generate. When inventory is included in the sale, it is quite likely that the seller has included at least part of it because he cannot sell it; if he could, he would sell it and remove the cash from the transaction. Thus, good inventory may be mixed with bad, and a wise buyer should pay for the first but not the second.

Reports of a firm's previous inventory turnover ratios may be poor indicators of a new owner's ability to get cash for the current inventory. Fire sales, to clear stale inventory at reduced prices before the sale of a business, increase reported inventory turnover, and therefore increase apparent value of the firm if anyone uses inventory turnover as an indication of the firm's value. But they do not increase the real, long-term value of the firm as a profit-producing machine. It could be that much of the inventory would turn over just fine, but the quick-selling part may be sold just prior to the business being transferred—and the cash would disappear with the seller—and that turnover could not be duplicated on a regular basis. A buyer must physically check the actual goods that are left for the new owners to sell. Any potential buyer must determine whether those goods are sellable or just taking up space. We need to carefully separate the available inventories into those that the new owners will be able to sell and those that they, too, are unlikely to be able to liquidate, then we need to put likely sale prices on them to determine their real value.

8.2.1.1.2 *Perishable Inventories* Some businesses, like newspapers, airlines, fruit and vegetable stores, motels, and bakeries, have a portion of their inventories that perishes daily. In valuing those firms, we need to look carefully at the perishables, to see if they can be managed in a way that reduces those write-offs; they could be hidden assets for a more skilled manager buying the firm.

Similarly, stale inventories can sometimes be recycled into side businesses, new markets, liquidated at conventional auctions, or sold on eBay or other online auctions. The relative skills of the seller and the buyer at managing or unlocking the value of these inventories (and other stale assets, like overdue receivables) can affect who would get the greater value from them after the transfer of ownership. In a perfect world, it might also affect who should own them after the transaction, and at what price.

8.2.1.2 FIXED TANGIBLE ASSETS Fixed tangible assets should be broken down into groups. First, consider those with readily available secondary markets, such as vehicles and buildings. One should hire independent appraisers for these assets if they are being purchased as part of the business; professional inspectors may also help determine their real condition and any hidden future costs. There are well-established techniques for this work. These are the easy assets to value.

Firm- or industry-specific assets are more difficult to value. Here the key concern is what they are worth to the purchasing business. If they are necessary for the business, their value should be determined on the basis of the cost to replace them. If they are surplus to the core business operations, their value should be based on the net amount that would likely be obtained from selling them. When the buyer already owns at least one similar business, one of the primary reasons for purchase is to get better economic use from existing assets. That may mean running the second firm's products on the existing firm's trucks, for example, in which case the second firm's trucks would be sold. Conversely, the purchase may be made, in part to get access to the second firm's tangible assets, like a prime real estate location. The value of these assets depends on the leverage they provide within the buyer's existing operations.

A Note on Depreciation

There are three main approaches to depreciation. An economist views deteriorations and decreased value of assets over time. An accountant views depreciation as the charge to allocate an asset's cost over its useful economic life. The IRS and tax planning views are similar in concept to the accountant's but toss in macro-economic efforts to increase expenditures on new capital in setting depreciation schedules. (There is also Section 179 of the U.S. Internal Revenue Code, which allows additional depreciation for individuals [i.e., firms] in year of purchase.)

Let's start with the economists' concept. Depreciation, in terms of its purpose in providing useful managerial information, should equal the realistic reduction in value of the assets, so that net book value, being purchase price minus depreciation, fairly reflects the current economic value of an asset.

Many people don't know what the real depreciation rate is. In addition, the IRS has standardized rules that may not accurately reflect either industry trends or the value of any specific piece of equipment. Many owners and their accountants, however, use the IRS rules to keep their accounting and tax-filing information simple.

The result for a buyer is that net book assets accurately reflect their *tax* value, not their economic value. What are they worth in productive work to the business? The IRS version bears an unknown resemblance to that value and should *not* be assumed to be an accurate estimate of it. The IRS is not the buyer, so the booked value of depreciation has to be reviewed, category by category, and sometimes item by item.

This problem is particularly true with closely held firms. Many keep their books based on tax laws and not GAAP. Hence, their fixed assets are written down much quicker than their actual value. This difference is one factor in getting a firm ready to sell—creating a GAAP-based accounting presentation because so many buyers still look at accounting values.

Some fully tax-depreciated equipment remains *very* valuable to a business—and some equipment with substantial remaining book value is so obsolete it has to be replaced. For an insightful discussion of the hidden values of equipment within a firm, see the management bestseller *The Goal*.[2]

[2] E. M. Goldratt and J. Cox, *The Goal: A Process of Ongoing Improvement*, 2nd rev. ed. (Great Barrington, Mass.: North River Press, 1992).

When the buyer does not have a great deal of personal industry experience, he is well advised to retain a consultant who does. That person should advise the prospective buyer on the value of the assets and ways to realize their value through the purchase and restructuring of the firm.

8.2.1.2.1 *Deferred Maintenance* When one is buying a going concern, the financial value of the business is based on its ability to produce future cash flows. Why bother with the value of specific assets? The main reason for being concerned is to be sure that they are in the same condition as advertised. The seller who plans ahead might think: "Why undertake routine maintenance on the fixed assets? The firm can save some money in the short run, increase my profits (extracted cash), and look more profitable to a potential buyer." On behalf of the buyer, asset quality must be checked carefully before determining a final price. For the buyer, that deferred maintenance would become a hidden liability, a double deduction against the artificially inflated profitability of the old firm.

In the example shown in table 8.1, we've held the level of sales constant, so that it is not a factor in the valuation. The table demonstrates what happens when we estimate value on the basis of profits as a ratio to the assets employed without addressing the issue of regular versus deferred maintenance. It shows specifically what happens when a seller defers maintenance and a buyer fails to notice. Profits are increased in the short run, depressed in the catch-up period. The apparent value of the firm fluctuates considerably, and a naive buyer would overpay for damaged assets and reduced long-term profits.

8.2.1.2.2 *Business Intelligence and Risk Reduction* For some buyers, another good reason to investigate the assets carefully may be the business intelligence gained. In most cases, the sellers have far more knowledge of the business than the buyers, creating an asymmetry that disadvantages the buyer.

Table 8.1 Impacts of Deferred Maintenance on Valuation

Valuation Items	Normal Operation	Deferred Maintenance	Catch-Up Year	Valuation Adjustments
Assets	$100,000	$100,000	$95,000	<$5,000>
Maintenance	$10,000/year	$5,000/year	$15,000	<$10,000>
Profits generated	$10,000	$15,000	$5,000	
Ratio (P/M)	10:10 = 1:1	15:5 = 3:1	5:15 = 1:3	
Value (P/Assets):	$= X$	$\cong 1.5X$	$\cong 0.5X$	$< = X$
Valuation impacts	Neutral case	Apparent value is increased 50%!	Value in first year is only 1/3 that presented by the DM seller	Ongoing value is only 2/3 of (claimed) DM value

By asking simple questions like "What do you use this for?" and "How often do you need to upgrade this software?" a prospective buyer can learn a great deal about not only the assets in the firm but also about the way they have been managed. In an important way, that is good for the seller, too: it is likely to reduce the risk-related discount the buyer will require to cover his lack of knowledge about these things.

8.2.1.3 INTANGIBLE ASSETS It is more difficult to put specific values on intangible assets. There are several points to consider. Is the business going to continue as a going concern, with minor changes, or is the purchase more strategic in nature, with the assets being acquired to fit into another ongoing business? In continuing the current business, major buyer considerations include client lists, business image, and so on. Those factors were discussed in earlier chapters. With a strategic purchase, the consideration is how well the operations and assets will fit into the acquiring business. Specific assets, like product or company image, are not as important—unless they are the reasons for the purchase.

One of the important intangible assets in many transactions is the "work in process" or WIPs. In manufacturing, and some service industries (like TV repair), there will be work under way on numerous contracts on the date of transfer of ownership. These assets may hold substantial value for both buyer and seller, and each may have a strong interest in ensuring the work is properly completed, billed, and collected. Sellers have invested time and materials in the WIP and would like to be paid for that embodied value; many sellers also want to ensure that the buyers honor the commitments the sellers had made to their customers. Buyers can use the completion of WIPs to cement relationships with the firm's existing customers and to quickly restart the firm's cash flow.

Both the value and the implied warranties in WIPs are often important parts of buy/sell negotiations. We've included them here, under intangible assets, because it is sometimes hard to be precise about the amount of value embedded in WIPs until they are sold and the fees collected. It is also hard to know for sure what liabilities are embedded in the warranties, real or implied, with the delivery of completed WIPs.

8.2.1.4 INTANGIBLE LIABILITIES In most purchases, the emphasis is on purchasing productive assets. After all, they create future cash flows. However, the *liabilities* incurred with a business purchase can have a profound effect on the price paid. The key liabilities are not so much the easy-to-measure ones like trade credit payables, because they are usually retained by the seller. They also do not include product liabilities, as they usually stay with the owner at the time the product was sold. If, however, the entire business is purchased or merged into an existing business, those types of liabilities come with the deal.

We would like to discuss two specific different types of potential liabilities. There may be many others. Our point is to get buyers thinking about parts of the sale/purchase contract that appear to be routine items—but which may be anything but routine under closer examination. Several of these routine items could end up becoming quite expensive.

8.2.1.4.1 *Environmental Compliance* First, let's consider *compliance with antipollution laws*. It is obvious today, in the United States and in most modern economies, that no firm is allowed to dump trash into a local river or exhaust noxious substances into the atmosphere. Furthermore, it should not be a surprise to know that toxic wastes cannot be dumped on the land behind the plant. But, what might come as a nasty surprise is that the buyer of a U.S. site can be held responsible for what previous owners did there many years before. The buyer can be forced to pay for the consequences and cleanup of dumping conducted by long-dead previous owners. As a result, any land that comes with a purchase must be inspected for environmental problems and bonded against any problems that might be found later. Those bonds should cover problems resulting, not just from the most recent seller, but issues arising from activities up to one hundred years earlier.

8.2.1.4.2 *Assumption of Unfavorable Contracts* Another form of liability arises from assumption of leases related to the business. Most of the time, these leases will be quite routine, but potential buyers should check them carefully. The firm could be liable for substantial long-term leases that are bleeding it. Many owners use leases to help finance their operations and preserve cash; some use leases to transfer funds from one family member or business unit to another, sometimes as a method of tax minimization. A new buyer should not find out after the deal is concluded that he or she is going to be financing the previous owners' children's college fund through inflated long-term lease payments on obsolete core machinery or overvalued real estate!

One wonders why some owners sell at what appear to be low prices. The following story was reported in the *Wall Street Journal* (April 3, 1995, B2–B3): A Microsoft programmer bought a laundromat as an investment. He did not check carefully on the obligations he was getting. His unemployed brother-in-law was hired to operate it. That was his second mistake. The brother-in-law did not work out. (There was a reason that he had been unemployed!) The buyer ended up running the business. The business did poorly because of a poor location. He could neither move nor liquidate the business because of the long-term lease commitment. To prevent an even bigger disaster, the programmer was forced to quit a position paying more than $100,000 per year, and forfeit over $250,000 in Microsoft stock options, to run an underperforming laundromat. Then he took on part-time work with no benefits, as a programmer back at Microsoft, to pay the family bills. This is a good example of why buyers hire competent attorneys to identify and investigate such contracts. It is up to the buyer to determine if there are potential problems, and to assess their negative impact on the value she or he is willing to offer for the firm. Conversely, it is the seller's responsibility to manage the firm and its assets in such a way as to minimize such liabilities. Not all sellers, however, know enough to do this, or care enough to do it well. Caveat emptor!

8.2.2 *Verifying Information to Value the Firm as a Going Concern*

After the assets and liabilities have been verified and valued, it is time to consider the business as a going concern. The major worries any buyer of a closely held firm faces are related to the credibility of the information presented by the seller. Is the information factually correct? Is it representative of the firm's actual performance? To what extent can past performance be projected into future profits? Some of the key items to verify are presented in table 8.2.

8.2.2.1 ACCURACY OF FINANCIAL DATA Few closely held firms have their statements audited by credible outside third parties. Most owners

Table 8.2 Checklist of Danger Signs for Buyers

- Recent changes in the firm's accountant or banker
- Recent changes in the firm's legal team
- Chaotic or missing financial statements and/or missing tax returns
- Seller unwilling to provide information about recent legal issues
- Seller uncomfortable discussing financial statements or not knowledgeable about the rules on which they are based (e.g., depreciation)
- Drops in capital budgeting or maintenance expenses
- High personnel turnover
- Discrepancies between historical or industry-standard inventory and what can be accounted for in the target firm
- Poor ratings with credit or consumer agencies
- Spin-off competitors
- Declining sales
- Arrangements with obscure leasing or other finance companies
- High levels of goodwill on the balance sheet, especially without receipts of value for the assets purchased
- Missing or out-of-date certifications (environmental, warranty, bidder, etc.)
- Missing documents from previous acquisitions, especially owner warranties
- Consumer complaints, especially above average levels and unresolved ones
- Lack of legal agreements for key employees (employment contracts, intellectual property rights, benefit packages, severance terms, etc.)
- Inadequate insurance
- Convoluted arrangements between the firm and the owner's family or friends
- Poor maintenance of facilities or equipment
- Underinvestment in training or research and development
- Idle assets
- Unusual overtime
- Abnormal recent sales history
- Inadequate explanations for profits, dividends, reinvestment policies
- Poor industry or community reputations
- Overreliance on owner as key person

cannot justify the expense to audit their own operations. The only closely held firms that usually have audited financial statements are ones that have outstanding loans backed by the SBA or other government agencies, the terms of which require audited statements. The financial statements of most closely held firms are compiled by the firm's accountant from data provided by the firm's owner/manager. Those statements rarely conform to GAAP, although this causes few problems because the specific rules used by the accountant are usually noted.

Does the seller appear comfortable and open in explaining the business to a potential buyer? Get the names and check with the firm's professional service providers (external accountant, lawyer, banker, insurance agent, auditor if there is one). One cannot afford to make mistakes based on poor information when one's entire wealth, reputation, and career are at stake. Talk with the firm's accountant, banker, insurance agent, and attorney on the quality of the data presented. Do they feel that the current owner/manager has been a "straight shooter" with them over the years? Be wary of recent changes in the firm's accountants, bankers, insurers, or attorneys. Try to find out who the previous ones were and contact them. To look for outside influences, the major customers and suppliers should also be interviewed.

Be especially wary of firms that change their support providers, particularly just prior to selling. There may be good reasons for such a change; and there may be an effort to cover a significant flaw. Sometimes, as an owner prepares a firm for sale, it becomes apparent that a different type of support professional is needed, compared to the ones who have been adequate for day-to-day operations. Private firms preparing for an IPO often change to support firms more familiar with the requirements for public companies. Among private firms, however, such changes may also signal strong disagreements between the owner and the support professional, and that possibility is too serious to overlook.

Probably the best data to verify are not those in a firm's financial statements, but the ones in its tax returns. Since the firm itself most likely does not pay taxes, being either a Subchapter S corporation or some form of limited partnership, the current owner/manager's returns should also be checked. Such a review provides three types of information. First, many times the firm's fixed assets are owned directly by the owner/manager, rather than the firm, usually for tax reasons. It's important for a buyer to know who really owns what. Second, in reviewing the tax returns, one gets a sense of how successful the business has been over the years in providing income and creating wealth for the current owner/manager. Finally, do the numbers look reasonable when compared to the firm's values or has the owner/manager been creating fiction in terms of tax deductions and reported income? If it appears that governments have been blatantly cheated out of due taxes, it is also possible that less than truthful information is being presented to potential buyers, or that hidden tax liabilities may be included in the package.

These reviews are designed to provide real information. They are also designed to help potential buyers decide how much they can trust the seller. The seller usually has much more information about the business that the buyer, so there is potential for abuse. Sellers provide certain formal and informal warranties about the condition of the business and its assets. How much a buyer will discount that information has much to do with the level of trust the seller can establish. Any lack of credibility in the information presented by the seller is likely to lead to an offsetting discount by the buyer as he tries to insure himself against misrepresentation. Many deals break down completely because the buyer loses all confidence in the seller, and discounts the value of the assets below anything the seller will accept.

8.2.2.2 MEANINGFULNESS OF FINANCIAL DATA Once the data have been studied, and they appear truthful—or have been adjusted to present a reasonably accurate picture—the next consideration is whether the statements are representative of the firm's potential future performance.

One of the things this book emphasizes to sellers is the value of planning ahead to avoid a position where a quick ownership change must be made. As a potential buyer of a business, this is something to remember from the other side of the transaction. When the owner/manager has just died after an accident or a short illness, there has been little time to get the firm ready for sale. It is going to be seen with all its warts, making it easier to judge—before even considering the fact that the inheriting owner/manager is more eager to sell the business. As a buyer, an even better bargain can usually be obtained if the owner/manager/trustee has recently died and there is no appointed heir to the firm. The trustee has a choice—invest the time and money needed to become an expert manager of the assets, or sell at a comparable discount to someone who is. For example, let's say a business is worth $1.5 million. The owner/manager dies and his wife, who has had nothing to do with the business, inherits. In her inexperienced hands, the business is no longer worth $1.5 million. What kind of investment would she need to make to develop the same expertise as that developed by her late husband in his thirty-five years in the industry? Without him, the business is worth less, and its value is likely to be discounted.

But what if the seller has taken our advice and planned ahead for this sale? One thing sellers may do to prepare for a sale is to manage their firms differently, paying closer attention to things that will make them look more attractive to buyers. Some of those modifications can be very helpful, real improvements in the business operations. Others may be short-term gains only, masking longer-term trouble.

One area of concern is with firms where temporary improvements, correctly reported, may nonetheless be indicators of future trouble. It is quite likely, for example, that a seller has modified the business' operations to produce financial results that make the business look better. Those financial improvements are not based on untruthful reporting but rather on actual changes in operations. Such changes often result in either of two impacts on the financial statements: improved revenues or decreased expenses.

8.2.2.2.1 *Recent Changes That Inflate Revenues* The easiest way to improve revenues over the short run is to increase prices at an amount slightly greater than one's competitors. Assuming that the firm's customers do not research the prices of all their options before each purchase, the physical volume of sales will stay constant in the short run. At slightly higher prices, revenue will increase and, with constant prices for the cost of goods sold, the gross profit margin will also increase. In the longer run, however, those customers will start to realize they are being exploited and business will be lost, ill will created, and so on. To buy such a firm based on its apparently improved performance, then have customers abandon it in droves, would be a serious mistake. Not only would revenues drop, but the cost of restoring goodwill would likely cause further declines in revenues (or increases in costs).

A related way to increase revenues in the short run is to extend greater trade credit. Easing the credit terms will allow for expanded sales. Does that make much sense? Earlier, it was noted that, in many sales of closely held firms, the seller keeps the trade receivables along with debts. Only the physical assets and the business name, organization, and so on are sold. The seller must collect these new marginal accounts along with regular accounts, meaning that some write-offs may occur. That does not seem to be in the seller's interest. Remember, however, that the seller is hoping that this greater short-run profit will be used by the buyer to determine both current earnings levels and also to estimate the firm's growth rate. An increase in the growth rate from 2% to 6% with a 20% capitalization rate, which is reasonable for a closely held firm, will increase value from 5.7 times to 7.5 times earnings. The overall gain in the resulting selling price would more than make up for a few extra bad debts in the assumed receivables. Consider table 8.3, which suggests a 33% valuation increase, using this method.

8.2.2.2.2 *Recent Changes That Deflate Expenses* Similarly, an owner/manager nearing retirement may cut expenses. Advertising can be reduced with little effect in the short run, but it will lower the firm's image in the longer run. Maintenance can be deferred on fixed assets with similar results. It is important to check the various expense accounts for changes over recent

Table 8.3 Impact of a Change of Credit Policy on Valuation

Item	Original Credit Policy	Easy Credit Policy
Sales	\$1,000,000	\$1,040,000
Growth rate	2%	6%
Capitalization	20%	20%
Net profit margin	10%	10%
Calculations	\$1,000,000 × 0.10/(0.20 − 0.02)	\$1,040,000 × 0.10/(0.20 − 0.06)
Value estimate	\$555,555	\$742,857

years. In today's world of computerized record-keeping, the expenses are easily split into various classes, making it easy to follow them over time. One of the more obvious indicators of short-term managerial tactics would be changes in managerial compensation. Although mentioned earlier, this clue should be reemphasized. An owner/manager wishing to make a business look better prior to selling could just decrease managerial compensation or drop nonperforming dependents from the payroll. This simple change, provided other things stayed more or less equal, would boost reported profits and enhance apparent performance margins—but it wouldn't have affected the underlying value of the firm, and should not affect its value to a buyer. It is just one more reminder that a potential acquisition's books should be examined with caution, and carefully recast before anyone places much confidence in them.

One way to assess an ongoing business is to compare its recent performance with the overall economy in which it operates. In valuing an established firm that is growing faster than its surrounding economy, one must ask why it is so effective and how long that superior performance will last. Does the firm have a unique product or service delivery? Why is it unique? How long can the business maintain its uniqueness? How much of the superior performance is due to the popularity of the selling owner—and will go with her when she leaves? If the critical idea can be relatively easily copied, the firm will likely not produce those excess returns for very long and will maintain its above-average growth rate for an even shorter period. A potential buyer must discount these returns to a shorter period as competitive forces can be expected to eat into the profits. This discount is particularly true for small firms that are unable to create a monopoly situation with protective entry barriers.

Even when assessing a firm without great growth potential, one that is earning a small but positive excess return, a buyer should always ask: "What am I missing? Why is the current owner selling this profitable business? Can I maintain (or improve) the current operation's performance?" A seller working in a given market is likely to know the local competitive environment better than any potential buyer. There is at least one reason the current owner is selling. The buyer must ascertain what is really happening with the firm. This need provides further rationale for checking with the firm's current service providers—accountant, attorney, insurer, and bankers—and its major business partners—primary vendors and key account customers.

Similarly, major operational changes should be reviewed carefully. Why would the current owner institute major changes in operations just prior to selling a business? It may be a good sign—a dynamic enterprise adapting to new opportunities—but it may also be a problem. To begin with, a business that is changing a lot is hard to value as a going concern. The firm is becoming different from the one that produced its history, the performance reflected in its financial statements. How can one tell what the reorganized firm is going to produce? Certainly not by projecting performance forward from the old firm's history! Since valuation is based on expected performance, the lack of a track record for a firm undergoing a major overhaul tends to radically diminish its going-concern value; there really is no going concern in the strict sense. Even the current owner is restructuring the assets, so why shouldn't a prospective buyer treat it the same way? It might best be valued as just the sum of its assets.

Many healthy businesses should go through transitions, restructurings, from time to time, and some will come up for sale during such a stage in their histories. Just because buyers discount the histories of such a firm doesn't mean the firm won't continue—or become more profitable for the buyer. It does mean that the historical performance may be steeply discounted, perhaps so deeply as to treat it as a pool of assets rather than a going concern. Among the ways to restore value to a firm in such a phase is a well-thought-out plan for the overhaul, something that lays out clearly the previous value of the firm, the restructuring process, and the expected future value of the revamped firm. Indeed, such a plan may even generate sufficient excitement to support a positive premium greater than the discontinuity discount—but it will need to be a good plan! Done right, it may have the value of both an established firm with evidence of the value of its assets, and a new venture with dynamic new growth potential.

8.2.2.3 VALUING PREDICTABLE CHANGE: DECLINE AND IMPROVEMENT Our final point here, about valuation of going concerns and their growth potential, deals with the other side of growth options. Firms showing exceptional growth should probably be discounted in value, relative to their straight-line projections, because the buyer is unlikely to be able to sustain the sellers' performance. Conversely, those firms earning inferior returns and showing growth less than that of the overall economy should be considered carefully for their untapped potential. Many of the latter candidate firms will be in shrinking industries or in no-growth locations where there is no exploitable potential (consider a premium car dealership on a small lot in a declining neighborhood). Some, however, are run by tired managers who have not kept up with their competitors. For a new owner, with properly revamped and updated operations, these firms could provide substantial opportunities. Whatever kind of firm one is considering, the decision to discount its prospects or increase them is fundamentally based on a judgment about which management team will be better able to get superior performance out of those assets. If the buyer has looked carefully at the way the seller is managing the assets and still believes she can do better, then the firm is probably worth more to the buyer (premium) than to the seller.

As one undertakes a valuation of a business, a key thing to remember is the incentive structures. Who expects to benefit from what? The seller has every incentive to make the business look as good as possible, to drive up the selling price. This principle is particularly true when the proposed sale is a strictly cash deal, since the buyer will have little recourse for a discount after the sale is concluded and the check cashed. A prospective buyer should look carefully at the data provided and question things that appear better than expected. Remember all the opportunities for improvements, but point out to the seller all the potential real puts that other competitors hold against the firm's future potential profits. The smart buyer will negotiate with as much of that knowledge as possible.

8.3 Know What You Can Pay

Let's say a business looks like it might be a profitable acquisition. Next, one must think about paying for it. Many potential buyers of closely held firms do not have sufficient resources to buy these businesses outright *and* provide the working capital to keep them running. We now present some points to remember when planning to get the business running "under new management" and paid for by the new owner.

8.3.1 *Financial Requirements to Run the Business Successfully: Working Capital*

Before determining how to pay the seller, the other capital requirements needed to run the business must be considered. Too often, businesses fail for lack of capital to cover necessary activities or purchases forgotten during the pricing process. The most obvious requirement is working capital. If the business is purchased as a sale of the assets, leaving a shell firm to the seller, most likely the shell (i.e., seller) will retain the debts, cash, and trade receivables. Inventory will most likely come with the business, but as a new customer, supplier credit is not guaranteed for the buyer. Cash purchases might be required for the first several months. A new owner, totally borrowed out to buy the business, will be unable to keep it going. While banks will lend against seasonal needs, they are not eager to lend the entire working capital needed.

If the firm sells on credit, it will probably be 45–60 days before cash comes in. Let's assume that cash will lag purchases by up to 60 days. That means that a buyer should have two months (at least) of working capital ready when she takes over the firm.

As a related need, how long will it be before the firm is actually running to projected capacity under the new ownership? While it is true that one reason businesses are purchased, rather than started from scratch, is to minimize startup time, even direct transfers are usually going to see some dip in operations until things are running smoothly again. This valley should be anticipated by holding in reserve another month or two worth of financing. Actual needs will vary from business to business. With a strong cash-paying clientele, a business like fast food is likely to see positive cash flow much sooner than a public sector consulting firm, for example, given the often extended payment histories of government agencies. A buyer may not need to have this cash available before the purchase, but he or she should have it lined up and approved. The likelihood is that it will be needed sooner, rather than later.

8.3.2 *Seller Financing*

8.3.2.1 A MORTGAGE ON THE BUSINESS TO STRETCH THE REPAYMENT TERMS Unless the firm is being purchased for strategic reasons, such as to obtain additional capacity quickly, fill out a product line, absorb a top management team, or eliminate a competitor, the new owner/manager usually has fresh ideas to make the business more profitable. They often require additional investments. It is therefore extremely important for the buyer to not get overextended by trying to pay off the previous owner too quickly. Planning for operations after the purchase becomes extremely important, just as important as planning for the actual purchase. Indeed, a common strategy is to make those highly profitable new investments a key part of the plan to retire the acquisition debt.

Earlier in this book, we talked about the importance of keeping the seller involved in the business until as much of his or her human capital as possible has been transferred. A simple way to accomplish this objective is to have him or her hold a mortgage on the business. This ongoing commitment to the firm's success is a major reason for getting sellers to finance the sale, instead of using outside financing. If the seller can be persuaded to take a long-term note for a significant portion of the purchase price, that may be a great way to accomplish two important goals. It can both reduce the cash flow dangers of a quick cash-out and maximize the transfer of reputation and other intangible assets to the new owners. An alternative may be to have a family member or family-controlled trust hold the longer term note. That approach works just as well financially but doesn't normally help with human capital issues. The exceptions occur when the buyer's extended family have a deep history in that kind of business, such as Dutch funeral parlors in New Jersey, Gujarati motel owners across the United States, or Asian or Greek restauranteurs.

8.3.2.2 WHEN THE SELLER WANTS A QUICK CASH-OUT All right, let's say we remembered to keep some funds in reserve for working capital and transition time, but buying the business will stretch us to the limit, and this seller wants an all-cash deal. What does a prospective buyer do?

Most business acquisitions are now either all-cash deals or financed over a period of one to two years. So much can change so quickly in the business world that it is very risky to trust someone else's management of a closely held firm to produce steady returns over long periods of time. Sellers, once they give up control of the operations, want cash.

There's good reason. One family we know sold its restaurant business and granted the buyer a ten-year deal. For the sellers, it amounted to a pension plan. The money would provide a steady income, with which they could finish building their family vacation home and settle into a comfortable retirement. They were tired of the restaurant business and didn't have the energy needed to deal with a rapidly changing environment. They were tired of the six-day-a-week demands of the business, the fourteen-hour days; they wanted to spend more time helping their adult children raise the grandchildren. It looked like a good deal. The buyer had the energy to convert the restaurant to meet the needs of a rapidly growing local minority group and to maintain service to an assured clientele.

Everything went well for a year or so. The sellers settled into retirement. Then, monthly payments started to slow; the buyer called, wanting to adjust the deal, to conserve some cash. He was running short of money after the renovations, and didn't have the money to pay all the bills. After two and half years, he simply stopped making any monthly payments and stopped maintaining the property. The sellers were forced to take legal action, seize the property, invest new money, and go back to running it themselves with a skeleton crew, a damaged property, and a crippled reputation. By the time we met them, they were very tired and desperate to get their lives back. They needed a new buyer, but the business wasn't worth what it had been. They were going to lose a lot of their equity, a chunk of their dream. But they weren't going to take back any financing for the next buyer!

While the original owner prefers the money sooner to later, even given a good interest rate, the buyer's biggest concern should be to make payments without sacrificing the business' future potential. That's in the interest of the seller, too. The rate of defaults on newly acquired businesses is quite high. The last thing the original owner/manager wants is to retire, move away from the area, and then have to take back the old firm when a default occurs. A smart seller, unable to get all cash, or unwilling to take the all-cash discount, has a strong incentive to make sure the buyer has sufficient funding to make the business successful, so the deferred payments can be completed.

In selling a closely held firm, what the seller wants is not necessarily what the seller gets. This situation is not like calling one's stockbroker to sell a $10,000 block of stock in a large public company. Most sellers will accept some sort of installment sale, particularly when they get a substantial down payment. This form of sale minimizes the seller's incentives to sell the business for more than it is worth. As will be shown in the next chapter, this type of sale can sometimes provide tax benefits to the seller through deferring the recognition of the gain.

Now suppose that one has $450,000 to pay for the name and tangible assets of an ongoing business with a selling price of $1 million. Careful estimates show that $250,000 will be needed for working capital, leaving $200,000 for a down payment. Suppose the remaining $800,000 is deemed to include $100,000 of specialized knowledge and goodwill, $650,000 of marketable real estate, and $50,000 of customized equipment, useful only in this business. Let's further suppose we find a bank willing to finance \$600,000 secured by the real estate, if the seller is willing to finance the remaining \$200,000. The seller agrees to finance that \$200,000 over two years at 10% interest on the unpaid balance. For the two-year seller's note, the annual payment calculates out to \$20,000 interest and \$100,000 principal for the first year, dropping to \$10,000 interest and the remaining \$100,000 principal due at the end of the second year. The ten-year bank note at 10% requires an additional \$97,650 per year. Can the new firm afford these terms?

The key is how much cash can be generated each year to pay interest and principal. Let's look at the value required. The owner/manager must also eat! Therefore, a minimum salary must be provided to cover personal expenses. We will assume that \$60,000 is required, and that this is calculated before income taxes. For the two loans, the interest expense portion, which is paid prior to taxes, is \$60,000 for the bank loan, and \$20,000 for the seller portion in the first year. The remaining principal repayment of \$37,650 for the bank loan and \$100,000 for the seller loan must be paid from after-tax profits. With the \$60,000 before tax required for living expenses, this puts the buyer into the 25% bracket for federal taxes (assuming the new owner is married and filing jointly). Then, in most areas, one must also pay state income and business taxes; we'll estimate those taxes at approximately 5% of gross taxable income. These charges raise the overall personal tax rate to 30% for this example.

As a result, to cover \$137,650 after taxes (\$37,650 for the principal on the bank loan and \$100,000 for the seller), the new owner must generate a before-tax income of \$137,650/(1 − 0.35%), or \$200,000, to make the principal portion of the payments. To that, we must add the first-year interest expense of \$80,000 and living expenses of \$60,000 for a total of \$340,000 for the first year! That is a lot of cash to expect from a \$1 million business, especially in its first year under new management.

8.3.2.3 DEPRECIATION EXPENSES AS SOURCES OF SHORT-TERM CASH

An aggressive buyer might view depreciation expense as a quick fix to provide a form of "tax-free cash." After all, depreciation expense merely lowers the taxable income. While we usually advise owners to treat their depreciation expense as the best initial estimate of their capital reinvestment budget, those funds could be diverted for other purposes, such as these payments. Suppose that depreciation expense for tax purposes averaged \$65,000 per year. If the new owner deferred all maintenance, that would add those \$65,000 to the reported profit and lower the required before-tax profit the business must generate to \$275,000.

Although this strategy might be considered for the two-year note in an emergency, it is hard to imagine any business going a full ten years without new investments and still remaining competitive. When they divert cash from the depreciation/reinvestment budget into principal payments, owners run their businesses into the ground.

8.3.3 *Outside Financing Considerations*

One way to minimize (or rather provide some flexibility to deal with) the problem of large cash flow requirements is to get outside financing. This option may be necessary if the original owner is unwilling to carry a note after the sale or at least one as large as the buyer's capital position would require. (Sellers of small closely held firms most always want to sell for cash, but rarely can get both a good price and such generous terms.) Outside financing comes in many forms. The most common options include selling equity positions, borrowing from family or other associates, or borrowing from institutions.

The key to determining the best source of financing is to consider what kind of business is being purchased and for what reason. Although opportunities come in many varieties, we will split the options along three dimensions: high-growth potential versus limited-growth opportunities; capital-intensive versus low-capital requirements; and IPO potential versus a firm that is likely to remain private (or be sold to another company). These factors will go a long way to determine the best funding source for buying—or starting a business from scratch. Table 8.4 lays out the basic matrix.

8.3.3.1 THE GROWTH DIMENSION High-growth opportunities provide a large upside potential for investors, making it relatively easy to obtain outside funding. A buyer with a need for additional financing will need to make it clear what the growth potential is. Initial funds from personal sources, and "love money" from friends and family, may not keep pace with the investment needs of a high-growth firm. Entrepreneurs in this situation need to line up the kinds of financial support they will need several months in advance. Identifying "angel" investors in their communities is an important step in the early stages. In this context, angels are wealthy individuals who finance new businesses for fun and profit. For more information on the activities and decision-making criteria of angel investors, one could start with Arthur Lipper's book.[3]

Angel investors sometimes have a longer-term objective than venture capital funds (that seek exits three to seven years away to cash out), but eventually these investors also want a return. They are sophisticated enough to know that, as minority shareholders in a closely held firm, they may be exploited by the owner/manager, and they try to protect themselves accordingly. They may use strong shareholder agreements, community networks, and frequent personal visits to constrain or punish wayward entrepreneurs. At the same time, good angels bring invaluable expertise, connections, and business savvy. They may also bring introductions to

[3] A. Lipper III, *The Guide for Venture Investing Angels: Financing and Investing in Private Companies* (Columbia: Missouri Innovation Center Publications, 1998).

Table 8.4 Sources of Funds by Type of Opportunity

	Growth Potential		Capital Requirements		Future Ownership	
Type of Money Sources	High	Low	Intensive	Low	Public	Private
Personal savings	Insufficient	Likely	Insufficient	Yes	Insufficient	Yes
Love money (family and friends)	Insufficient	Likely	Insufficient	Possible	Insufficient	Maybe
Banks	Special	Conventional	Part of mix	Conventional	Probable	Conventional?
Angels	Possible	No	Insufficient	Why?	Not for long	Maybe
Venture capital	Convertible	No	Possible	No	Possible	Not very likely
Public markets	Potential	No	Maybe	No	Yes	No

venture capital firms with deeper, syndicated, resources that can help a firm grow toward public markets.

The expertise that these outside financiers can bring to a new business should not be overlooked. They are usually experts in the industries in which they invest. They must see something in this business that makes them feel it can earn excess returns. From their experience, they can see that the firm can do something that is valuable in the marketplace. The owner/manager is often too busy with the daily trials and problems of operating the business to focus on these strategic aspects. Outside investors can help entrepreneurs learn to delegate management chores, and keep their sights raised on the larger potential of the business. They can also be invaluable in introducing entrepreneurs to the people they will need as the business grows—more sophisticated managers, service providers, and investors.

8.3.3.2 INFORMATION COSTS OF ILLIQUIDITY AND MINORITY SHAREHOLDERS Offsetting the information cost of illiquidity is the benefit of control that comes to the current manager of a closely held firm. Earlier in this book, we discussed those benefits. For the typical owner/manager, the value of control more than offsets the cost of having an illiquid investment, even when selling the business. For smaller firms that would not attract much market following, the control benefits probably outweigh the lost market information costs from not being public.

Where these costs do become important is when a closely held firm has minority or outside investors. They receive none of the control benefits of ownership but suffer from all of the costs of illiquidity: inability to sell, costs of equity sales, and lack of information. Furthermore, if the manager owns over 50% of the business, the returns to minority shareholders exist entirely at the manager's mercy. Unless the funds are invested with the expectation of a non-financial reward, such as helping a family member, successful investing in closely held firms requires a different kind of analytical expertise and a higher level of direct participation than investing in stock-market securities.

These investors are the ones most subject to the 30–35% discount in value for lack of liquidity, discussed in detail in chapter 7. Traders set the market price. Since majority shareholders generally do not trade in their shares, the traders are almost always the minority shareholders, and they pay a heavy penalty for their position. Thus, the value of a closely held firm can easily appear to be 30–35% less than that of a comparable public firm. The inside owner/manager receives all the benefits of ownership, including the ability to set salaries and consume perks, without having to consider or worry about market discipline to control his or her behavior. Both groups, insiders and outside minority shareholders, lose from the lack of market-provided information.

Third-party investors in closely held firms face a substantial illiquidity problem. To overcome that, normal market rationality suggests that they should demand a higher discount, for example, taking a larger equity stake for the value of their investments. Not all angels make their decisions purely on the basis of economic rationality, however. Economic potential, the excitement of involvement with dynamic entrepreneurs, the ability to strengthen communities they care about, and many other criteria may also play roles.[4]

8.3.3.3 CAPITAL INTENSITY The more capital-intensive the firm, the greater the likelihood it will need multiple sources of financial support. Mixes of debt and equity will likely be required.

It is important to find (at least) one bank with the ability to provide the various kinds of debt financing that the firm is expected to need. This strategy means that the managers of growth firms should begin early to cultivate larger, or more business-oriented, banks for at least some of their financial needs. Firms with modest capital requirements can afford to shop among local banks.

Similarly, on the equity side of the firm, the development of a diverse capital structure and the ability to bring in different kinds of investors will be important if a firm is expected to grow rapidly. Development of the financial systems and acumen needed to satisfy increasingly sophisticated and demanding investors is important in capital-intensive growth firms.

8.3.3.4 PUBLIC OR PRIVATE OWNERSHIP PLANS? If the long-term goal is to create a public firm, venture capitalists and angels may be interested in investing. On the positive side, they bring expertise to the operation in the form of specific industry, marketing, and financial knowledge. On the downside, they may want to be in a position of control, particularly if things go poorly. They usually want to be able, in the extreme situation, to shut down the business, recycle the remaining assets, and minimize their losses. On the upside, venture capitalists sometimes want to be in a position to force the firm to go public. This step allows them and their backers to cash out, or create a "liquidity event" to exchange their illiquid, closely held positions for marketable stock, if no premium corporate buyer can be found. The returns are tax-free until owners sell their shares and then are taxed as capital gains. A new owner/manager should consider this financing option when going public is a desirable strategic outcome.

The use of angels and venture capitalists is a fine strategy if the business has a reasonable chance of developing into a public firm or a buyout by a

[4] For additional information about angels, also known as informal venture capitalists, see R. T. Harrison and C. M. Mason, eds., *Informal Venture Capital: Evaluating the Impact of Business Introduction Services* (London: Woodhead-Faulkner/Prentice Hall, 1996). Many other books have been produced in the decade since this one. For a good update on current activities in this market in the United States, see the June 1, 2005, global broadcast of the MIT Enterprise Forum on angel markets, available online at http://enterpriseforum.mit.edu/network/broadcasts/200506/index.html.

public company. However, what about the other good opportunities? Alternatively, suppose that the business will be run directly by the new owner, becoming his or her primary employment? The question becomes how to finance that kind of purchase. Private debt is usually preferred, with funds borrowed from sophisticated investors. First, consider the positive aspects. The interest expense is tax-deductible. It has a finite maturity, meaning that it will eventually be paid off. The type of individuals investing realize the risk and charge accordingly, but they are also flexible, often taking payment early if things go better than expected or restructuring deals when things do not work out as expected. The last thing they really want to do is take over and run or liquidate the business. Still, these deals are increasingly structured as a kind of convertible debt financing, so they can take over when things really do not work out. These angel investors are most likely successful people running their own closely held businesses, sometimes including professional practices such as medicine, law, and accounting. They have a natural aversion to public financial markets. They would rather invest their surplus wealth where they can see it at work.

8.4 Reorganizing the Business

Once the amount to pay has been decided, and it looks like the financing can be arranged, it is time to consider the specific legal organization for the soon-to-be-acquired business. The two major (defensive) objectives are to minimize future taxes and protect one's other assets against unforeseen happenings. As with other business decisions, the costs involved must be considered. Normally, one does not hire the top law firm in town to set up the organization of a million-dollar business. But most owners do need legal help to properly organize a business, and getting that done right does cost money. After that, we need to make sure the accounts are well organized, and then address the normal requirements for running a successful business. In the first part of this section, we discuss the various legal/taxable forms the business may take. In the second part, we review the various business services a business buyer needs to organize.

8.4.1 *Organize to Maximize and Protect Wealth*

The most common objectives in organizing a firm are to maximize the expected after-tax benefits from the business while protecting oneself against unforeseen liabilities. The benefits are defined after both business and personal taxes, which include taxes on income as well as self-employment taxes. The potential liabilities include both those against the business and personal ones arising from the business.

There are many different business formats, each creating slightly different tax obligations. They can be reduced to those formats providing (or not providing) limited liability and those formats requiring double taxation of company profits as well as shareholder receipts or flowing all profits directly to the owners for taxation in their hands. There are three traditional forms of business organizations in Western countries: proprietorship, partnership, and corporation.[5]

Traditional partnerships are treated much like proprietorships. Organizations with various kinds of limitations on the liabilities of the owners include LLPs, Subchapter S corporations, and regular corporations. Table 8.5 highlights the major differences between the various business organization forms.

8.4.1.1 PROPRIETORSHIPS AND REGULAR PARTNERSHIPS

A proprietorship is merely an extension of an individual. It has no limited liability, and owners of sole proprietorships pay taxes as individuals. A proprietorship is easy to form, usually with no specific registration required.

The regular partnership is the same as the proprietorship, except it is two or more individuals or corporations. It pays no taxes as an entity; all profits and liabilities flow through to the partners. With "joint and several" liability exposure, the entire wealth position of each partner is at risk. That extended liability usually makes this form unacceptable unless the partners have equal (the best being zero) outside wealth. For any partnership, it is important for both the IRS and the partners to spell out in writing the nature of the organization and the individual responsibilities. Even when a partnership starts as a very small operation by close friends, the potential for misunderstanding grows as it encounters more customers, suppliers, partners, and other participants. We encourage the development of partnership agreements—and their frequent review and revision.

8.4.1.2 CORPORATIONS (C-CORPS)

In the United States, due to constitutional provisions, corporations are chartered by the state governments. Most small closely held firms are chartered in the state in which they have most of their operations. The corporate form offers limited shareholder liability, but exposes the firm to taxes on the business profits. Those taxes are computed on profits after the owner/manager's "reasonable salary." (In a proprietorship or partnership, there is no separate salary paid to owners—they simply own the profits or losses, and hence pay personal income taxes on their shares of the profits.)

[5] One could argue that the limited partnership (LP) is a traditional form where there is at least one general partner who is at risk and limited partners who are only at risk for the amount invested in the partnership. However, with partnership tax laws creating passive income since the 1986 U.S. Tax Reform Act, this form of business has no tax advantage. Furthermore, the more recent forms called LLPs and LLCs offer more flexibility and liability protection for all partners compared to the limited partnership.

Table 8.5 Summary of Organization Characteristics

Liability exposure	Regular C Corporation	Subchapter S Corporation	Limited Liability Partnership	Traditional Partnership and Proprietorship
Liability exposure	Limited	Limited	Limited[a]	Unlimited
Income taxes	Firm pays taxes after managers' wages	Profits flow through to owners after managers' wages	Profits flow through to owners before managers' wages	Profits flow through to owners before managers' wages
Qualified pension plans	Yes	Yes	Yes	Yes
Group health	Yes	Yes	Yes	Yes
Other benefits: group disability, medical reimbursement, disability plans, cafeteria plans, deferred compensation	Yes	No	No	No

[a] If any partner is guilty of fraud, the veil can be pierced, making all partners liable.

The limited liability of the corporation is not always as good as it might seem. When most closely held firms borrow money, at least initially, the principal owners must cosign the loan agreements—essentially backing the company with their personal assets. Financial institutions usually insist that owners take personal liability for the debts of the corporation, at least until the corporation has assets and a track record to justify it being treated as a separate entity for real business purposes. Many entrepreneurs work very hard in their first few years to establish their firms as separate creditworthy operations to remove that personal liability for the firm's behavior. Until then, however, the corporate form doesn't really shield them from those responsibilities, although it may shield them from other creditors and some legal attacks.

8.4.1.3 SUBCHAPTER S CORPORATIONS To avoid double taxation but still obtain limited liability, several hybrid business formats are available in the United States. The oldest is the Subchapter S corporation (S-corp), so called because it is governed by Subchapter S of the Internal Revenue Code. To become an S-corp, a firm obtains a regular corporate charter and then petitions the IRS for Subchapter S status.

When individual U.S. citizens (or permanent residents) own a closely held firm, it likely meets the Subchapter S qualifications. S-corps pay executive wages like regular corporations, but any remaining profits flow through to the owners for taxation whether the profits are retained in the firm or paid out. This arrangement works well for firms that pay out all profits. The tax implications are quite complex, however, for S-corps that retain profits to be used as working capital, then later paid out as dividends. By law, dividends are deemed to be paid first from current (taxable) profits, and then from retained (previously taxed) ones. Since the owners have to pay taxes on the profits as they occur, whether or not they have been extracted from the firm, all retained profits from prior years have already been taxed. Payments from that pool would therefore be treated as untaxed, simple returns of capital. Future dividends are only preferred by investors if they are larger, so the key issue is the firm's ability to reinvest at greater than the required rate of return. If it can, other things being equal, it makes economic sense for the owners to pay the taxes and leave the profits in the firm. If not, the rational choice is to withdraw the profits as they occur.

Subchapter S also has restrictive rules that apply when a company provides fringe benefits, other than qualified retirement plans and death benefits, for shareholder-employees owning more than 2% of the equity. These restrictions are present in all business forms except the regular taxpaying, or "C," corporations.

One of the important benefits American companies provide to employees, including shareholder-employees, is group health expenses. Those expenses have been only partially deductible by the firm but, effective with the 2003 reporting year, are now fully deductible. However, full deduction of other types of fringe benefits is available only to regular taxpaying C corporations. These issues remain important matters of ongoing discussion, subject to change by Congress, so check with a current tax professional for the latest rules.

8.4.1.4 LIMITED LIABILITY PARTNERSHIPS AND CORPORATIONS (LLPS AND LLCS) To get around the IRS requirements to qualify for Subchapter S status, available only to U.S. citizens and legal permanent residents, and to avoid the withdrawal of retained profits, the LLP (or in some states the LLC) was created.[6] After being introduced in Wyoming in 1975, this innovation had spread to more than forty-five other American states by 2006. Under LLP/LLC rules, firms are registered with the Secretary of State in the state where most of their business is transacted. They receive limited liability protection when operating in other states as well. What they avoid is the cost of getting a corporate charter, qualifying with the IRS, and maintaining the complex tax books required by Subchapter S firms. As long as they are structured properly, LLPs and LLCs will be treated by the IRS as partnerships for tax purposes. Although they also have restrictions on employee benefits, like those for S-corps,

[6] Some states have both, where the LLP is a limited liability partnership and the LLC is treated more like a regular corporation.

regular partnerships and proprietorships, by 2006 LLP/LLCs had become the preferred organizational form for closely held firms. Compared to C-corps, they have the advantage of single taxation and they are more flexible than S-corps.

8.4.1.5 CHOOSING A TAX-MINIMIZATION STRATEGY Under current U.S. tax rates, it is advantageous for shareholders if a successful firm pays taxes as a corporation when the firm needs to retain money for reinvestment. Consider first a reasonably successful firm where the owner/manager's personal marginal tax rate is assumed to be 30% and the unchanged corporate tax rates are 15% on the first $50,000 and 25% on the next $25,000 before increasing to 34%. By retaining the first $75,000 of profits in the firm, $8,750 in taxes would be saved. After that, the personal income tax rate is lower, so it would be smart to increase wages to a level that would maximize retained profits at $75,000.

With an extremely successful firm, and an owner/manager paying corporate taxes at 34% and personal taxes at 35%, the double-taxation option looks preferable, saving 1% of all profits before taxes. In fact, any time the corporate tax rate is less than the personal tax rate, it will be the owner/manager's advantage to reinvest through the corporation. An example is shown in table 8.6. These are among the reasons that closely held firms rarely pay dividends, even in their corporate forms, and why major investors tend to all be on the payroll in some way, even if only as board members.

A problem arises with the taxes payable when the firm is sold or funds are withdrawn as dividends. The regular corporate format gives the government another tax bite, as ordinary (personal income) taxes on the dividends and as a double (instead of single) tax on the gain from the sale of the firm. The specific issues associated with this kind of cash-out exit are discussed in chapter 9. In today's tax framework, owners are almost always better served when they organize their firms as single-tax entities.[7] More important in the long run, however, is the level of taxation on the future sale of the business, which we defer discussing in detail until the next chapter. The differences can be highlighted here, with an example shown in table 8.7.

8.4.1.6 THE COSTS OF LIABILITY PROTECTION Costs are always a consideration in organizing the business. If the individual or group starting a business has little or no wealth outside the firm, liability protection is not that important. If the business runs into trouble, they have no

[7] If the business has outside investors and the total paid-in capital is less than $1 million the firm should consider registering as a 1244 corporation. This format allows the shareholders to write off losses as ordinary losses at their regular tax rate instead of the normal capital losses (at the 15% capital gain/loss rate) if the firm goes bankrupt. These provisions are limited to $100,000 per year, for persons married and filing joint returns, but can be carried forward.

Table 8.6 Double-Taxation Scenario: Firm Earns $5M, Needs $2M for New Investments

	Subchapter S Corporation	Regular Corporation
Corporate tax	$0	$1.7M
Reinvestment	$2M	$2M
Dividend payout	$3M	$1.3M
10% shareholder receives	$300,000	$130,000
Pays personal taxes at 35%	$175,000	$44,200
Net to shareholder	$125,000	$85,800

Table 8.7 Exit Tax Differences Scenario: Firm Is Started for $1M, Retains $3M (for Book Value of $4M), Is Sold for $6M

	Subchapter S Corporation	Regular Corporation
Corporate tax at 34%	$0	$680,000
Owner receives	$6M	$5,320,000
Amount previously taxed	$4M	$1M
Pays capital gain taxes at 20% on rest	$400,000	$864,000
Net to shareholder	$5.6M	$4,456,000

outside assets that need to be protected from creditors. After all, individuals can still file for bankruptcy more easily than businesses can, despite the changes of 2005. It is probably not worth the additional cost and frustration in dealing with government rules and bureaucrats to obtain a limited liability format—particularly as proprietorships or regular partnerships have the preferred tax position.

What business owners must remember is to change the business format if success builds up after a few years. By then, they have wealth to protect!

8.4.1.7 DIFFERENCES BETWEEN STATES The discussion here has covered only federal taxes and liability considerations. Each state has slightly different taxing methods and allows different organizational forms. Some of them can be quite expensive. In New York City, for example, unincorporated businesses must pay business taxes, and then the owners are taxed again on the net income they receive. In Pennsylvania, firms are assessed a minimum franchise tax for doing business in the state. In Pennsylvania, LLPs are recognized only as LLCs and must pay regular corporate income taxes. It is important to consider specific state taxes and regulations when selecting the organizational form for a new firm.

8.4.2 *Outside Service Providers*

Although their usage can vary widely between businesses, every business needs at least four different service providers: attorney, accountant, banker, and insurance agent. Their services are necessary for most businesses to operate successfully, which is why we feel they should be discussed here. They should also be put in place before the business is purchased to help with the process—each can help structure the transaction and new firm in ways to improve the odds of success. Since buyers most likely have their own advisors, they are faced with the choice of relying on the seller's current or former advisors, using their own, or developing a third set. Let's briefly review their functions and what attributes the acquiring owner/ manager should seek.

8.4.2.1 LAWYERS An attorney is needed initially to assist with the due diligence process, especially in a thorough review of the selling firm's contracts and other legal assets and liabilities. After that, legal experts can help organize the business and review any contracts between other owners and outsiders. It is important to establish in writing all contracts between owners for two reasons. First, the tax collector might question the organization or distribution of profits, particularly in a situation where a person in a lower tax bracket gets what might appear to be a greater portion of the profits. Such circumstances may occur in income-splitting arrangements among family members, with lower-tax children receiving substantial income. Second, partners in successful firms sometimes have fallings out. With a tightly written partnership or shareholders' agreement, it becomes cheaper to resolve those issues. In the future, the firm will quite often need legal counsel for any number of issues. Medium-sized firms will probably find it advantageous to maintain legal counsel on retainer, so they can work with attorneys who develop familiarity with their circumstances and values.

8.4.2.2 ACCOUNTANTS For a prospective buyer of an existing firm, good accounting support is essential, particularly with the process of reviewing the financial statements, verifying their assumptions and meanings, and recasting them to show what the prospective acquisition would look like if managed by the buyer. As the acquisition proceeds, a good accountant can help the buyer understand the implications of various negotiating options, both for the businesses involved and for his or her own personal wealth and tax positions. Once the deal is set, accounting help will be useful in setting up the reorganized firm, and in developing a system of performance measurements that give the new managers the ability to understand and control operations according to their own style.

A good accountant provides several important services to the owner of a small, closely held firm, including tax advice and general financial advice. Audited financial statements are generally a low priority for most owners of closely held firms. Audited statements are rarely needed, except for government-secured loans such as SBA loans, in which case audit capabilities become important.

Taxes must be paid regularly, however, and financial management and planning are ongoing concerns. A good accountant is essential to help the owner make sure these functions are carried out properly and in a timely manner. Although regular bookkeeping is usually a staff function even in smaller firms, an outside accountant can provide good value by helping the owner set up an accounting system that helps her understand the financial health of the firm. The same accountant may also train the bookkeeper to enter the data correctly, and review that person's work to ensure accuracy. A third useful function is to perform analyses and interpretations of the financial data. Accountants also prepare financial statements for the owners, for their bankers, and for tax purposes. Teaching inexperienced owners how to read and interpret their own financial statements can be an invaluable role for a good accountant. As an advisor and sounding board for alternative business investments, an accountant can serve as a critical ally of an owner/manager.

Business owners and potential owners should interview several accountants before making a selection. The kind of accountant required will vary with the complexity of the firm, and with the complexity of the owners' personal financial situation. Does the accountant have a good understanding of finance or is he or she just a glorified bookkeeper? Does the accountant stay current with tax laws and know how to reference the latest rulings? If not, one might as well just use a standard off-the-shelf tax package and do one's own taxes.

We assume that the firm maintains its own books for routine matters, such as purchases and payments, payroll, and receivables and collections. Unlike large firms, small, closely held firms cannot maintain different staff groups to handle ordering goods, receiving them, and paying for goods or selling goods, collecting receivables, and depositing funds. Depending on the size of the firm and the number of transactions that have to be recorded, the owner may have to do all those things herself. As the firm grows, a mixture of part-time and full-time service providers may be used.

Internal accountants or bookkeepers must be bonded against theft. For that matter, the external ones must be bonded as well if they actually handle the firm's money for any of these functions. Bonding certifies that the person has not been arrested for theft, as well as insuring against possible future theft.

8.4.2.3 BANKERS Most buyers will choose to acquire a firm that costs more than the cash they have on hand, so most acquisitions are done with at least partial bank funding. There are several important roles for the bankers. One is to review the buyer's financial position, and determine how much additional debt can be supported by that buyer. The next step may be to consider how much new debt can be supported if the acquisition is successful, essentially lining up the postdeal financing.

In the course of due diligence, the selling firm's bankers should be contacted to determine their level of interest in serving the firm once it is purchased and reorganized. The process of that review may identify significant issues about the liabilities and opportunities the acquisition will encounter. One of the considerations to be addressed is the continuation or restructuring of existing lines of credit, margin allowances, credit card authorities, and other financial arrangements. Based on those discussions, the buyer needs to decide which banking relationships to carry forward from her existing operation, which to retain from the acquired firm, and which new ones need to be created for the reorganized firm to succeed and grow as she plans.

In selecting a banker, the key considerations are convenience and understanding. The first factor is rather straightforward. Is the bank easily accessible to make deposits and handle routine transactions? For a small closely held firm, having an armored truck pick up the daily receipts is a bit too expensive! Therefore, it is important to have easy and safe access to the bank, particularly if frequent deposits of cash receipts are required.

What the owner of a closely held firm must consider is the ease of borrowing from the bank at a reasonable cost, and the availability of more specialized banking services like credit card authorization, international money transfers, and letters of credit. It is also important that the chosen bank have the ability and willingness to provide the financial services the firm needs as it grows. Given the limitations imposed by the Federal Deposit Insurance Corporation (FDIC), local banks may not have the capital to adequately support the needs of a rapidly growing firm. Establishing handoff or changeover relationships with larger regional or national banks may be a requirement.

To be an effective financial partner of the firm, the banker must understand the business well. With many large banks, even those that advertise themselves as being friendly to small new firms, this is nearly impossible. By the time that an owner/manager gets a banker fully conversant with the firm's needs, the banker often gets transferred to a different location. This change necessitates training a new banker, and the frustrating cycle continues. For this reason, many small firms find that money is cheaper and relationships closer when dealing with a small, particularly local, bank. That said, many large banks are trying hard to create special units and provide special staff and training to grow their business with small and medium-sized enterprises.

8.4.2.4 INSURANCE AGENTS Another important set of service providers deals with insurance. Businesses need a variety of insurance products, with the details often depending on their particular industries. Finding a good insurance agent can be more difficult than finding the other three service providers.

Unfortunately, many insurance agents are shortsighted in dealing with new small firms, failing to realize that although the initial fees are small, these firms may grow over time, requiring greater coverage and creating the core of a successful insurance practice. Next, many agents deal with just a few products or are only competitive on the price of a few products. This limitation can require several different insurance agents to provide coverage—one for health coverage, another for the vehicles, a third for general liability, and then another for fire protection, and so on. The owner of a closely held firm needs to ensure that he or she has a full package. It is much easier to deal with one agency, provided that agency can give good service across the full range of the owner's needs.

Even with limited corporate liability protecting one's personal assets, all but the largest, self-insured, businesses usually have insurance. The key question is what is adequate coverage. A traditional rule of thumb was to not insure for more than the firm's net worth. A $2 million business would have coverage to $2 million. The firm can still be sued for greater amounts, however. If it has $2 million in coverage and has a $4 million judgment against it, the insurance carrier will pay $2 million and the owner/manager will pay the remainder and lose all his equity in the business! Furthermore, in many cases, the owner/manager can be personally sued even with a limited liability form of business, making insurance an extremely important consideration. Although one should not insure specific assets for more than they are worth, covering the overall business for liability is a different issue, because it involves the owner's livelihood and equity.

Money can be saved on insurance costs at the lower end. With vehicle insurance, for example, a higher deductible pays for itself as the insurance company doesn't have to incur costs and get involved with minor fender-benders. Conversely, increased coverage at the upper end may be a good idea. The cost of additional coverage in moving from $50,000 per accident up to $500,000 is not large, even though those big claims are the ones an owner should worry about.

Even with limited liability for the business, many lawsuits, particularly with closely held firms, will name the individual owner/manager as well. Protection from those liabilities requires personal liability insurance. One way an owner/manager can protect herself against this type of claim is to have no personal assets in her own name. Place the family cars and house in the spouse's name (if the marriage is strong). Put as much money as possible into qualified retirement plans, because creditors cannot attack this money. (The infamous O. J. Simpson used this technique. Even though he lost the civil lawsuit, the Brown and Goldman families cannot get any of his NFL retirement money.) As owners and their firms mature, it becomes ever more important to protect those assets.

8.4.2.5 OTHER PROVIDERS OF SERVICES TO OWNERS OF CLOSELY HELD FIRMS Although the above four kinds of providers are likely to be found supporting every successful private firm, there is a host of other service providers available. Their value depends on the talents of the owner and the needs of the business. They include: advertising, marketing, Web site design and operation, telecommunications, supply chain management, personnel, payroll, and so on. If an owner outsources everything, and pays full market price for all these services, he is unlikely to remain competitive, so selectivity is important. For a buyer, the key is to understand what he already has, in his own talents and in any existing enterprises, that can economically add value to the firm being acquired. That synergy factor can make the seller's assets more productive in the hands of the buyer. Only when those capabilities are understood should he begin assessing what the new enterprise needs and how those additional resources can be added to the mix.

8.4.2.6 COMMON CONSIDERATIONS In selecting a provider for any of these services, common attributes should be considered. Does the provider deal with other firms in the same or similar industries? There are many industry-specific regulations that experienced service providers will know. In addition, a good service provider can help an owner understand the competitive environment.

Does the service provider deal with other businesses of similar size? A service provider who deals only with extremely small businesses can usually not see the complexities and unique issues facing a larger organization. Those providers usually provide common "cookie-cutter" solutions for everyone because the typical client's small budget does not allow for customized attention. On the other hand, providers of these services for much larger firms are likely to charge higher rates to cover a greater overhead cost. For their smaller clients, the service agency may provide inferior service—it's hard to justify spending as much time getting to know the special needs of a firm that generates $2,000 in annual fees as it is to understand one that generates $100,000 a year.

Is the provider familiar with the specific laws and taxes in the states in which the business operates? This consideration is particularly important when a firm is located close to a state line. Local providers may operate in several states, but may know well only the specific rules of one of the states. When the acquisition brings the buyer into new markets and regulatory jurisdictions, that kind of knowledge is very valuable. Is it something that would cause the buyer to retain (or replace) the firms that provided those services to the seller?

The final consideration is selecting a provider with whom the new owner is comfortable working. Given the intensity of crises that hit small firms, one of the obvious requirements is the professionalism of the service provider in doing routine things, like returning calls promptly. It is also important that the service provider be someone with whom the owner/manager feels comfortable discussing the firm's, and possibly his personal, situation. Confidence and trust are values that are earned over long relationships; they start best between people who respect each other's professionalism and integrity.

These service providers should be lined up when buying the business. Remember, if one does not work out, the firm can always hire someone else. Over the long haul, veteran owners will develop long-standing relationships with their providers. Those relationships are intangible, but still very valuable, assets as owners contemplate expansion by acquisition. That confidence in well-nurtured relationships is one of the main reasons many buyers bring with them their established service teams—and one reason for the seller's support professionals to be concerned about their impending loss of the account. Buyers have the opportunity to carefully assess both sets of professionals, drawing the best from each.

8.5 Buying In? Remember to Price the Exit

The process of buying the business has been reviewed and understood. Is it not time to put this book away and get on with the business? Not quite yet, not if one is really interested in maximizing one's wealth. We must proceed to discuss exits. Although the exit is often the farthest thought from a buyer's mind at the time of acquisition, it can affect the value of the purchase option today. The two major factors that must be considered are the put option to close the business if it is not successful, and the transaction costs that will be incurred when exiting the business in the future.

8.5.1 *The "Put" Options: What Will Be Left If the Losses Have to Be Cut*

We never really want to consider failure when starting something new, but we should. In academia, there are options for students to drop a course that is going poorly or for faculty to take a visiting position to try out a new school. In business, there are options to exit a business quickly and cheaply through sale or liquidation.

One thing to consider in the process of buying or starting a business is the use of unique talents or assets. These might provide great excess returns, but they can also increase the cost and difficulty of exiting the business. They should be appraised on entry because they can affect the value. Recall the story earlier in this chapter about the person entering the laundromat business as a part-time venture while he pursued a career at Microsoft. The business required a reasonable investment, but the major hidden cost was its long-term lease on the property. It had a poor location, which is why the former owner wanted out. The new owner could not find a buyer. The lack of a put option to exit the business cost him dearly. That story also points out the importance of considering all the costs.

One could argue that a put option is just a fancy phrase for "selling costs." The difference is really in the circumstances. One sells when the business has run its course for the current owner and it is time to move on to other activities. An owner closes a business that has performed poorly and it is not worth pursuing. Then why should anyone worry about selling, a regular sale, when entering a business? It could affect the value that one is willing to pay. Consider a business in a declining rural area or a rotting inner city. It has been successful, but now has little future value, making its sale difficult and its price depressed. Or one might have a unique talent, such as that of an artist, making it difficult to find a buyer with similar talents to carry on the business. These factors increase the cost of exiting the future business with anything near what it is worth to its current owner. They should be considered when valuing an initial opportunity to go into business, since they affect the entrepreneur's ability to exit with the equity created by pouring energy and talent into the development of the business.

8.5.2 *Cash Producers and Residual Values*

The purchase price of the business can be considered as having two components. The first, discussed extensively in earlier chapters as well as this one, is the potential of the business to produce regular profits on the investment. We've discussed various techniques by which future expected profits can be estimated, then reduced to a present value. The second component of the value of the business is its residual value at the point of exit. That also needs to be estimated and discounted to the present.

Consider the following scenarios. Firm A has a specialized asset in the knowledge of its artist/owner. When that artist exits the business, much of the value of the business will go with her. The residual value is probably not that of a going concern, whereas the value of the concern to the artist/owner is substantial. No other owner, working without this artist's talents, is likely to find it worth nearly as much. There is little residual value here.

Firm B is a strong growth firm in a dynamic market. It has the kind of R&D team that continues to attract great new talent, and that team spins out market-leading new products on a regular basis. A young dynamic management team is being well groomed by the founding team, and by the venture capitalists who are ushering it toward an IPO. Strong alliances are in place both up and down the supply chain. When the founder retires next year, the residual value of the firm may even rise.

Indeed, the market valuation of many growth companies is based on the value of their future exit, not their current profit-making capabilities. Some high-tech firms have no reliable record of profitability, yet they are worth billions. Their value is largely based on the expectation of a profitable exit. That contrasts sharply with Firm A, where the premium value of the firm exits with the retiring seller. Most businesses will lie somewhere between these two examples, and the real mix is important to their value. What kind of value will a buyer be able to retain or create? When will that value become apparent to the investors who will eventually buy the business from him?

The price an investor should pay for a firm depends a great deal on what kinds of returns are expected—and when. That includes both profits on ongoing operations, and the residual value at the time of exit. A potential buyer must consider how he is likely to exit the business prior to determining its value to him. He must think like a seller to be a good buyer. Those are the kinds of issues addressed in the next chapter of this book.

8.6 Selling and Buying

"As I see it," began Tom, "we have basically three smart choices in front of each of us. Which one we should pick depends on our assessment of where we can get the greatest overall returns, financial and otherwise."

"What three choices do you see?" Mike was curious to see how his friend had come to understand their situation.

Tom dove in. "The first is to keep plowing money back into the business. That makes sense if it looks like the best investment return—and if the family and I want to keep doing this. In our case, that means Tracey should go into the MBA program, learn something about retailing and general operations, build her networks among people who might become our suppliers, or our buying partners. And we'd look at ways to keep improving the business, maybe growing it, adding a new location or two as she gets her feet under her, and as I can still help."

"Not a bad plan," said Mike. "What are your other two options?"

"Plan B would be to sell the whole thing soon, cash out, put the money into some sort of investment pool, and live off the proceeds. I don't think I *want* to retire yet, so I'm not keen on that one. Besides, I don't think we'd get enough to put the kids through college, live comfortably, and so on. So, Plan B is our least likely option, one I'd trigger only if we can't see anything better to do with the equity we've built."

"OK, I see. Plan A is to keep pouring everything back into the business. Plan B is to take it all out. Can I guess that Plan C is to take some of it out?" Mike supposed.

Tom grinned that wry, lopsided grin of his. "Right. Plan C is that I keep running the business the best I can, reinvesting selectively—to make sure we don't get run over, and to support the family as it is. At the same time, we withdraw bits and pieces to cover the college costs, and to begin the process of seeding new opportunities post-MBA for Tracey. She likes the store, but really wants to explore other opportunities too. I think she's going to be a great entrepreneur someday, and it's too early to tell if this business will be her launching pad—or when. Same for the other two. It may be that one or two of them take over this business, while the other one launches something new. Realistically, we're probably five to ten years away from that fork in the road, so we have time to prepare."

"Have you seen anything else that you think can do better for you than what you have right now?" Mike was wrestling with the same question and wanted to know what his friend had observed.

"No." It was obvious from his tone that Tom had thought this one through. "Celia and I have talked about it, and run some numbers. We've thought about the changes involved, and we come to the same conclusion every time: We're better off running the business we currently own. In the last few months, as you and I have gone through this process of learning about the investment side of owning our companies, I think I've learned to run the business better, to find ways to make more money, and waste less, than I was doing before. I can do better financially right where I am. That doesn't mean something great won't come along tomorrow. If it does, I'm more likely to recognize it. For the immediate future, however, my plan is to keep buying more of the business I've got, while pulling out something to create a future investment fund that will allow us to go out and buy something different for Trace and the other kids, if that's what they want. Meanwhile, I've also got quite a few ideas about improving the future sale value of this business, so that Celia and I get properly rewarded when we do decide to cash out."

"Bravo!" exclaimed Mike. "That sounds like a pretty darned good plan! Pris and I have been talking about the same things, although Billy and Michelle are a bit younger. And I think our situation is different from yours in one fundamental way. While there seems to be an unlimited future for retail operations in this country, manufacturing is under growing pressure from lower wage countries. We used to be able to compete on technology, but some of our overseas competitors have technologies at least as good as ours—and are buying better replacements. And they pay a lot less for their engineering and production staffs. Transportation costs are dropping, so that line of defense is thinning out too. I'm not seeing many opportunities to reinvest at the kinds of margins you are."

"Does that mean you're going to sell and join me in the retail sector?!" Tom sounded surprised, and a bit excited. Maybe he was beginning to think about the potential for a joint venture, a business in which they might be partners. That would be an exciting way for the friends to go forward, applying their different skills to a common venture.

"Not exactly." Mike didn't sound as enthusiastic about that possibility. "It doesn't look like there's much of a market for the manufacturing side of our business. My guess is that it is one of those not-a-going-concern things we discussed several months ago. We can make money at it, although not much the way it is working now, but our reinvestment costs are going to be low as well. The distribution side of the business looks better, especially if we let our competitors overseas invest in the new machinery. Then we'll import from them for U.S. markets. I just don't see the point of putting big money into new production equipment in this country."

Tom looked worried for his friend, partly because the strategy seemed less than a winner, and partly because Mike seemed to be a bit depressed about it, instead of his usual enthusiastic self. "Is that good enough, Mike? How will you maintain your markets if your customers see that the products are being made by other people? How do you get your equity out—whenever you want to do that?"

"Oh, we have a few other options up our sleeves!" replied Mike with a hint of a smile. "What I've learned over these months is that I have to look a lot harder for value-added things we can make. I'm going to push harder for new products, things we can make and add to our lines, and protect them with patents if we have to. Those might be things we can sell to our overseas partners, getting royalties back. We're also going to take a look at buying parts of those companies, giving us footholds for lower-cost manufacturing in lower-cost countries. 'Backward integration' is what the Professor called it, I think. We're also going to be looking at higher value custom production runs for special customers, in a sense narrowing our key client list. I know that's a risk, but one I think I can manage, and one I think we're ready to take. Some of the products I can already foresee are ones that allow us to import components, add some of our own, and do final assembly and distribution here. We'll ship the base production overseas and use our higher priced talent and existing machinery to do more high-value stuff."

"What's your plan for the kids, and for your retirement?" Tom still wasn't sure that Mike's plan added up to a full deal.

Mike hesitated. They were old friends and shared much, but he wasn't sure he wanted to tell Tom the details of his last conversation with Priscilla and their financial advisor. "That's something we're still working on," he eventually said. "One thing I think is clear is that we have to put more aside for the kids' college expenses. Billy starts this fall, and Michelle is a couple of years away. The likelihood is that one or the other is going to need support through grad school, so we're starting to think we might be on the hook for more than ten years of college. With that and the investment issues, we're going to reduce expenses at home and work, and put more cash aside into investment accounts. That will give us the flexibility I now see we need to make selective business investments, as well as to build our kid-and-retirement funds."

Tom realized he should not push for more information at this time, and the conversation lapsed into silence for a few seconds before one of the younger kids ran up. "Daddy, Uncle Mike, would you come out and pitch for us?"

9
The Exit Strategy

9.0 So, How Do I Cash Out of This Business?

Priscilla called Tom. That didn't happen often, and hardly ever during business hours. He could tell it was urgent; Mike's wife was upset. What had happened?

"It's Mike. He had his annual physical a couple of days ago, and Dr. Singh saw something he didn't like. He called Mike back for a stress test this morning, and Mike failed it, badly. Dr. Singh sent him straight to the Cardiac Center, and it sounds like he's headed for one of those big bypass operations first thing tomorrow morning. Tom, what do we do? The doctor said he's going to be away from work for quite a while and definitely shouldn't be planning to go back to the high-stress role of company owner anytime soon. I'm so worried about him, and about our future."

He could tell she was on the verge of panic, tears, probably both. "All right, Pris, first we help Mike. Then, we'll deal with the business. Did he leave Andy in charge?"

"Yes—she's been his deputy for the last couple of years, and does a good job keeping the place running whenever we take a short vacation. But Tom, his will leaves the business to me, and I know I can't run it. Andy's already called this morning with an urgent question about one of our major accounts, and I couldn't even understand the issue. I guess I'm not in any mood to focus on the business, but still—"

"Steady, Pris." Tom tried to project a calm he wasn't sure he felt. "Steady. We are talking about a bypass here, not the reading of his will."

"I know, I know, but that's the only plan we have! We never really thought about him leaving the business, so we just set up the will to make sure it was covered. He's been so tied up in that business for the last fifteen years that it's been impossible for him to really think about leaving. His idea of retirement was always fifteen to twenty years away, so he hasn't really thought about how it would happen. Now we have to come up with a better plan, and we have to do it immediately. Tom, I have to get Mike out of that business, and I hope it's not too late. Can you help me?"

"Of course. I can turn some things over to Tracey and my staff for the next few days, and help you and Andy while we sort out the longer-term options. Let's not involve Mike until he's ready, but we can get some things done in the meantime. I've been thinking a bit about this myself recently. But first, let's take care of Mike. I'll meet you at the hospital."

BASIC EXIT STRATEGIES: THE THREE OPTIONS In this chapter, we will discuss the importance of maintaining an exit strategy for the owner(s) of a closely held firm. Except for the smallest of businesses, a major component of a good exit plan is knowledge about the value of the business. It is important for the owner/manager to have a realistic strategy. He or she cannot expect to work until age eighty and then have a grandchild take over—although we know of at least one joyful instance where that happened. Even if more realistic assumptions are made, such as retiring at sixty-five (or fifty), some things do not work out as expected; one should always be prepared to leave the business. Having an exit strategy for the business is a little like having a will. Everyone who runs his or her own business should have both. The exit strategy, like the will, can be changed anytime the circumstances change. It is not set in stone but is a continuously evolving process. One never knows when one's time is about to run out, whether by heart attack or accident, but the arrangements should have been made to allow the business to continue with as little interruption as possible. That's the best way to preserve the value the owner created in the business, and it is also one definition of a going concern.

An exit strategy can take one of three broad approaches. These are not necessarily mutually exclusive exits but rather factors that must be considered in developing the process. First, the owners can consider going public, or selling the firm to widely dispersed third-party investors. This step creates a market for the firm's equity, changing market valuation into a fairly easy exercise. It also reduces the need for a customized exit strategy. For the founder and principal shareholders, owning part of a public firm allows them to give away or sell small increments of their equity every year to children or whomever they please. It also allows them to will their equity in a more manageable form, or to sell portions of it whenever they wish for estate planning or personal purposes. Going public is, however, expensive in many ways, and difficult both before and after. Those liquidity benefits are not free! Most owners of closely held firms choose not to go public.

Assuming the firm will remain closely held, two broad exit strategies exist. The firm can be sold to outsiders in an arm's-length transaction, or it can be sold or given to insiders, including the original owners' heirs, partners, or employees. The considerations associated with those two exit strategies are treated in the second and third sections.

The final section discusses special issues arising when one is trying to handle firms with joint ownership. Quite often, two or more principals start a business together; in other cases, new partners or shareholders join the firm as it grows. Joint ownership brings additional items to consider when developing an exit strategy.

9.1 Why Go Public? Why Not?

Before looking at other exit strategies for owners of closely held firms, we must consider the option that changes closely held status to widely held—taking the firm public. It is the most visible exit for an entrepreneurial founder, one that is held in high, sometimes mythical, regard by much of the business media. Going public is, however, an exceedingly uncommon outcome. Only 13,000 American firms are public—out of about 20 million. That makes for a ratio of less than one in a thousand. Rare and extreme though it may be, the Initial Public Offering (IPO) is nonetheless an important option, so let's consider it first, then proceed to the more common exit strategies.

9.1.1 *The Value of Market Feedback*

A transition to public ownership (i.e., widely held and traded on public stock markets) provides several major benefits for the owners of closely held firms. First, the value of the firm becomes defined by the market. The principal owner no longer has to wonder what the business is worth, since the market values it daily. The market's perception of news released and decisions made becomes immediately apparent as the stock price adjusts to reflect the market consciousness.

This process of providing information to the public, and seeing it judged and incorporated into a public valuation, is one of the major reasons why public companies are valued higher than comparable private companies. Public ownership creates market information that the firm can use in making decisions. The market considers thousands of different firms and how they interrelate, something no individual can track. The market mechanism provides more feedback to a firm's managers. The scrutiny of investors and investment advisors increases accountability by broadening the base of observers. Their collective intelligence is reflected in feedback not generally available to private firms.

We should note that if this book were about valuing *public* firms, this chapter on exit strategies would not be necessary because the rational firm follows the best market value—or at least most people assume it does. There are, of course, imperfections in information, in analysts' perception and use of that information, in market reactions to information, and so on—which is why some people make more money in public market investments than others do. Public markets are far from perfect communicators of value—but they work more effectively for more people than do private markets.

9.1.2 *Confirmation of Going Concern Status*

Second, although a public firm CEO must worry about who will be his or her replacement some day, the business will almost always continue as a going concern. There is no need for a firm to worry about an exit strategy because of a single individual. Public firms are more closely regulated, with a need for publication of their Minutes. The Board of Directors is responsible to the shareholders for ensuring continuity in leadership and performance and, to that end, makes changes in the management team, including replacing CEOs. The Directors are liable for their management of the firm, and shareholder activists hold them to that.

There is no assurance, of course, that a public firm will continue indefinitely. Being a going concern and having public market liquidity are no guarantees of permanent or independent existence. Investors and other companies make buyout offers to the shareholders of public firms. There is considerable turnover, considerable dynamism, among public companies. Few, however, are liquidated for asset values.

9.1.3 *The Value of Liquidity*

Third, a public firm also can give ownership stakes to key employees in the business. That reality of shared ownership usually improves morale, commitment, and performance. The liquidity and prestige of publicly traded shares can help a firm attract and retain good employees when there's a competitive market for good managers.

It is also very valuable to owners, as they are able to value their holdings independently. That market allows those holdings to be used as collateral, because lending agencies have a market value with which to benchmark the collateral—and a market into which they can sell the collateral if need be. That process dramatically reduces their costs of lending and makes such loans against equity easier (and cheaper).

The liquidity of public equity further helps owners diversify their portfolios. Most owners of closely held businesses tend to have much of their lifetime equity tied up in their businesses. If anything goes wrong with the business, family net worth can suffer badly. With their holdings converted into equity in a public firm, they can cash out part of their holdings and diversity their wealth. That diversification should increase the likelihood of their wealth surviving adverse events, on the principle that adversity is unlikely to equally affect different investments.

9.1.4 *Downsides of an IPO*

There are downsides, however, in owning a public firm. The more apparent problems for smaller firms include substantial out-of-pocket costs for SEC compliance, double taxation, and the required publication of information on the firm's performance (financial statements) and the managers' salaries (proxy statements for shareholders). Managers of public firms must deal with two entirely new classes of stakeholders: the arm's-length independent shareholders; and regulatory bodies such as the SEC.

For a smaller firm going public, publication of key financial data can be both embarrassing and costly. Studies have show that small public firms usually pay much lower salaries than even smaller private firms. When the private firm goes public, it must often adjust its salaries and find other ways to compensate executives. Essential operating executives must set aside time to deal with shareholder inquiries, because an investor relations department is too expensive for smaller public firms. That distraction can affect the performance of those executives in other areas of the firm's operations.

9.1.4.1 THINLY TRADED SHARES Stock options have little value in a privately held firm unless going public is contemplated, but stock shares can be given to key employees of a closely held firm even when it is private. The problem is, what is the private firm worth? Having this minority position might be all right during one's tenure as an active manager, but what happens when one leaves either to work elsewhere or to retire? Some well-known firms, such as UPS until recently, faced this dilemma. The employees had to sell their shares back to the firm when they left, because there was no public market for the shares. Their value was determined by the firm's formula instead of by market prices. This valuation method was probably more fair than leaving a small number of minority shareholders with no real market value, but the lack of liquidity and external valuation certainly reduced the value of the shares.

A *bulletin board* trading firm specializes in making markets for small, thinly traded securities. Kohler, the plumbing fixtures company, is an example of firms with frozen minority positions. When they traded, the shares of that closely owned firm changed hands at around $100,000 per share—and that is no typo! Around 1999, the firm made an offer to repurchase outstanding shares for $49,000 per share. Offended, the holders refused to sell, and the market makers, knowing the position of the firm's insiders, refused to pay more than the firm's offer price. The losers in such situations are the frozen minority shareholders.

Ownership positions are only valuable when the owner can sell at the market value. Adverse incentives are created in giving shares to valuable employees and then limiting the marketability of the shares. If the only way they can realize the value of the shares is through a change of the majority, then such frozen positions are incentives for a change in ownership.

9.1.4.2 MARKET FEEDBACK REFLECTS AN INDUSTRY MORE THAN A FIRM A market provides information about a business only when the latter is large enough to attract a market following. Take the example of Zell's liquidity, presented in chapter 7, in the discussion on the required rate of return. Sam Zell expounded on the importance of the market to tell him that REITs had overexpanded. He compared the situation in 1998 with the early 1990 downturn in real estate. Two key points emerge. First, Zell's own business, which he operates and in which he owns a substantial position, is worth several billion dollars. It is not a small closely held firm. Second, he compared the industry's position between the two times. The public ownership positions in all the REITs gave the whole industry a market following. As an owner of a closely held firm, one can still learn from the market by viewing how one's public competitors are doing as a group. For a small firm that is public, it is unlikely that the market will provide any firm-specific information. If the firm is not covered by several analysts, and if it does not trade widely, then each trade may be motivated by different circumstances, making it hard to decipher management feedback from the trading price.

9.1.4.3 INABILITY TO ATTRACT COMPETITIVE TALENT Small public firms with thinly traded stocks are also handicapped when it comes to attracting managerial talent. Top executives will worry about falling out of the "loop" if they leave to run a small firm. How can they move up to a larger firm? Smaller firms often have to groom their own new managers and the replacements for their founders. It is difficult to attract top outside executives without selling them the business.

9.1.4.4 HIGH TRANSACTION COSTS FOR THINLY TRADED STOCKS Small public firms do have continuous market values—but how meaningful are they? They attract little market following because of their small size. This thin market results in high trading costs when their shares are traded. The spread between the bid and ask prices for firms valued between $5 million and $15 million averaged 8.7% in a recent sample of 123 firms.[1] That spread in turn makes their published market prices not very dependable because of the thinness of the markets. When stocks are rarely traded, the specific circumstances surrounding a particular transaction may have a lot of influence over the striking price—and those circumstances may not apply to the next trade. Consequently, it is difficult to establish the market value of such shares when there is no broad market. When the managers and other insiders own a controlling interest, the market price will be discounted for the insiders' control. These discounts appear to run between 25% and 35%, as discussed in chapter 7.

Thus, all the reasons that Bill Gates and Paul Allen took Microsoft public do not hold for all small public firms. Although they still own significant positions, Gates and Allen no longer have more than 50% of Microsoft's

[1] Based on a run from Trade and Quote trading tapes (commonly referred to as TAQ). Trade and Quote is a data service from the New York Stock Exchange. See www.nysedata.com/nysedata/InformationProducts/DelayedHistoricalData/blabla/tabid/201/Default.aspx for more information (accessed October 11, 2005).

shares. Their firm's huge size now attracts a market following, and information is definitely reflected immediately in its share price. IPOs are worth considering if a firm needs access to public capital pools, and has the size and story to attract a good public following. Most owners of small firms find that, when the costs and benefits are reviewed, it is better to stay private.

9.2 Selling the Business outside the Family

A business has been built over the years. The children have developed their own careers. The owner's spouse has seen more than enough of this business and would like both of them to retire. This situation is not unusual; it is the norm. Of every one hundred family-owned businesses, by far the dominant form of business throughout the world, only a third are transferred to the next generation of the owner's family.[2] As most closely held businesses are family owned, this simple statistic reminds us that two-thirds of them change ownership through sales to outsiders, or through dissolution and sales of assets. These sales should be arranged to obtain as much after-tax money as possible for the owners with as little risk as possible. This section reviews some of the factors to consider when selling a business to non–family members. In the following section, we'll address insider options.

The real process of selling a business well is outlined in table 9.1. It is a many-step process, with a lot of value contingent on doing things well along the way.

9.2.1 *Direct or Brokered?*

One of the important early steps is to decide how the business will be sold. Conceptually, it is like selling a house. A critical step is finding qualified buyers. The two main choices are "by owner" or through a business broker. In the case of some franchised firms, another option may be to sell back to the franchisor, or within the network of existing or qualified franchisees.

9.2.1.1 FOR SALE BY OWNER To sell a business directly, ads are taken out in business publications such as the *Wall Street Journal* if the opportunity can attract national attention, or local publications if it cannot. Many areas now have local business publications, such as *Crain's* weekly business papers or magazines, and there are also local newspapers. Finally, one gets the word out that the business is up for sale through mentioning it to friends, associates, service and professional clubs, church congregations, and so on.

These channels are inexpensive; many are free of direct charges. The challenge to an owner trying to sell this way is to release enough information

[2] As reported in Jeffrey A. Tannenbaum, "The Front Lines," *Wall Street Journal*, July 9, 1999, p. B1.

Table 9.1 General Process for Selling a Business Well

- Conduct soul-searching to determine why the owner is considering a sale—and what life on the other side of a sale should look like.
- Sort out what the owner wants to get out of the sale—and what she or he doesn't want (e.g., peace, cash/annuity, relief from duties and responsibilities, estate planning, trust funds, tenure for employees, care for customers, family brand name, community honor, an ongoing role of some sort, opportunities for children or grandchildren).
- Clean up the business, so that it can be readied for sale.
- Remove owner idiosyncrasies from the payroll and operations.
- Recast the books as if it were independently owned.
- Paint, landscape, tidy.
- Figure out what's really for sale, and what the owner or heirs wish to retain (e.g., business operations, name, real estate, vehicles, furniture, equipment, contracts).
- Identify and consider the taxation implications of various options.
- Conduct market research to see who is buying the kind of assets the owners wish to sell, and what kinds of money and terms they are offering.
- Prepare listing documents that do *not* identify the actual firm or seller (which means the seller needs a confidential go-between).
- Prepare disclosure documents (work with a good attorney and accountant).
- Estimate reasonable values under various terms, for qualification and negotiating purposes.
- Reexamine the decision to sell versus invest more, especially if minor investments can significantly improve the near-term value.
- Examine non-arm's-length potential buyers, like family or employees, suppliers or buyers, to see if any have the potential interest and wherewithal to buy.
- Conduct an auction. Advertise to reach the most likely audiences of bidders.
- Choose the best terms.
- Work out the best deal you can.
- If you can't make that work, go on to bid #2, and so on, until one works out or the list of good bids is exhausted.
- If no bids are satisfactory, pull it off the market, reassess, remanage, and restart.

to attract the right potential buyers, while keeping the time-wasters away—and not give away damaging information to either competitors or potential negotiating opponents.

There are many risks associated with such a direct approach, including loss of key suppliers, customers, and employees. Notifying the world that key management is about to change, without also announcing the new owners and their credibility, is an open invitation for competitors to raid the firm. If an owner decides to sell the firm himself, discretion is a very important attribute. Identifying the right networks and using them skillfully is also important.

9.2.1.2 USING A BUSINESS BROKER/INVESTMENT BANKER The other option is to work with a business broker, sometimes known as an *investment banker*. These firms usually specialize in certain types of businesses and areas of the country. One can start with the Yellow Pages, but better results can often be obtained through a seller's attorney or accounting firm. A further advantage of this route is that these professionals are usually good at keeping secrets and exercising discretion. In addition, they can serve as intermediaries, buffering the seller from curious inquiries. Business brokers have the experience of numerous transactions, focused market research skills, expert accounting and restructuring knowledge, large databases of potential buyers, and other services for owners, usually in return for a percentage of the final price. Good services are not cheap—but they can make a substantial difference in the selling price. They can also make a huge difference in the cash-out, after-tax value, and in the legal protection offered to an inexperienced seller.

9.2.2 *The Market for Good Secondhand Businesses*

Regardless of the approach taken, one should not expect a fast sale. How long does it take to sell a house? Compare a rather uniform item such as a house, with easily identifiable characteristics, to the peculiarities of even a simple business. It is important to plan ahead. For the best results, start the process several years prior to a scheduled retirement date. That should provide the time to look for the best offer without being desperate to sell. One does not want to be in the position of having to take the first offer. If a potential buyer senses desperation, then his or her approach may well be to come in with a very low offer. Buyers are, after all, investors, and investors know that a lower initial price makes profit more likely.

9.2.2.1 WHO ARE THE BUYERS? Sellers need to know what kind of buyer is likely to pay them the best price for their businesses. Setting aside the category of "fool,"[3] let's consider the kinds of buyers and the types of firms for which they would be most suited. The key, as always in this book, is to discriminate between inferior, average, and superior buyers. Where is a seller likely to find the *best* deal?

For example, the best buyers of businesses not being sold as going concerns, that is, asset sales, are most likely to be owners of similar businesses, into which those assets can be easily merged and made productive. Now, there may be circumstances in which the other local owners do not need those assets. Conversely, there may be circumstances in which the assets would have higher value to new startups, regional firms, or even large companies.

Early-stage, high-potential firms, on the other hand, are least likely to be sold for a premium to other startup operators. Those owners are often cash-poor, and not as able as the founding entrepreneurs to realize the value

[3] Although people sometimes make bad deals, some people win lotteries, and some people inherit wealth, we've always found it wiser to assume than someone with the interest and money to buy a business got there by being a smart businessperson. The best assumption is always that a buyer is capable—at least until the cash is fully transferred!

inherent in the founders' entrepreneurial vision. Top-dollar sales of this kind are likely to come from larger firms.

We've identified six types of firms for sale, and cross-referenced them by four kinds of buyers. The most and least likely premium buyers are identified in table 9.2.

9.2.2.2 SELLERS GET BETTER PRICES WHEN THEY REDUCE THE BUYERS' RISKS

The seller who wants as much cash as possible must find a buyer—who likely wants to pay as little as possible. Nevertheless, potential buyers are always concerned about risks. One of the major categories of risk is ignorance, what they don't know about the firm. Remember—we're discussing an arm's-length buyer, not an employee who knows the business, warts and all.

9.2.2.2.1 *The Price of Deception and the Reward for Transparency*

Any potential buyer will be worried about the odds against taking delivery of whatever the seller is promising. For the seller cashing out of this business, there is little incentive to be totally honest. Most sellers find it much easier on their consciences to cheat a stranger than to deceive someone with whom they have been dealing over a long time, even when the formal relationship is about to end.

Most potential buyers are aware of these incentives and are rightfully skeptical when reviewing a firm's books. This incentive to cheat must be minimized by the buyers through the sales contract. The price the seller receives is likely to be closely related to how well the buyer feels those risks have been addressed. Every seller therefore has an incentive to consider ways he can best reduce the buyer's perceived risks while still maximizing his own value. There is no magical answer—this is one of those tough trade-off zones—but there are useful ways to organize the sale to achieve higher value for both buyer and seller.

Table 9.2 Most Likely and Unlikely Buyers, by Type of Sale

	Best Buyers, by Type of Firm			
	Business Novices	Local Business Owners	Regional Firms	Large Companies
Assets	Maybe	Likely	Maybe	Maybe
Small, stable, no growth	Likely	Maybe	Unlikely	No
Early stage, high growth potential	Unlikely	Possible	Maybe	Maybe
Local franchise	Likely	Yes	Maybe	Unlikely
Regional or product middle contender	No	Unlikely	Likely	Maybe
Well-defined leader in key market niche	No	Maybe	Maybe	Likely

9.2.2.2.2 *Human Capital: The Value of Knowledge Transferred* Closely related to this issue is the seller's *human capital*. In many businesses, as discussed in chapter 2, specific business knowledge has been built up over the years. Although the seller can let the new owner acquire this knowledge the hard way, she will usually get paid more for the business if the new owner's learning curve is shortened and softened. The seller can transfer human capital to the buyer, and get paid for it, either through a transition period where the departing owner serves as a consultant to the new owner, or as part of the selling price itself. The specific approach to packaging and delivering this knowledge should be part of the sale negotiations.

This firm-specific capital is of little or no use to the seller exiting the business because the buyer will almost surely require a *noncompete* clause in the contract. These parts of the contract usually state that the seller cannot start a similar business for a time period, such as two years, or within some area, such as fifty miles, of the existing business. Although their enforcement can be difficult, these legal restrictions provide some insurance that the seller is not just relocating the businesses by selling the original location. The buyer must also worry about a seller who formally sells the business to one party but encourages all the customers to go to a different party after the sale. The seller needs to keep in mind that the buyer is worried about the bad things that can happen.

Ask anyone who has started a business what it was like at the beginning. All the entrepreneur's wealth (and then some) was put into the business. If that business failed, it would have been a disaster for the entrepreneur. The new buyer shares those fears. The more fearful the buyer is of these things, the less capital she is likely to risk in an early cash payment, and the more she will retain in reserve to deal with anticipated problems. Fearful buyers will want to minimize the initial payment and maximize the long-term performance clauses. The more a seller can reduce those perceptions of risk, the easier it will be to persuade the buyer to move value (and cash) into the front end of the deal.

9.2.3 *Tax Strategy While Operating the Business: Double or Single?*

Sellers usually try to structure sales to get the most money, as soon as possible, after taxes. This objective requires careful planning in organizing the business for tax purposes well before it becomes time to consider selling. There are two basic ways that a closely held firm can be structured for taxes. It can be operated as a regular C corporation, which pays taxes as a business before its shareholders pay again on any dividends they receive. Alternatively, the firm can be formed as a single-tax entity, such as a partnership, or Subchapter S corporation. More recently, owners have the additional option of using a Limited Liability Company (LLC) or Limited Liability Partnership (LLP), in which all profits annually flow through to the owners, who then pay the taxes at their personal income tax rates.

At first glance, paying taxes once sure looks better than paying taxes twice. But one must look closely. When taxes are paid twice (regular or C corporation), all the wages and benefits paid to the owner/manager are tax-deductible (for the business)—including medical insurance and contributions to retirement plans. These benefits must also be made available to all employees, however, not just the controlling shareholder, to be deducted by the corporation. Furthermore, the IRS goes to great lengths, particularly with retirement plans, to make sure that they do not just benefit the highly paid workers in a firm, a group that most obviously includes the owner/manager. Although they can be deducted from taxable income as business expenses, those employee benefits are still expenses, still costs to the business. Do they pay for themselves in reduced taxes and increased employee morale, productivity, and loyalty? That's the trade-off.

The major consideration deals with paying taxes and not the tax-deductible benefits. Suppose our firm needs to retain at least a portion of its profits for future expansion. (Note: if no additional equity is needed in the business, a U.S. firm is always better off with a single taxation status.) Is an owner better off taking the money out as personal income, paying the personal tax, then reinvesting what's left—or should she pay the corporate tax and retain the after-tax residual in the firm for reinvestment?

We need to think about this in terms of the tax rates on income earned by the firm, and whether the owner is better off having it taxed inside the firm or outside. The first $50,000 of a U.S. firm's taxable income is taxed at a 15% rate, and the next $25,000 is taxed at 25%. Furthermore, if the firm is quite successful, the owner/manager could easily be in the 35% marginal tax bracket for personal income. Income between $75,001 and $100,000 is taxed at 34% in the business, so it would still be worth more left in the business, with a tax savings of 1% ($250).[4] When the funds are going to be retained in the business for the foreseeable future, as reinvestments, the owner's advantage is better served by leaving the first $100,000 in the firm and paying tax on it at the corporate rates.

Above that level, a tax-smart small closely held firm would never pay dividends—just continue to increase the salary of its owner/manager to pay out surplus funds. On the first $100,000 of taxable profits, a single taxation entity would leave the recipients paying taxes of 0.35 × $100,000, or $35,000.[5]

[4] Taxable income over $100,000 is taxed at 39% up to $335,000 taxable income before dropping to the 34% rate. This eliminates the advantage of the 15% rate on the first $50,000 and the 25% rate on the next $25,000 of taxable income. Unless the firm is hugely profitable, it is cheaper to pay wages after $100,000 of taxable income than corporate taxes at a 39% marginal tax rate.

[5] This analysis assumes that self-employment taxes are being avoided. At this salary level, the owner/manager is paying the maximum retirement and is now only paying the 2.9% Medicare tax. This is still an additional $2,900 When a reasonable salary is paid the owner/manager of a Subchapter S corporation, the self-employment taxes are avoided on the profits.

A double-taxation entity would pay taxes of only $22,250, for a tax savings of $13,750/year.

9.2.4 *Tax Strategy When Exiting for Stock*

When a firm is taken public, or merged into a public firm in return for a tax-free stock transfer, the tax saving still exists. In these situations, the selling owner/manager takes stock in a publicly traded firm. He or she will have no tax liability until the received stock is sold. At that point, the seller will pay a capital gains tax, set for 2006 at a 15% maximum rate, on the difference between the selling price of the shares and the former owner/manager's tax basis at the time of the merger/IPO.

The tax base varies, however. In the double-taxation situation, the owner's tax base would be the total original investment he made into the business, divided by the number of shares. If the firm had prospered greatly, that base could reflect a very large difference and become a substantial tax bill. In the single-taxation situation, the base would be the total equity of the firm at the time of the sale or merger, divided by the number of shares. Because personal taxes had already been paid on those funds, the capital gains tax would apply only to the change in value that occurred after the sale. The slightly higher tax base for the single-taxation owner would probably not justify paying the higher taxes on the retained funds at the personal rates instead of the lower corporate rates.

This taxation framework for a merger or stock sale to a public company is similar to the one that would become effective if the business were taken public. The firms with real IPO potential are a very small subset of all closely held firms. To the owner/manager, however, either option may involve retaining or giving up managerial control, and that may be at least as important as the tax implications. Some entrepreneurs are happy to give up control of a venture to managers with the assets to make the venture continue to grow; others are less inclined to move on to other ventures. Given the similarity of the tax implications, those managerial issues need to be addressed first.

In either event, the key issues are the establishment of a new tax base, derived from the value placed on the firm at the time of sale, and the appreciation or depreciation that occurs between that point and the time the shares in the public company are sold.

9.2.5 *Taxes When Exiting for Cash*

The situation is different when the owner/manager expects to sell the business for cash, the way most closely held firms will probably be sold. At that stage, whether the business was organized as a C corporation or as a flow-through entity will make a *big* difference! Unfortunately, the tax savings from the lower rates under double taxation can become very problematic when it comes time to cash out of the business.

9.2.5.1 IMPACTS OF SINGLE-TAX OR DOUBLE-TAX VEHICLES Suppose that a firm has $500,000 of the owners' initial invested capital and an additional $800,000 of retained earnings. A buyer is willing to pay $1.5 million. If the firm were organized as anything but a C corporation for tax purposes, the sellers would have a capital gain of the selling price minus their tax basis ($1,500,000 − $1,300,000), or $200,000 in this example. At a 15% capital gains rate, this would leave the sellers $1,500,000 − (0.15 − 200,000) or $1,470,000 after taxes. Seems reasonable, doesn't it? The owners get their reinvested money back, because it was previously taxed, and pay tax on the residual capital gain.

The owners of a regular taxpaying C corporation, however, would continue to be subject to double taxation. First, the firm would pay a gains tax on the same $200,000 gain. Because gains are taxed at basically the same rate as ordinary income for corporations, this rate would be 34%—assuming the firm had enough other profits to be entirely in the 34% tax bracket for that year. That $68,000 in taxes would be subtracted from the total sale price to give a net amount to shareholders of $1,432,000. The shareholders would then be subject to a capital gains tax on the difference over their original investment in the business ($1,432,000 − $500,000) = $932,000. Figuring capital gains tax at 15%, the sellers would have to pay an additional $139,800 in taxes, leaving them a net of $1,292,200. That sum is $177,800 less than they would receive if the firm were organized as a flow-through firm. Table 9.3 shows the trade-offs and their tax implications.

This difference in taxes on the sale of a business has existed since the repeal of the General Holdings rule in the 1986 U.S. Tax Reform Act and is one of the principal factors behind the widespread conversion of C corporations into S corporations and LLCs.

Table 9.3 Comparison of Capital Gains in Flow-Through versus C Corporations

Item	Flow-Through Firm	C Corporation
Initial investment	$500,000	$500,000
Retained earnings	$800,000	$800,000
Sale price	$1,500,000	$1,500,000
Portion subject to corp. capital gains	$0	$200,000
Tax on crop. capital gains @ 34%	$0	$68,000
Pretax income to shareholders	n/a	$1,432,000
Tax-paid capital returned to shareholders	$1,300,000	$500,000
Capital gains by shareholders	$200,000	$932,000
Capital gains tax on shareholder gains @ 15%	$30,000	$139,800
Net proceeds to shareholders	$1,470,000	$1,292,200

9.2.5.2 TAX DEFERRALS For the same $1.5 million purchase price, one way to reduce or postpone the tax burden might be to sell the business on an installment plan. In this example, equal payments will be made at the end of each year for five years, after an initial down payment of $400,000 at the time of sale. Let's assume the discount rate for the payments has been set at 8%. To calculate the annual payments, the residual $1,100,000 being financed (after the first payment) is divided by the present value of an annuity for five years at 8% (= 3.9927). This formula produces an annual payment of $1,100,000/3.9927 or $275,500.

The five equal installments of $275,500 consist of both interest income (on which the seller will pay ordinary tax) and repayment of principal. The principal includes both the tax base (prepaid) and the capital gain on which capital gains tax must be paid. The interest income is calculated as the difference between the total of the five payments, $1,377,500, and the amount owed of $1,100,000, for an interest component over five years of $275,500.

For a Subchapter S sale under the installment method, taxes would be due as follows. In the year of sale, 4/15 of the principal is collected, so 4/15 of the capital gain is recognized for taxes. Because the capital gain is $200,000, that makes the portion of the gain recognized in the first year equal to $200,000 × 4/15 = $53,300. Over the next five years, capital gains on the remaining ($200,000 − $53,300) = $146,700 need to be recognized. That amount is spread evenly over the five years as ($146,700)/5 = $29,340 to be recognized each year. We also have to recognize the interest income each year, calculated as $275,500/5 or $55,100 per year. The IRS does allow a straight-line recognition of interest income on installment sales. The remaining $220,400 received each year is simply a return of the owners' capital on which taxes had been previously paid.

The tax savings might not exist if the income earner faces constant tax rates over time, so any expected variation in tax rates has to be taken into consideration. The installment sale provides the new owner with additional time to raise (or earn) the funds. In many cases, those additional funds are raised from the ongoing operations of the firm, including times when the new owner takes a lower salary and transfers a portion of the total owner's compensation into debt reduction.

A wise seller should not structure a deal to rely on payments greater than the business can be expected to generate as after-tax profits. Remember, for the buyer of the business, the annual payments of principal are not tax-deductible. Only the interest portion is deductible. As discussed in chapter 8, this need to make the payments may provide some modest assurance to the buyer that the business is what is advertised, but can hardly be relied on. It is the buyer's responsibility to make the payments, from whatever sources he has, not the seller's job to ensure the business will carry the payments.

9.2.5.3 CHARITABLE REMAINDER TRUSTS The latest wrinkle to avoid the tax collector is to give the business to charity! Now, Americans have always been able to give wealth tax-free to qualifying charities, but this new approach still produces wealth for the original owner/founder. This approach works best when the business would create a large capital gain if sold, yet the owner has a substantial expected time before death. Through donating the business to a charity, the capital gains tax can be avoided (similar to donating any appreciated asset to charity). Then, the charity, which does not know how to run the business, reorganizes it as a limited partnership with the original owner/manager maintaining a 3% ownership as the general partner. This situation is treated as only a temporary stage while the sale is completed to an independent third party.

The original owner/manager gets paid through a charitable remainder trust. The value obtained from the eventual sale goes into a trust from which the seller receives the income for the remainder of the owner's and spouse's joint lives. With 8% as the expected return on the money in trust, approximately 15% of the business' value ends up with the charity, and the remainder gets paid out to the founder and spouse over their expected joint lives.

Good advice on tax strategies is always recommended. U.S. tax laws change frequently, and the Internal Revenue Code has become very complicated. After-tax wealth is one of the primary objectives of a sale; good advisors can be very valuable in helping owners reach that objective. Conversely, bad advice, or aggressiveness to the point of fraud, can be very expensive. Therefore, one should check with an expert on trusts for the latest rulings and corresponding IRS treatment before proceeding.

9.3 Insider Sales and Transfers

The seller's objective in an outside sale is usually to obtain as much after-tax money as possible. For a sale to family insiders, that objective is sometimes reversed. Under these circumstances, the current and future owners both want to transfer as much of the value of the business as possible to the heirs, with the minimum tax liability for both generations. With most transfers, this means minimizing taxes by convincing the tax collector that the firm has a small value. This section covers some ways to facilitate such ownership transfers. First, however, the owner/manager should consider a few related factors, such as who will get the business and when the best time to transfer it would be. These matters are not always as simple as they seem at first glance.

9.3.1 *Considerations in Transfer Planning*

Before getting into the specifics of who gets what, it is important that the owner/manager determine what his or her wishes are. Should all the children share equally in the wealth? Who will run the business? Are they prepared to handle the entire operation? Has a tentative date been set for the current principal to retire?

One of the most difficult tasks for a business owner is to give up the general manager's role. He or she is known for building the business; many aspects of personal and social identity are tied up in that relationship between person and firm. For long-standing owners, the firm is more than a good living—it is also a central fact of the person's life. An often-told story, now part of the folklore of the family business community, is about an eighty-five-year-old business owner calling his sixty-year-old son into his office. The elderly patriarch was going to tell his heir that he had finally decided to retire in just a few more years, only to have his son preempt him by announcing his own retirement! The son, after forty years in the firm, had given up waiting for the top slot. The father, by denying his loyal son that opportunity, faced the prospect of losing his available successor. There is much bitter truth in that ironic and tragic situation.

Special Note on Family Firms

This book is not designed to directly address the many interesting and worthwhile issues involved with the transfer of family firms. Readers wishing more information in that area are referred to the following organizations.

USA: The Family Firm Institute, Inc. 200 Lincoln Street, #201 Boston, MA 02111 Tel: 617 482–3045 Fax: 617 482–3049 www.ffi.org

Canada: Canadian Association of Family Enterprises; 1388 C Cornwall Road Oakville, ON L6J 7W5 Toll free: 1-(866)-849-0099 Tel: 416-538-9992 Fax: 416-538-9556. www.cafenational.org

Europe and rest of world: Family Business Network; 23, ch. de Bellerive, P.O. Box 915, 1001 Lausanne Switzerland; Tel: +41 21 618 0223. www.fbn-i.org

A related decision is whether or not the successor is ready for the challenges of managing the firm. One problem that most owner/managers face in operating a closely held firm is delegating responsibility. Many continue to make all the important decisions until the day they die. For many firms, that owner's reluctance to delegate effectively is one of the main reasons they did not grow into larger public firms. It is also one of the major reasons why only 30% of family firms make successful transfers to their next generations; the heirs are not adequately prepared to make the critical business decisions. Because we want to focus on the ownership transfer problem and not the management problems of family businesses, we assume that the principal's retirement date has been set and the replacement is ready.

Ignoring tax implications for the moment, the easiest approach is to just distribute shares equally to all the children. The problem is that there is usually a wide range of interest, participation, and talent among the members of succeeding generations. Although the active participants may be given a few more shares, unfortunately, that configuration may be the least preferable for all parties. The active shareholder/managers have to carry the burden of the inactive shareholders, and the inactive holders may have much of their inherited wealth tied up in a firm in which they have little expertise or authority.

9.3.1.1 SCENARIO A: CARRYING THE BURDEN In one situation we know, wealthy parents divided their company's shares in five equal parts and gave 20% to each of their four children. The older son took over full-time management of the firm, and it did well enough to afford him a comfortable lifestyle. However, because each of his siblings also shared in the ownership, his good work also afforded them comfortable lifestyles—without having to contribute any time or talent to the management of the firm. Until one of his sisters joined the firm (and became a very capable senior executive), the CEO found himself in the position of doing all the family's work for 20% of the benefits. Though he didn't complain, being grateful for his gift, one has to wonder how long sibling relations would stay harmonious with such an unfair distribution of burden and reward. This scenario is one the family business community calls equal, but not equitable.

9.3.1.2 SCENARIO B: FROZEN OUT Conversely, the situation when the most active child is granted effective control of the firm, and his or her siblings have their inheritances tied up in minority shareholdings, can look good but also has its problems. Except for the active participants, this inheritance sometimes turns out to be rather worthless. The problem does not emerge immediately but rather over time after the original (now retired) owner/manager dies. The "chief" child controls the business and gets to allocate the distribution of all the wealth, usually in the form of salaries, for reasons noted elsewhere in this book. Since closely held firms rarely pay dividends, there is little or no cash return to the siblings. Furthermore, as the stock is closely held, there is no market for it, so the minority shareholders have no way to sell it and get their equity out. Once the original owner dies, minority siblings and their children who do not earn their salaries will likely not have jobs with the firm. The new principal owner/manager's children and spouse may have top-paying positions, even if they do not contribute productively to the firm. The unproductive children probably make almost as much as any hard-working children. One friend in this situation reflected that about the only benefit he ever received from the stock in his grandfather's firm was tickets to the Kentucky Derby every year. His cousins in the controlling family, on the other hand, had top-paying jobs with little responsibility. Results vary, of course, with family relationships and individuals' senses of responsibility.

9.3.1.3 OTHER SCENARIOS: RESOLVING THE CONFLICTS A common way to get around these problems is to give an equal number of shares to each child, but retain the controlling interest. Consider the simplest case, with just two children. If they each get 49%, the original owner maintains the tie-breaker with 2%. The *Wall Street Journal* once ran an article about Marshall Paisner, who was then going around the country making speeches about leaving a legacy rather than an inheritance.[6] Such a plan may run well as long as the senior Paisner is around, but eventually he will die and then his wife, the children's mother, will have to serve as the tie-breaker. Eventually, she will pass that controlling 2% on to someone. The tie-breaker formula also works successfully if the siblings agree on major decisions and can work out their differences. In other words, any scheme can be made to work if the key players have talent for being team players and not just individual entrepreneurs. The problem is that they have been raised in an environment that tends to lionize individual entrepreneurs who want to "call their own shots."

This situation occurred recently in a large food wholesaler in the southeastern United States. Each brother thought he should run the business after Dad died. They both worked long, hard hours, as do almost all successful self-employed businesspeople. As with the Paisners, after Dad died, Mom got his 2% of the stock. She was not active in the business and hated being in a position of settling disputes between her sons. The older brother, who was also Mom's favorite, convinced her to sell him the 2% so she would not have to worry about business decisions. That transfer gave him 51% and effective control. The younger brother did not fare very well under that arrangement. Eventually, the firm was split into two pieces, with the younger brother getting the smaller part, plus cash. Despite Dad's intention that the brothers would benefit from continuation of the firm he had built, their personal conflicts forced a breakup that resulted in each running a smaller and weaker firm.

9.3.1.4 EQUAL OR EQUITABLE? The best approach is to plan ahead well before death or retirement. This strategy becomes particularly important when tax consequences are considered. The owner/manager has to decide which dependents must be provided for when he or she retires or dies. One's spouse is the most common direct beneficiary. After those obligations are addressed, how should the remaining wealth be distributed? Most parents want to distribute their wealth equally to their children. However, a major portion of the owner/manager's wealth is usually tied up in the business, and this consolidated and illiquid position can cause major difficulties in transferring wealth to those who do not participate in the business. We have just shown that one generally does not want to give nonparticipants minority equity ownership positions that are practically worthless in a closely held firm.

[6] This story was the feature of Jeffrey A. Tannenbaum, "The Front Lines," *Wall Street Journal*, July 9, 1999.

9.3.1.4.1 *Borrowing to Fund Cash-Outs* A firm can borrow the money to buy out the outside children, but managers must be careful to avoid a high leverage strategy that will overburden the continuing heirs and damage the firm's future flexibility. When an owner/manager plans ahead, payout values can be established and the payments made from operating earnings over longer time periods.

9.3.1.4.2 *Dividing Up the Assets* Do the children working in the business get along? Perhaps the better question is, Can they be expected to get along after the current owner is gone? Some businesses can easily be split into parts, such as the Paisners' business of car washes and convenience stores. If the children were raised to be like their parents, independent and self-motivated, it may be difficult for them to work with each other as equals on a long-run basis. Splitting the business may be a good strategy.

A good example of ways to resolve these issues came to us from a pair of foreign students. This brother and sister had two much older brothers. One (B1) was being groomed to run the main business, and the other (B2) had developed his own car dealership. Now, the youngest brother (B3) wanted to work in the family's main business, but his sister (S) was not at all interested. The father, who then was around seventy, had the main business valued by an outsider appraiser. This procedure established an amount that the family then used to estimate the inheritance of the daughter and her brother with the car dealership. She and he were given that sum as cash payments, and the other two brothers (B1 and B3) were given the business. Older brother (B1) was fifteen years older than his younger sibling partner, so there was no question that B1 was going to run the business. The problem will arise, however, when the older brother reaches retirement age and the younger brother feels that he should take over the operations of the business. Will the older sibling let his younger brother take control, or will he try to pass control to his own son? One need only remember the recent acts of King Hussein of Jordan, who transferred the succession from his brother to his son as he literally lay on his deathbed, to see the kinds of difficult issues that may arise.

This example raises several important points. First, the owner/founder had the business valued when he was getting ready to hand over operating decisions to the eldest son. At that time, the value represented what the father had built during his career. He made plans to distribute that value equally to his four children, with two of the gifts in equity and two in cash. Doing this as he was preparing to retire gave him ample time to obtain any financing needed to pay the outside children. Further increases in the firm's value after the sons take over will reflect the next generation's decisions; the family members participating in those decisions should rightfully receive credit for the value they create (or lose).

9.3.1.4.3 *Do We Have Enough to Go Around?* Finally, some businesses provide a good return for the original owner/manager but are not large enough to provide the same lifestyle for several adult heirs. In many cases, these businesses are just an extension of the owner/manager's talents and do not represent a separate ongoing entity. In a few cases, they could be a separate entity but with very limited potential for an increase in size sufficient to support more than one family in the next generation. When planning an equitable transfer to the next generation, this limitation creates one of the trickier situations.

The fairest way is to value the earnings stream that the business provides to the owner's human capital and investment in the business. From this value, subtract what a comparable manager could earn elsewhere. It is important to assess the options as if equal time and effort were put into both endeavors. It is also important to account for the different fringe benefits that employment provides versus owning one's own business. This "equivalent skill" salary is then capitalized over the same period and at the same discount rate. Any excess income being earned in self-employment represents the business' net value. If there are four children, then the one taking the business should pay the others three-fourths of the "business' value." Most likely, the payment would be in the form of a business loan from the siblings because that is what they would receive as their inheritance.

In some cases, the well-analyzed value will turn out to be zero—or even negative! In those circumstances, the current owner is actually taking a discount over his or her market value to enjoy the privileges and style of self-employment, but there is no net financial value to the firm. In an economically rational world, it would be unlikely that any of the heirs would find it attractive to take over. There are some pretty important emotional reasons, however, and such events do occur. One of the more common examples of this nonrational behavior occurs with family farms.

EXHIBIT 9.A: WHEN EQUALITY IS *NOT* AN EQUITABLE SOLUTION! A CASE STORY A great way to think about the differences in equality and equity comes from the following case story, often used in family business workshops.

Mom and Dad are trying to retire from their business. Let's say it is worth $10 million. If they divide the value equally, each of their four children gets $2.5 million in cash and the business is sold to an outside party. Alternatively, each child could be given 25% of the shares. Those are the equal options. However...

Older son has been working in the business for nearly twenty years and has prepared himself carefully to take over. He is ready and eager to take on the firm. Selling it to an outsider would disinherit him, and his skills would not be worth as much to either the new owner or the open market. Saddling him with 75% control in the hands of his disinterested or incompetent siblings (more below) hardly seems right. Equal treatment for him would be most unfair.

Older daughter has been a national-caliber athlete and is just making the transition to coaching. She's never been interested in the business, but has also never made much money in her career—and probably won't. Her parents have supported her career with a modest supplementary stipend, and she's been happy with that. She's not very interested in the money. Neither of the equal solutions suits her very well.

Second son shows flashes of competence if not outright brilliance—when he's sober and clean, and bothers to show up for work. For most of his adult life, however, he's managed about six productive months every three years. This playboy means well, but giving him money usually means he spends more time on drugs or in rehab than he does on the job. His parents worry that just giving him money will mean that he soon burns through it and is left with nothing. Forcing his aberrant behavior on his older brother seems cruel to the older son. Neither equal solution appears right for this (sometimes) black sheep of the family—or his siblings.

Second daughter is happily married, raising several young children, a volunteer pillar of her communities, and struggling to help her husband make the mortgage payments on their suburban home. She, too, has little interest in the business and no preparation for either managerial or governance responsibilities. Cash would help her, but she and her husband are leery of sudden unearned wealth—and feeling like she's the one who has the financial security. The prospect has challenged their marriage in a way no one wants. For her, too, the equal solutions don't look very good.

Thus we reach a point at which equal treatment of the kids is profoundly unfair and unloving in each case. This is definitely *not* what the parents want to leave as their legacy.

At this point, we usually turn it back over to the participants in the workshop to create equitable (fair) solutions. Here's the best set we've seen emerge so far.

1. Recapitalize the business with a 75% mortgage.
2. The other 25% represents the older son's inheritance. Give him 100% of the shares in the firm, and let him earn the rest of the equity by paying off the debt and building from there.
3. Use a third of the cash (i.e., 25% of the value of the firm) to create an annuity trust fund for the older daughter, managed by a stable financial institution, to provide her with a reliable supplementary income.
4. For the younger daughter, offer to pay off the rest of her family's mortgage, and put the rest of her share of the cash into trust funds for her children.
5. Finally, for the second son, buy him a small resort that he will have to manage well to maintain a lifestyle he'd like.

These outcomes, each different, represent equal love in the parents' legacy. They are equitable in that they give each child something important and valuable in his or her special circumstances. The conversion between emotional equality and financial equity is rarely going to be simple.

9.3.2 *Minimizing Gift and Estate Taxes*

The basic methods of distributing business assets and other wealth to one's heirs are straightforward. The financing may be challenging, but can usually be handled with advance planning. The complex part comes in avoiding (if possible) or at least minimizing the proportion of the wealth transfer diverted into taxes. In the United States and most other countries, people pay gift and/or death taxes at some minimum threshold. What we want to do now is consider some of the ways to minimize those taxes.[7]

This review is designed to get us thinking about possible ways to structure the ownership transfer to accomplish specific objectives. A complete discussion of this topic would be enough to fill another book. While the specific rules noted in this section are those of the United States, most of the basic concepts also hold in other countries. Also, remember that this review covers only U.S. federal tax implications. Many states also tax estates and many tax them at a higher relative rate than comparable state and federal income taxes. Someone getting ready to start enacting a wealth transfer should certainly contact legal counsel. A good tax accountant could also be invaluable.

The current U.S. tax framework covering transfers of wealth to others is a complex combination of gift and death taxes. Still, every business owner should have some basic feel for how it works. When transferring the ownership of a closely held firm to our chosen heirs, we can plan and realize our objectives better if we understand the various ways to minimize the effect of those taxes.

The U.S. federal government taxes the givers of gifts made over a lifetime (gift tax) and the residual wealth or estate when they die (inheritance tax). The givers have usually already paid taxes on these monies. The recipients pay no taxes because the funds or stocks are gifts received and not income earned by the recipients.

[7] There is a growing movement in the United States to abolish estate taxes, but few people are convinced they will completely disappear. Whatever the situation is, it will likely have a large effect on the way owner/managers plan their estates. In this area, it is especially important to check with your tax specialist for the current laws as they apply to your estate planning. The examples in this book are based on the 2006 taxes and rates, which under current law will reappear in 2011, even though most people expect Congress to change the tax laws before that. Further, all the proposed changes maintain the basic concept of a joint gift/estate tax but at much higher exemption levels and lower tax rates.

Unlike income taxes, where married people usually file joint tax returns, these are individual taxes. Each person pays them after various exemptions. The first principle is that no taxes are paid on gifts to a spouse and no estate taxes are paid on money left to one's spouse. This exemption assumes that both are U.S. citizens. If the surviving party is a resident alien, the transfer is limited to $120,000 prior to taxes (based on 2006 rates). At first glance, the easiest way to minimize taxes would be to leave one's wealth to the spouse, tax-free. The problem is that taxes must be paid on the full estate when the surviving spouse dies.

The government does not start taxing the first dollar of gifts or estates. There are sizable exclusions. In 2006, the exempt level was $2 million and was expected to rise further in coming years. The vast majority of Americans have estates of less than $2 million in net value, so these gift and estate taxes are not a consideration (although they are starting to affect middle-income people who have saved well for their retirements).

For the successful small business owner, however, this limit becomes a major obstacle when trying to transfer a business to one's heirs. Because individuals get the exclusion, just leaving the entire estate to one's spouse wastes a $2 million deduction. With federal estate taxes quickly climbing to 46%, that would be a major loss! Suppose that the taxable estate was $6 million and no taxable gifts had been made. If it is taxed as if 50% belonged to each spouse, the tax would be $780,800 each or $1,562,600 total. On the other hand, if it is taxed solely to the surviving spouse, the tax is $2,275,800, which is $714,200 higher! This loss of value to the heirs results from a combination of the estate losing a $2 million deduction and the rate schedule rising as values increase. To leave the estate, or in this case the business, entirely to one's spouse can result in a substantial jump in the eventual taxes and a real loss of wealth for the family.

The other easy way to reduce future estate taxes is through planned giving. The tax laws allow a gift to any individual of $12,000 per year (2006 rate). The amount can be doubled to $24,000 if it is elected to be given jointly with the spouse—even when the money or property is entirely from one of them. These gifts do not count against any lifetime giving allowance. The only condition is that the amounts must actually be given with no strings attached. In tax terms, it must be a *completed gift*. If the recipient is a minor, the money can be placed into a trust for the child until he or she turns twenty-one. The excluded gift amounts can be extended by making direct payments to universities for tuition payments or to hospitals and doctors for medical payments. Suppose that you are worth $10 million and are married with two children. Gifts of $48,000 per year may not look that generous, but over twenty-five years of giving they would add up to $1,200,000 or 12% of the estate. Doing it this way would avoid inheritance taxes at a 50% rate, saving the heirs $600,000. Now, if those two children have provided four grandchildren, an additional $96,000 can be given away each year without tax consequences, leading to a transfer of an additional $2.4 million, and avoidance of $1.2 million more in estate taxes.

The next factor to consider is that less tax is paid when giving wealth away when alive than in paying taxes after one dies. Consider a single person with a $3 million taxable estate. After death in 2002, a tax of $780,800 would be imposed on the estate, as shown in the earlier example, leaving $2,219,200 for the heirs. Suppose instead the owner had given to the children the same after-tax value four years earlier. After the $11,000-per-year exemption for each gift (based on the effective rate in 2002), and the $1 million exclusion for the unified credit for gifts or at death, the remaining $1,446,000 is also gifted. The tax calculated on the $1,446,000 is $532,000, meaning that a total value of $2,468,000 could be passed through to the heirs. This early giving saves $248,800 in gift and estate taxes. The government is aware of that savings, of course, and tries to recapture some of that value by requiring that any gifts made within three years of death be added back into the estate to calculate the taxes payable. One should not wait before disposing of wealth if one wants the heirs to receive its full value.

This section has presented a simplified introduction to some of the key issues around estate taxes. It has been presented primarily to discuss strategies to transfer a closely held business while minimizing taxes. Consideration must also be made to ensure that the retiring owner/manager has sufficient income after retirement and that the founder's widow or widower will also be covered. Charitable donations can be made that lower the taxable estate and funeral expenses, legal fees, and outstanding debts are deducted to determine the final taxable value of an estate. Our objective here has been merely to point out how the unified gift and estate taxes are implemented and how the allowances can be used to lower the total tax obligation. Other things being equal, a lower tax obligation means a larger transfer to the owner's chosen beneficiaries.

9.3.3 *Transferring Ownership to Minimize Gift and Estate Taxes*

A basic understanding of the unified gift and estate taxes is necessary to appreciate many of the strategies involved in transferring the ownership of a closely held firm from one generation to the next. The key is to be aware of various techniques and how they work. The details require good legal and tax assistance to be sure that all approaches are considered. Some attorneys want to use the same technique for every situation, just varying the particulars, when quite often a different approach might work better. The owner/manager of the business should consider the strategies well before retirement to have the time needed to minimize the total tax obligation.

The firm's value must be established for each of these approaches. Furthermore, to minimize potential problems with the tax collector, the valuation requires an independent appraiser. The government must have some confidence that the firm's value is at least approximately what the owners claim. As an example, to demonstrate the different approaches, an appraisal of $10 million will be used, along with an individual owner who is married and has two children.

9.3.3.1 MAXIMIZE ALLOWABLE ANNUAL GIFTS The first step is to give $24,000/year to each child, assuming a married donor. But some owner/managers cannot spare that kind of cash. No problem. Start giving away the firm, which is why it was appraised. Divide the firm up into enough shares that each one might be worth $1, $10, $100, or $1,000. Then give each child enough shares to add up to $24,000 worth of stock in the company. Because the owner/manager still has controlling interest of the business after the gifts, the minority shares are not as valuable. The IRS allows a 35% discount, so the firm is valued at only $6,500,000 for the minority shares. The annual gifts of $48,000 for our two-child example now represent 0.738% of the firm, instead of 0.480%. The reason for the minority interest discount is that a minority shareholder in a closely held firm is totally at the mercy of its principal owner/manager. Why that assumption holds in this situation may be a bit puzzling, but we'll take the tax advantage, regardless of its logic.

9.3.3.2 USE THE UNIFIED GIFT AND ESTATE CREDIT The owner/manager and spouse should also consider using the unified gift and estate credit. Starting in 2002, it was equivalent to giving $1 million. Remember that this exemption is over and above the basic $24,000/year jointly given to each child. If the owner/manager and spouse together make gifts of $1.024 million in equity to each child, that would amount to total gifts of 31.5% of the business, based on the 35% minority discount and the tax-free allowance of $24,000 per year.

Two purposes are served with these gifts. First, they lower the taxable estate when the time comes to pay the inheritance taxes. Second, any future appreciation in the value of this part of the business is exempt from estate taxes. Suppose the business' value increases to $15 million over the next ten years. All the gains in the value of the equity transferred to the two children when it was worth only $10 million are exempt from taxes. The more a business is expected to appreciate over time, the more important it is to transfer it early to minimize gift and estate taxes.

9.3.3.3 INSTALLMENT PLANS AND APPRECIATED VALUES Another approach to minimize taxes is to sell the business on an installment plan. An installment sale is always a good consideration, and it is a particularly good approach when the business is expected to appreciate in value. The taxable amount is based on the value at the time the deal was initiated. Selling when the business is only worth $10 million transfers the expected $5 million appreciation to the children with no taxes.

Suppose that the owner/manager did not transfer the business prior to the increase in value, but a substantial portion of the business had been gifted to the children. The original owner still worries about covering his or her living costs in retirement. The best strategy now is to sell the business to the children using a contingent installment sale. The first factor is that the business must be valued and it has appreciated in value to $15 million. Let's assume that the original owner/manager is now seventy years old and still owns 55% of this $15 million business, for a $8,250,000 value (after deducting twenty years' worth of annual gifts of $24,000 in stock to each child). The rest of the business is sold to the children on a fifteen-year installment contract, the maximum term allowed, contingent on the original owner/manager or spouse living. When he dies, the payments stop. In a regular installment sale, any remaining payments would go into the estate, but this is classified as a self-canceling note, because the beneficiaries would be designated as the same people as the payees.

In the original example of an arm's-length sale of the business, we suggested a discount rate of 8% to bring the long-term value back to present value. In this family transfer case, a higher rate (or a higher nominal sales price) must be used because it is a contingent sale. This procedure keeps the IRS from viewing it as a gift designed to avoid taxes. Let's make it a 10% rate. Over fifteen years, this rate would lead to an annual payment of $1,085,000 per year, for total payment of $16,270,000. Of the payments, 49.3% would be interest, and that should be claimed as a business tax deduction by the new owners (the children). In addition, the seller can forgive $24,000 of the payments each year with no tax consequences, as long as he or she lives, because there are two children and a single owner, with a predeceased spouse, in this example. Assuming that he or she dies prior to ninety years of age, the remaining debt is forgiven and does not go into the estate. If the seller lives to be ninety or older, of course, the debt will have been repaid and the ownership fully transferred.

9.3.3.4 LIMITED PARTNERSHIPS Another option to minimize taxes when transferring ownership is to use a limited partnership. This technique only works when the children do not want to run the business. If they are materially participating in the firm's operations, the IRS will not recognize this form of transfer for its favorable tax treatment. The original owner/manager remains the general partner, still running the business. Children receive ownership positions, with a minority interest discount even when they have over 50% ownership. Once the ownership position is transferred, the entire business is sold, triggering capital gains treatment.

9.3.3.5 DEFERRED PAYMENT OF ESTATE TAXES AND THE MILLION-DOLLAR DEDUCTION The final consideration deals with paying estate taxes resulting from a closely held firm. Let's suppose the owner/manager of the $10 million firm dies before starting to divest the ownership position, and the heirs want to maintain the business in the family but do not have sufficient liquidity to pay the taxes. There are several provisions in the tax code to alleviate this situation. First, installment payments on the estate taxes can be made over a ten-year period, after a five-year postponement. Second, interest must be paid on the amounts owed, but it is substantially subsidized. A 2% interest rate applies to the taxes attributable to the first $1 million of taxable value. Any value owed over that first million carries an interest rate equal to 45% of the regular tax-underpayment interest rate.

Third, a family-owned business can also qualify for a deduction under Section 2033A of the tax code, which gives an additional estate deduction of $1 million or the value of the business, whichever is smaller. To qualify, the deceased's interest in the business must be greater than 50% of the adjusted gross estate, and it must pass to family members. The heirs may trigger tax recapture, however, if they sell the business, quit being active participants in it, or move it offshore. As always, heirs of the owner should check their plans with a competent tax advisor for the specific laws in effect at the time.

9.4 Jointly Owned Businesses

The joint owners of a closely held firm, whether a corporation or a partnership, with two or more equal owners, must make some additional decisions. What happens if one or more of the principal owners becomes incapacitated or dies? Protecting the firm and the investments of the principals against the consequences of such mishaps usually entails some form of a buy/sell agreement, plus a method of financing it. It will involve the sale of the withdrawn partner's stake. As with any sale, the value of the firm must first be determined before a fair price can be assessed.

9.4.1 *Repurchase of an Incapacitated Partner's Shares*

A typical closely held firm with joint ownership has an agreement that allows the surviving owners to buy out the interest held by the disabled partner or estate of the deceased co-owner. This arrangement minimizes disruption in the business when these events occur, preserving value for all participants, including the heirs of the departing partner. A current valuation is needed to ensure a fair arrangement among the parties. The survivors will not want to overpay, and the deceased's estate must get a fair value. Finally, a current valuation is also needed to settle the estate taxes.

Based on the valuation of the business, the owners may decide to have the firm carry life and disability insurance on each partner. This protection can be set up several different ways, which an insurance agent can explain. The key issue is that the amount of insurance to be paid at death or disability must equal the value of that owner's share of the business. The firm, or its owners in the case of the single-tax entities, make after-tax payments on this insurance. It is not a tax deduction. As a result, when a claim is paid, the recipient (the firm in this case) pays no income tax on the amount received. That amount is then used to pay the deceased's estate for that person's share of the business. When shares are repurchased after a death, the payment goes into the person's estate for estate tax purposes. Life insurance receipts are exempt from income taxes but not from inheritance taxes.

Insurance (or annuities) may also be purchased to provide the heirs with sufficient funds to pay the estate taxes—to ensure they are able to continue to operate the business.

9.4.2 *Key Man and Business Interruption Insurance*

A variation on those insurance programs is provided by "key man" insurance. In most firms, especially smaller ones, one or more individuals are really important to the continued successful operation of the firm. It may be true that "no person is essential," but the absence of some people can be devastating. To ensure against those kinds of catastrophes, key man insurance was developed.

In most forms, it provides funds to immediately hire an interim executive to replace the one lost through death or disablement. It can provide the funding for a temporary CEO, for example, if the owner/manager is, say, struck by lightning on the golf course. Then, it may also provide funding for a more extended search for a long-term replacement executive. Once that executive is in place, the insurance coverage ends, and the firm resumes paying for its own talent. Key man insurance helps ensure that the interruptions in the firm's business, due to tragedy among its officers, are minimized.

Business interruption insurance serves some similar purposes. Often written to cover a wider range of disruptions, its purpose is to cover a firm's cash flow requirements when disasters occur. Key man is a special category of business interruption insurance.

One of the important features of these kinds of insurance is that they bring to a firm additional expertise in disaster management. Although a firm may want such insurance, few can afford to pay for uncontrolled risks. Insurance firms are experts in controlling and minimizing risks. A good agent can help an owner/manager or partnership identify its most expensive risks—and work to reduce their exposure. It can significantly improve management of the firm, and further increase the likelihood that the value created by its entrepreneurs will pass on to their designated heirs.

9.5 An Exit Plan Emerges

"Let's review the options." As interim CEO and President, Tom led off the discussion at the meeting of the Board of Mike's company. Mike was present as Chairman, although they had agreed that Tom would manage the meeting. Priscilla, a minority shareholder, was a Director and Secretary-Treasurer of the corporation. Celia and Tracey were present as guests.

"Let's start by ruling out some of the options. One way for the owners of a private company to extract their equity and get out of management responsibility is to sell the company to public investors. Going public doesn't look like a workable option here. Mike's company isn't really big enough, at that $5 million level, to sell on one of the bigger exchanges, and Mike's not in condition to do all the work that would be required of the selling CEO. The costs are significant, and the company's growth prospects, especially without Mike's full involvement, aren't IPO caliber, so stock-market investors aren't likely to value it highly. Does everyone agree that an IPO is not the right plan, at least at this time?"

All the heads nodded. Tracey was looking very tense, quite uncomfortable as the only member of the next generation in the room, yet extremely curious about this process, and very pleased to have been invited. She had spent some of her summer semester on a special assignment to use her business school knowledge to assess the options facing Mike and his family. Mike was looking frail; he had lost a lot of weight during the recovery period and was still sorting out what he was going to be able to do with his post-heart-operation life. The wives, Priscilla and Celia, were anxious, each in her own way. Priscilla was fearful for Mike's health and wanted him out of the business as soon as possible, yet realized that their financial ability had been hurt with his illness. They needed to find a way to support the family, and she knew she wouldn't be able to pick up the business and run it in Mike's place. Celia cared deeply for her longtime friends and wanted a safe and sound solution for them—and she was worried that she could be in Priscilla's place at any time. Tom was comfortable in his leadership role, but walking gently with his friends and family. The decisions were not his to make, but he could help a lot in this situation.

"That leaves several other options. Let's see what else we can rule out, then find the best available strategy among what's left." Tom laid out his plan for the meeting. "The other end of the scale is to put the business up for sale as is. From what I can see, from what Andy and Mike have been telling me, and from Tracey's consulting report, the business, as is, would not bring a very good price. Although revenues are pretty good, margins are thinning and the investment value of the firm right now would not produce enough for Mike and Pris and their kids to live on. A lot of the value of the firm lies in the skills of the employees—including Mike—and in their ability to get older machines to produce things that new owners would be unlikely to be able to design or sell. As a pile of assets, it wouldn't produce much. As a going concern, it is more valuable—but we have to have the right people to run it. I believe it would be a mistake to liquidate the assets at this time."

Again the heads all nodded, some more reluctantly than others. Pris knew this agreement meant they were not going to make a quick, clean break from the burdens of the business, and she worried that the ongoing stress might cause a relapse in Mike's recovery—or that the firm might flounder without his full effort or expertise devoted to it. It was a set of risks she understood they had to take, but she was not thrilled by the prospects.

"That cuts down the options," Tom concluded. "The primary choice is to continue to run the business as is, with Andy handling the day-to-day operations for bonus pay, and all of us serving as a kind of collective CEO. That's not a long-term solution, of course, so we need to be working on an additional plan as well. And we have to tell the workers at the company something that gives them hope of a good future, or we'll start losing the skilled people that make the place valuable. Their confidence is essential, or this will be just a pile of old assets."

Tom continued: "The second choice, as outlined in Tracey's report, is to find an interim CEO. Since she raised that idea a couple of weeks ago, I've made some discreet enquiries around the area. Most people are like me—never heard of the thing. But a few, usually the most senior people, seemed to take it as a normal question. A couple of them seemed to think there would be quite a few capable people available."

Mike indicated he wanted to say something. In a voice still reduced by his recent experience, he said, "After the first few years, I did a review of insurance policies. Without being arrogant, it was clear to me that the business might falter badly if I was killed or incapacitated. Since it was our primary source of support for the family, I bought key man insurance, and have maintained that policy ever since. We have insurance to cover six months of a hired executive, if you can find one who can do the job. This seems like a good time to make use of that."

Tom nodded in agreement. "Am I right that none of us is ready, willing, and able to take on the job at this time?" All heads nodded, Tracey's among them. She knew she wasn't ready. "Are we also agreed that Andy is a good manager, but not the CEO we need?"

Pris leaned forward. "Andy has been a rock for me. She knows the plant well, knows the workers, some of the customers. She's been really good since Mike's operation, taking care of the details, but I think she's feeling the strain. Her usual good humor is getting thin, and I'm hearing more answers like 'Mrs. P, I don't know what Mike would do about that.' I'm getting concerned that she's not able to bring in the work we need to keep the plant running and everyone busy. And I don't want her to take on responsibilities she's not ready to handle."

"Is there anyone else in the company ready to do the job?" Tom didn't want to put any strain on Mike, but this was a question he needed to answer.

Mike thought for a moment. "No, I don't think so. Billy and Michelle are interested in the company, probably have some useful abilities, but they are many years away from being ready to run it successfully. Frank, the young guy we hired in Sales and Marketing a couple of years ago, has potential, but he's also several years away from knowing the business well enough to run it. Everyone else is pretty well in his or her right job now. I think we are going to have to go outside."

"What does everyone else think?" Tom asked, looking slowly around the room.

Celia quickly threw up her hands. "I could never do that, and the kids need me."

Pris also declined. "I've done what I can the last few weeks, but I know that I'm not able to run this company at the level Mike could, at the level it needs to be run. There are just too many things I don't understand. It's been an interesting challenge, and I'm less scared now than I was. I even confess I've learned a lot. Some days have been really great. I know I can help, but I also know I'm not the CEO the company needs."

Tracey stepped in quickly. "It's been a thrill to be involved, to help as much as I can. I know I'm never going to forget this summer; I've learned so much! I am now sure that I want to be in business, but I also know I have much more to learn before I can run a company properly. I might be ready in ten years!" She smiled, and the others reflected her nervous enthusiasm in their own ways.

Tom stated: "I've enjoyed helping, too. I've learned a lot about that business, about myself, about all of you, and I think I'm a better manager and a happier guy as a result. I also know that I don't know enough about Mike's kind of business to run it really well—and that my own business needs me—more every day I'm away from it."

"Doc says I'm out for another six months at least, and probably forever," said Mike softly. "I just get so wrapped up in the challenges, I won't let go. That's what it takes; that's why I've been good—and that's why he thinks I can't work like that anymore."

"All right, I think we're agreed. First, the business will continue. Second, while each of us may have a role to play, we need to hire an interim CEO." Tom ticked off the conclusions. "I know a couple of investment bankers, from meeting them at the club, and one of them specializes in private firms. There's a lawyer there, too, who seems to know a fair bit about this part of the market. And I know a couple of guys who have put money into venture capital funds. I'll call each of them, discreetly, and see if their networks can turn up any candidates for an interim CEO to run the company until either Mike is ready to come back, or we move further down the line toward selling it."

"We should meet again in a couple of weeks." And with that, the Board adjourned.

10

What We Know, Where to Go Next

10.0 A Different Way of Managing a Business

Mike, Tom, Pris, and Celia were sitting in the living room, enjoying the glow of the good meal and the mellow effect of the port. Mike was out of hospital, safely through the bypass operation, adjusting to a new diet and new ways of living. The business questions weren't settled yet, but the transition was under way.

"You know, Tom," Mike drawled, "when the Professor showed up at the Chamber luncheon a year ago, I almost didn't go. His topic sounded pretty boring. Something caught my eye, and I thought—what the heck, it is always good to see the other owners and hear the latest rumors. I'm amazed at how much we've learned since."

Tom thought for a moment. "It has completely changed the way I think about my occupation, my work, the business and financial parts of our lives. I used to think it was all about marketing, making deals, building revenues and profits. Now I understand those things are all part of the operating side of a business. The strategy part is about successful investing, about deciding what kinds of things increase our families' wealth."

"For my part," Celia piped in, "I've become more comfortable with the role of the business in our family. Before this valuation stuff started, business was something the guys did. They went out every day, did their things, and sometimes brought home the money. What went on, I didn't understand—and still don't really—but the hard part was I couldn't understand how to plan our household. I didn't know what money I could count on, what would happen if things went wrong. I was always nervous about overspending—or denying the kids things." Celia's comments had Pris nodding in vigorous agreement.

All four agreed that managing the businesses as investments, thinking about increasing their value every year, had helped them in many ways.

"Just the same, there's a lot we don't know yet." Mike still looked a little fragile, yet calm in a way no one would have anticipated a few months earlier. "I've learned to find good tax and investment advisors, and to ask them much better questions. As we move toward selling the business, I'm learning how to prepare it for sale, and how to recognize a good offer when it comes. I'm also starting to think how we will manage the proceeds, how to reinvest in things that take less stressful work on my part."

Tom agreed. "At the same time, I find I'm managing my own business, and helping manage yours, in different ways. What's important has changed, along with my performance indicators. I find myself asking different questions about the choices we face, and paying attention to different things. It's a different way of managing. Another twenty years, and I might get pretty good at this!"

Everybody laughed, but there was a nervous tremor underlying the giggles. Was it really a joke? Was he serious? Would that scenario be a good thing—or not?

WHERE ARE WE IN THIS LEARNING PROCESS? The basic processes needed to value a closely held firm have now been addressed. What we need to ask ourselves at this point is what we have learned. The answer consists of four parts: ideas that should be incorporated when estimating value in general; ideas that should be considered in valuing a closely held firm; choices that have to be resolved in the valuation process; and changes in the way we manage and invest in closely held firms. This closing chapter summarizes these key topics.

NO SIMPLE FORMULAS Before we start, one missing item should be discussed. This book contains no summary formula for doing a valuation of a business. We have not presented any such formula because no single valuation process can be applied to all businesses. First, we have to determine whether a firm should be valued as a going concern or as a sum of its parts. Then we must project the expected future returns. After that come questions about risk assessment, investment alternatives, inflation effects, tax issues, estate planning, and legacy intentions.

The Mona Lisa was not painted by connecting dots! Similarly, one cannot properly value a business by merely filling in the blanks, adding annual totals, dividing to get present value, and summing over time to get—presto!—the value of a firm. An accurate valuation of a small retailer worth something in the $100,000s is different than a small manufacturer, which is different than a closely held service provider, which in turn may be radically different than a small dot-com that was worth something in the mere low billions of dollars (in 2000)! Good valuations take numerous, sometimes interdependent, factors into consideration. This summary reviews the key points to be considered, not a formula to be followed.

10.1 What Has Been Learned about Valuation in General?

While the premise of this book has been the need to develop specialized techniques for valuing closely held firms, there is much to be learned from valuation techniques in general. Many of the principles discussed here apply to public firms, private firms, real estate, intellectual property, and other kinds of investment property.

10.1.1 *Look Forward*

The most important point about valuation is to always remember to look forward. A firm is worth what it can produce in the future. The past investments into the business, whether paid-in capital or retained earnings, are just history. With a going concern, the present value of expected future cash flows defines the value of the firm. With the non-going concern, the values of assets are determined by what they can do in the future, not their historical cost. Any valuator of a closely held firm who starts with the book value of a firm's assets, and then considers adjustments, should be fired immediately if a realistic estimate of value is desired. We have to start with current market value, based on future earning potential, not history.

10.1.2 *Use Historical Data Properly*

That emphasis on future earning potential does not mean that historical data are totally worthless. After all, in predicting future performance, a major factor to be considered is how well the firm has performed in recent years. A firm with five years of increasing profits can more likely justify predictions of short-term growth in free cash flows than a firm that has lost money over the past five years. What one should *not* consider, however, are the comparative book values of the two firms when assessing their relative values. Those historical data are meaningless in this context.

Historical performance is the best starting point for a neutral case forecast. History, as was argued earlier in the book, shows what management was able to do with the firm's previous collection of assets. Given reasonable stability in management, assets, and competition, that track record is the default scenario for the future. Good valuation, however, challenges those assumptions, to see what might be improving or deteriorating, and adjusts the neutral scenario to better fit the facts. Hence, we take historical performance as a baseline. The more data-rich that baseline is, the more robust the forecasts that can be built on it. Thus, a dot-com firm with no operating history is more difficult to assess than GE (formed in 1892) or the Hudson Bay Company (chartered in 1673); the baseline projections of a dot-com startup have few provable data, so the resulting projections are much less stable than they are for companies with well-established track records.

10.1.3 *Where Are the Value-Added Returns and What Is Causing Them?*

On the second point, above-average returns must be earned on future investments to create value greater than an investor could expect from investing in the market of public firms. A firm is worth more than the capitalized value of its projected free cash flow when it is expected to earn a rate of return on its future investments greater than its required rate of return (which is used to capitalize the current earnings). It may be earning substantially greater returns on its current investments; its ROE may be much greater than its required rate of return (which is the owner/manager's opportunity cost). If there are no future opportunities giving above-average rates of return, however, the owner/manager would be just as well off investing the profits in the stock market as reinvesting in the business.

In fact, some planners suggest that such an owner would be *better* off shifting free cash to angel investments or the stock market because those investments will help diversify his or her portfolio. In that way of thinking, the same expected returns with a diversified portfolio reduces risk and makes such an investment strategy more attractive. The argument is controversial, however. A person who knows his or her business very well has considerable advantages when selecting investments in that business—but probably has no advantages as a stock-market investor. These two options are not easily compared due to that large difference in the investor's expertise.

Wealth-oriented owner/managers should identify future investments that will earn excess rates of return before estimating an above-average value for their firms. What justification is there for an above-market multiple? Although historical returns are, for the most part, just history, it is quite possible that a firm earning above-average rates of return on its current investments will be likely to earn above-average returns in the future. But what has caused those above-average returns in the past? Will that cause continue in the future? Will it grow or shrink? We have to be especially careful about situations where the cause of the above-average return is the retiring owner! A typical, very successful, firm probably earns well-above-average returns on its current investments and can expect smaller returns on its future investments as competitive pressures limit future opportunities.

Conversely, it is difficult to justify a valuation reflecting future above-average returns for a firm with a strong track record of earning only its required rate of return on current assets. Further down the scale, a firm with an inferior track record as an investment vehicle will likely be sold for a below-average price. There are special circumstances, when a special asset, such as a choice location, contract, or piece of intellectual property, can command a premium from one or more buyers. Those are, however, the exceptions that prove the general principle.

10.1.4 *Impacts of Inflation*

Inflation decreases value and causes estimation problems. The decrease in value results from the depreciation tax shield determined on each asset's historical cost. The estimation problems result from inflation increases in the replacement cost of assets and increased working capital requirements. By basing valuation estimates on cash flow from operations, we can adjust for these inflation problems. Alternatively, correction factors can be developed to make adjustments directly to the profit forecasts.

10.1.5 *Risk and Reward*

The key concept of *required return* addresses the riskiness of the business. The systematic risk is the most important component, because an owner can always match this risk level through investing directly in a public stock market.[1] The valuation is based on the discounted free cash flows to equity holders. To be comparable, the risk assessment must measure firms with similar leverage or debt usage levels. These principles hold true for valuation of both public and closely held firms.

10.1.6 *The Basic Valuation Scenario*

With that information, we can lay out the basic data required for a valuation estimate.

1. Basic facts: What is this business doing?
2. Comparative frame: What other firms do similar business? How are they performing?
3. How does our target firm compare on performance measures?
4. What kinds of prices have owners of the benchmark firms been receiving on public and private markets?
5. What special circumstances apply, to justify an increased or decreased baseline valuation?
6. What kinds of buyers would most appreciate the premium assets of the target firm? What kinds of premiums do they pay for such special situations?

[1] It is important to note, however, that large public companies and small closely held firms may be radically different in their abilities to manage those risks. Closely held firms are supposed to be more nimble, but may also be more fragile due to their smaller management teams and less diversified suppliers, customers, assets, and governance and management systems.

10.2 What Has Been Learned about Valuing Closely Held Firms?

Some of the valuation issues discussed in this book are not applicable to public firms. Indeed, the focus of the book has been on demonstrating the differences, and on showing how valuation models need to be overhauled when applied to closely held firms. Here's a summary of the key issues that apply to valuation of closely held firms.

10.2.1 *Lack of Separation between Owner and Manager*

In closely held firms, little or no separation exists between owners and managers. Most of the uniqueness in valuing a closely held firm results from this convergence. Does an ongoing business concern exist or is this business just an extension of a self-employed individual? Many closely held firms do not really represent separate ongoing businesses.

10.2.2 *Focus on Maximizing After-Tax Wealth*

An owner/manager normally operates a firm to maximize personal satisfaction. That satisfaction can take many forms, but its financial manifestation is most often measured in terms of after-tax wealth. Retained wealth is determined after both business and personal taxes have been paid, because it is the residual that the owner/manager can use to fund objectives of his or her own choosing.

10.2.3 *Financial Statements Reflect the Owner's Preferences*

Owners of closely held firms have some legal latitude to organize their businesses according to their own preferences. As a result, the financial statements of their firms reflect many such personal choices. Unlike the statements of public companies, which have to follow strict standards to ensure their comparability, those of closely held firms may need extensive recasting before they can be meaningfully analyzed by third parties. The stated asset values, profits, wages, and other benefits must be adjusted before we can use them with any hope of accurately estimating a firm's value. The adjusted values should reflect the firm's profit after corporate taxes, and after market wages and benefits are paid to professional managers. Other data reflecting the perks and idiosyncrasies of the current owner also need to be adjusted to reflect more common practices. Only then can data from a going concern be used to fairly value the company as it should appear to a neutral observer. Those recast statements become the baseline from which negotiations can proceed.

We should note that most buyers of closely held firms are not neutral investors. They are motivated by their ability to make use of the assets of the firm being acquired. They are therefore likely to make a secondary recasting of the financial statements, to show themselves how that firm, or its assets, might perform under their management, in association with other investments they control, within their taxation situation. They make their investment decisions on the basis of what the firm will be worth to them, in their contexts.

10.2.4 *The Value of Assets in Non-Going Concerns*

Non-going concerns are valued as assets, both tangible and intangible. The market value of those assets depends on what they can add to the market value of other firms. Intangible assets include anything of value that the owner/manager has developed over time—business name, reputation, customers, business organization, intellectual property, and so on—which is not tangible. These assets are worth what it would cost a new business to replicate them, including both the out-of-pocket costs and the opportunity cost of the time needed to get started.

10.2.5 *Intellectual Capital and the Current Owner*

The owner/manager's special talents were most likely the cause of any superior returns the firm earned, at least on investments during its early years. Will these returns continue if the business is sold? When the value of the firm is calculated, a key question becomes how much of the value comes from the business or the owner/manager's personal talents. Unfortunately, this component cannot be determined with certainty until a new manager runs the business. It can be affected by the way the transfer takes place. A sudden departure or death of the owner will dramatically reduce the next owner's ability to pick up the *intellectual capital*, or knowledge, of his predecessor. A smooth handoff, however, can be accomplished if there is sufficient time and goodwill, during which most of the value is transferred. In the latter case, the business is worth more to the new owner than it would be without that handoff.

10.2.6 *The Dangers of Unknown Competitors*

Small closely held firms sell at a low multiple of earnings. An unknown real *put* exists against all businesses from unknown and unseen potential competition. Firms possessing new ideas, products, licenses, or marketing techniques exercise this put when they enter an established firm's market. This put, or what some people have called the "Wal-Mart liquidator" risk, exists in all firms. It is larger in small firms because they have fewer resources with which to view the big picture, to give them the time they need to adapt and defend themselves. The put is also larger in closely held firms because no market feedback exists from securities markets. Small closely held firms face a double whammy and an increased discount on their value.

10.2.7 *The Illiquidity Discount*

Lack of liquidity creates another cost for closely held firms beyond the risks of new competition. Rational investors require a substantial premium in returns (or discount in purchase price) to compensate for the lack of liquidity and information that public markets bring to a business.

10.2.8 *Ethical Incentives*

Conflicting incentives exist at the time of a closely held firm's sale. Unlike public firms where ongoing reputation is a factor, most sales of closely held firms represent a one-time transaction between buyer and seller. As a result, each party has an incentive to cheat the other. That ethical conflict can be minimized in various ways, including sound due diligence work on each side, and a transfer arrangement that spreads the payout over time.

10.3 What's Left to Learn about Valuing Closely Held Firms?

As much as we've covered in this book, there is also much left uncovered. In some cases, that's a matter of space available. We have not gone into the details of the technical financial models, for example, nor have we provided reams of background data or endless references to the scholarly literature.

Several important topics would benefit from additional discussion and research. Even as we have provided the best information and insight we have about ways to deal with these topics, we've been noting that we do not yet have really satisfactory ways of addressing several of them. Some of the key items are highlighted here. While we have cautioned readers throughout this book that valuation of closely held firms has to be based on many assumptions, these additional notes should leave us all the more wary about glib and simplistic solutions.

10.3.1 *How Markets Value Growth*

How should we estimate the value of growth opportunities? Conceptually, the value of a growth opportunity is equal to the net present value of future investment returns. What many people do not understand is how these values are assessed in the marketplace.

Real growth, for which premium valuations apply, is founded on a firm's ability to earn above-average returns on future investments. When owners reinvest in their firms and earn only the normal or required rate of return, we can call that routine expansion, and it earns a *normal* market valuation. Failure to invest at or above the required rate of return will, naturally, lead to a below-average valuation.

These are key points for businesspeople who too often think that simple retained earnings and additional investment are always good. It matters a great deal how effectively those retained earnings are invested in new business opportunities.

Several years ago, we witnessed dot-com firms selling for huge multiples of their revenues, before they earned any profits at all—and then we watched as many of those inflated values collapsed to zero. How did investors come to put such high market values on such unproven business opportunities—and then change their minds so radically? Why were those growth opportunities worth so much in 1999 and so little in 2002? Although some observers dismiss the dot-com phenomenon as a once-in-a-lifetime aberration of market hysteria, so many fortunes were made and lost that it behooves us to pay closer attention. As investment flowed into dot-coms and then burned, all other sectors of the economy were affected. Entrepreneurs changed their strategies in radical directions, sometimes for the better, and so did investors.

10.3.2 *What Is a Firm's Correct Discount Rate?*

What is the specific discount rate we should use to value a business? In this book, we have shown how to use several different rates, each one reasonable under its circumstances—but we could have gone up or down a couple of percentage points and still been reasonable. Inside that range, it can make quite a big difference what rate one chooses. So what's the *right* rate?

Conceptually, the right discount rate equals the risk-free time value of money, plus the market-risk premium, plus an illiquidity premium. The firm's price of risk should equal the firm's systematic market risk times the market price of risk.

The problem is that smaller firms appear to require greater rates of return than their market risk alone would justify. Furthermore, the cost of illiquidity also appears to be greater than a rational investor would expect. Those two observations suggest that the current approach to the rational valuation model is incomplete. It needs to be adjusted for real market behavior that lies outside our current definitions.

The question is: What should we do about this here? One way to address the problem is to adjust valuations in accordance with these caveats. That approach means some sort of discount should be applied to the required rate of return, and the illiquidity discount should be adjusted too. But how much? Our hunch is that these adjustments are nonlinear, that is, they increase as the firm size drops, and as non-economic and nonmarket factors increase as components in the purchase decision. As they say in academic circles, that's a great subject for the next round of research!

10.3.3 *What Really Is a Going Concern?*

What are the specific criteria for a going concern? What specific attributes must be present to value a closely held business as a going concern instead of as specific assets? The simple answer is that there is no simple rule—it depends on numerous factors, including the way the firm is currently managed, the market for secondhand businesses of its type, and the market for its assets.

At least at the beginning of the valuation process, most closely held firms should be valued both ways. Some of their components may be more valuable to different buyers, even if the core business continues as a going concern. How should specific intangibles be valued? A customer list is usually valuable. The question becomes what specific amount should be attached to that asset. The criterion is the cost of reproducing the asset without buying the firm (or the list). That procedure sets an alternative market-based price.

10.3.4 *How Should the Cost of Future Competition Be Estimated?*

What is the cost of the "Wal-Mart liquidator" put? It is obvious to anyone in American retailing that when Wal-Mart moves into an area, things will never be the same again. There are many other fields where the entry of powerful competitors may force liquidation or radical restructuring on existing businesses. When those events will occur and exactly how they will unfold is unknown. How should those unforeseen events affect the value of existing firms?

Smaller businesses have fewer resources to counteract these competitive events, and closely held firms get no stock-market feedback, so they tend to be seen as most at risk. Still, to complete a valuation, a specific value must be placed on this risk. How likely is it? Are any consolidators active in this sector? What territories are in their strategic plans? What has happened to the local firms when Big Boxes have entered their markets? There are some effective defenses, as current research is beginning to show. How well is the subject firm being managed, specifically in terms of its ability to cope with national or global competitors entering its markets? These factors make a substantial difference in the real value of closely held firms.

10.3.5 *The Valuator's Crystal Ball*

In going forward to value firms, we must remember to look to the future and consider what might happen. Consider both the good (or future real options) and the bad (future real puts) against a profit stream. The future is going to look a lot like the past—only different, as a wag once said. The valuator's challenge is to know what parts of the past to project forward and how to make reasonable estimates of the parts that will change.

Valuations are just forecasts of the price that would be earned if the firm were put on the market. Good valuations should be conditional and probabilistic. They are based on many assumptions, some more firmly supported than others. If one or more of those assumptions is violated, the valuation might change. We need to know the key assumptions and sensitivities, and when we see something in that group change, we need to reconsider the valuation. Thus, things like confidence intervals, key assumptions, and sensitivity analyses make sense.

It is also apparent that valuation is at least partly abstract, because it is initially done without taking into consideration the particular circumstances of the most likely buyers. As a deal moves forward, and one or more real buyers emerge, the buyers' specific values can be plugged into the valuation to produce a more realistic estimate of sale price and conditions.

At several points, trade-offs between price and economic conditions have been noted. As interest rates rise and fall, investors will change their valuation of the earnings potential of firms. Higher interest rates increase the emphasis on shorter-term, more certain payoffs; lower rates allow more value for longer-term growth prospects.

Finally, we have inserted many caveats about changing tax and legal environments. The importance of good, current advice will remain high. As critical rules of any game are changed, good captains and coaches review their strategies and adjust accordingly.

10.4 Implications for the Management of Closely Held Firms

Let us conclude by stating what we did not even try to do in this book. There are two important topics, related to the valuation of closely held firms, which we deliberately avoided.

This book has been written from the standpoint of an imminent sale, focusing on the present value of a firm, as it is. We have addressed the question: How do I figure out what this business is worth? It assumes that the current state of the business is the state in which it will be valued and sold. Therefore, we have more or less conceded that the average 35% discount forfeited by owners of closely held firms would apply, with the potential for significant variations above and below that level in individual cases.

That discount continues to grate on us, however. Even as we acknowledge its existence, and can (sometimes) rationalize it, we find it deplorable that entrepreneurs are so poorly rewarded for their efforts. In this book, we have had our hands full dealing with the status quo, but we know that there are many things owners can do to reduce, eliminate, or reverse that discount.

There is much that can be done by managers to improve the value of a closely held firm in the years before its sale. We suspect that there is even more entrepreneurs can do, when designing and building firms, to ensure that they receive a premium for their efforts when they choose to exit. Those, as they say, are subjects for another day.

10.5 Lessons Learned?

After dinner, they retired to Mike's study and made themselves comfortable in front of the fire. Mike was still a bit pale, and smaller than before, but stronger in other ways. He was putting in four-hour work days, although not usually at the plant. The interim CEO was working out pretty well, and the business was beginning to thrive again. They had even won a few new contracts, and the repositioning strategy he had worked out before the heart operation was starting to show results.

The Professor said, "Well, that was a wonderful dinner, Mike. Pris is a great cook, and I can see you've come to enjoy some things culinary, too! That salad you concocted was worth seconds."

"Well, Professor, my life has changed a lot in the last six months. This mortality thing wasn't something I'd ever really thought about, maybe something I feared too much to face, but things are working out okay. People have been really helpful, especially my family, and Tom here—and your guidance has helped us deal more rationally with some pretty big issues. I had been running the business to beat competitors and support the family, but now I see it much more as an investment that has to be managed to produce returns. With that change in perspective, I'm learning to run it better, and it is beginning to produce a better income for us with less direct effort on my part. In hindsight, I was doing a lot of no-income things."

"Very good," the Professor nodded. "I sometimes wonder how much better this economy could perform if more business owners thought and worked as you are now doing. When you originally came to me," he continued, "you both wanted to know what your businesses were worth. We've been working together for more than a year now. Do you have your answers yet?" His face was calm, but his eyes were twinkling with friendly amusement.

Mike and Tom paused. Neither of them had a number. They looked down, into the fire, avoiding eye contact with each other as much as with the Professor. After all this time and effort, after all the new insights, all the "Eureka!" moments, after all the improvements they had made in their companies, after all the consulting fees they had paid the Professor—had they failed? Like the fire, the value of their firms could be seen and measured, but couldn't be easily grasped or frozen into a single number.

Tom broke the silence. "I don't know! I know a lot more than I did. I can see the things that are valuable, versus those that don't add value. I have a better long-term strategy for me and for my family—and Mike's even further ahead of me on those scores. I understand some of the processes of value creation, but I don't have a bottom-line number. I don't even know if I could work through the process to get a solid bottom-line number!" After a quick glance at the others, he continued to stare into the fire. The Professor waited.

Mike thought about it for a minute. "Well, I don't either, but I do have some ballpark estimates, some rough figures. I have some idea what we have to do to pay our family for its investment, and our managers and staff for their talents, and our suppliers for their contributions. And I have a much better appreciation for the kinds of products, the kinds of services we have to provide to get paid enough to take care of all these people. That adds up to gross revenues, and margins I understand better. I can now take those margins, those returns to investment and talent, and create a very rough version of the Professor's investment model. I understand, I think, some of those discount rates and ROIs, so I could plug them in and get a rough approximation of what the company is worth to us. I know those numbers can bounce around, depending on the economy, and the assumptions we use, so only a ballpark makes sense anyway. I have a better understanding of our exit options, of the kinds of buyers that might exist and what they might offer for the company. It's still not very pretty, but I do have a much better sense of what I can do to make it better. With all of that, and a lot of help from you two and the rest of our families, I've been able to work out a strategy that works for us. In that sense, yeah, I guess I have learned a lot about the value of my business, even though I can't put a specific price tag on it tonight."

"Excellent!" exclaimed the Professor, clapping his hands. "The only time a specific number is important is when you actually have a firm offer to purchase in front of you. Since neither of you is planning on selling tomorrow, you have no need of a specific number. What's more important for the time being is exactly what you are doing—managing the businesses so that you make value-adding decisions, so that your investment choices are well-informed by a sense of value."

Mike and Tom were staring at him, sheepish and happy grins spreading across their faces. "So, Professor, have we passed this course after all?"

Appendix 1

Glossary

Accrual: Accounting system whereby financial transactions are presumed to take place at the time they are confirmed; for example, Sales are counted as Revenue as soon as the product is shipped. Compare to Cash method, which counts Sales as Revenues only when the customer's check clears the bank.

Angel investors: *See* Venture capital, informal.

Assets: *Tangible* assets have actual physical existence such as land, real estate, machinery, or cash. *Intangible* assets have no physical existence, such as reputation, staff loyalty, goodwill, trademarks, and patents.

Audit: A method of reviewing financial statements, using a statistical sampling procedure, designed to ferret out any systematic errors. Methods are governed by professional bodies.

Audited statements: Financial statements on which an audit has been conducted. Accompanied by a certification that the statement appears to be free from material errors, and signed by a certified auditor.

Base case: Valuation analyses always start with a *base case.* It is a scenario that assumes the subject of the valuation is a mature firm with no new investment opportunities. Then the valuators can introduce variations that adapt the base case ever more closely to resemble the real firm under consideration. Also known as *baseline case.*

Beta: A measure of the investment risk associated with a publicly listed stock, based on its volatility relative to the market as a whole. In technical terms, beta is the regression coefficient of a firm's returns versus the market's, an indication of the stock's systematic risk. Its volatility is its standard deviation of returns, which is called its total risk.

Blue Book: Kelley Blue Book is a survey of used auto prices at both wholesale and retail level (online at www.kbb.com).

Bulletin board trading firm: Specializes in making markets for small, thinly traded securities. Bulletin board (BB) firms are those too small to appear even on NASDAQ. Either their trading volume is too low, like Kohler; the business is too little; or their share price is less than $1. BBs also include a lot of preferred issues of larger firms that just do not trade often. The name comes from initially posting bids and asks on bulletin boards. Now they are traded over computer screens, similar to NASDAQ firms.

Cash flow (CF): The real movement of money through a firm, equivalent to a personal checkbook approach. Approximated by adding depreciation back into profits, and adjusting payables and receivables to count only cash that actually moves through the firm's accounts during the stated time period. With *adjusted free cash flow* (AFCF), free cash flows are adjusted for the owner/managers' opportunity cost of working elsewhere instead of actual cash benefits paid. *Discounted cash flow* (DCF) is the present value of cash flows. *Free cash flow* (FCF) is the cash flow generated by operations after undertaking new investments.

Cash method of accounting: Revenues and expenses are recognized when cash is actually paid. As example, sales on credit are recognized when cash is collected. This system is used in most small firms.

Contingent claims analysis: Evaluates opportunities like options where they are undertaken if profitable in future and rejected otherwise.

Contribution margin: Difference between selling price and cost of goods sold (or variable costs) for items sold.

Corporation: A C corporation is a regular taxpaying corporation with a state charter. An S corporation has special tax status granted by IRS to qualifying corporations that gives tax status similar to partnerships. *See also* LLC.

Current cost value: What it currently costs to obtain an asset as opposed to its initial or historical cost.

Delisting (from a public stock exchange): Firms that sell for less than $1 per share are dropped or delisted by the NYSE and the NASDAQ.

Depreciation tax shield: The reduction in taxable income from depreciation expense.

Discount: Reduction in value for specific conditions, such as minority shareholdings, or illiquidity.

Discount rate: Rate such as interest rate or required rate of return to discount future cash flows to present values.

Dividend substitutes: Alternative ways of extracting value from a firm, such as above-market salaries, perks, income-splitting with family members, and some personal uses of company assets. Shareholders in public firms are generally restricted to receiving their portions of free cash flow in the form of dividends (or capital gains, if the surplus is retained in the firm).

Due diligence: Examination of situation to be sure it is correct. Usually refers to research undertaken by buyers or their agents when buying a firm or making a loan, to be sure that the presented facts are correct, or to correct them so the prospective buyer or lender has a clear picture of the condition of the firm and its assets.

EPS: Earnings per share, a common way to standardize measures of financial performance, especially useful for public companies that have market-defined values for their shares.

Excess cash: Cash generated by a firm in excess of its requirements for operations and investments to maintain its present level of performance.

Excess returns: Returns greater than the required rate of return. For example, if the required rate of return is 14% and the firm earns 18%, it makes a 4%

excess rate of return. (Since the terms *monopoly* or *value from excess returns* carry negative implications, we usually see the alternative term *market value added* or MVA to describe the same increase in value.)

Expected joint life: When the last person of a couple is expected to die, based on actuarial tables.

Family firm: Various definitions have been offered, but the key aspects include ownership of a firm being controlled by one or more families and/or having multiple members of a family active in management of the firm. This is the dominant form of business organization in the world; more than 90% of all businesses are classified as family firms.

FASB: Financial Accounting Standards Board, principal regulator of accounting standards in the United States.

FIFO: First In, First Out. Used in inventory management, it describes a system of a simple queue; the goods are used in the order they are received. This method means that most goods are held in inventory for approximately the same length of time.

Fisher's formula for inflation: The Fisher relationship for inflation between the required nominal return, the required real return, and the expected rate of inflation is defined as: $(1 + \text{Nominal Return}) = (1 + \text{Expected Rate of Inflation}) \times (1 + \text{Real Return})$.

Free cash flow: Profits from operations, minus the cost of all investments required to maintain those profits.

Future investments: Represent investments in the future, usually providing excess returns, that a firm can undertake.

GAAP: Generally Accepted Accounting Principles, the common set of standards and procedures by which audited financial statements are prepared. Public companies must conform to these rules, with any deviations carefully noted and explained. Private companies are not so tightly constrained, and readers of financial statements from closely held firms should *not* presume that they conform to GAAP.

Going concern: Assumes that the firm will continue indefinitely into the future. To be considered a going concern under GAAP, it must be generating sufficient funds to pay its obligations. Same as ongoing concern.

Gordon's growth model: $V = \text{Free Cash Flow}/(R - G)$, where $V = \text{value}$, $R = \text{required rate of return}$, and $G = \text{rate of growth in free cash flow}$.

Inflation: Increase in prices over time.

Intellectual capital: Specialized knowledge. Thomas Stewart defines it this way: "Intellectual capital is the sum of everything everybody in a company knows that gives it a competitive edge. Unlike the assets with which business people and accountants are familiar—land, factories, equipment, cash—intellectual capital is intangible. It is the knowledge of a workforce: The training and intuition of a team of chemists who discover a billion-dollar new drug or the know-how of workmen who come up with a thousand different ways to improve the efficiency of a factory. It is the electronic network that transports information at warp speed through a company, so that it can react to the market faster than its rivals. It is the collaboration—the shared learning—between a company and its customers, which forges a bond between them that brings the customer back again and again. In a sentence:

Intellectual capital is intellectual material—knowledge, information, intellectual property, experience—that can be put to use to create wealth. It is collective brainpower. It's hard to identify and harder still to deploy effectively" (from *Intellectual Capital: The New Wealth of Organizations* [New York: Currency/Doubleday, 1997]; also available online at http://members.aol.com/thosstew/forward.html).

IPO: Initial public offering, the first time a firm's stock is made available to the general investing public through a regulated stock exchange. Changes the rules under which management can operate the firm.

IRS: Internal Revenue Service, tax collection agency of the U.S. federal government. Has determined that there is no specific valuation methodology that suits all firms. Also granter of Subchapter S status.

Leverage: Generally, the ratio of debt to equity. An alternative usage is the total assets under control, relative to the amount of equity held.

Liability limited organizations: An *LLC* is a limited liability corporation. An *LLP* is a limited liability partnership. *See also* Partnerships.

Lump sum: One-time payment of the entire value.

MACRS depreciation: Modified Accelerated Class Recovery System. An accounting system used in the United States to depreciate assets for tax purposes. A result of the 1986 Tax Reform Act.

Maintenance investments: Investments required to maintain a firm's current level of performance.

Monopoly: A condition whereby a company has an exclusive hold on a market, without direct competitors. Usually caused by either a new or different product, or a production process that is significantly cheaper than those of competitors. In a true monopoly, competitors are prohibited from entering the product market. (Since the terms *monopoly* and *value from excess returns* carry negative implications, we usually see the alternative term *market value added* or MVA to describe the same increase in value.)

Monopoly rent: Rent contracted − (Required rate of return × Asset value).

MVA: Market value added = Market value − Value invested.

NPV: Net present value; *see also* Present value.

Nominal rate: Real rate plus expected inflation. Also known as *contracted rate.*

Ongoing concern: *See* Going concern.

Options: On a security, a call option is the right to buy the underlying security at a preset fixed price during a given time period (American option) or at a specific time (European option). The put option gives its holder the right to sell at a preset price. Another meaning of the word—more common, at least outside the financial community—is simply any available choice or opportunity.

Owner's compensation: Total value of compensation provided to the owner; includes salary, perks, and other benefits.

Partnerships: *General partner*: Partner with unlimited liabilities, usually also with managerial responsibility for the enterprise. *Limited liability partnership (LLP)*: More modern form, offering more liability protection for all partners. *Limited partner*: Member of a partnership, whose liabilities are limited to the value of the investment made by that partner. *Limited partnership*: Traditional form of partnership in the United States, with a general partner who operates the organization and shoulders the risk, and limited partners whose risk is limited to the size of their investment. *Managing partner*: Member of a partnership with executive responsibilities. *Regular partnership*: Simple form of organization with two or more parties sharing in the liabilities. May be divided with different percentages. No limits to liability for any partner, that is, joint and several liability applies.

Premium buyer: One who is willing to pay an above-market price for a closely held firm or its assets, usually due to values outside that firm, such as a strategic fit with the buyer's operations.

Present value: Process of discounting that brings future (or past) expenses or revenues into a standard form, valued at a specific date (usually the present), where they become readily comparable.

Profits: Revenues minus Expenses, as determined by GAAP.

Proprietorship (sole): A firm owned by an individual with unlimited liability.

Put: "An option contract that provides the option holder the right, but not the obligation, to sell (or put) an optioned asset to the option writer at the strike price within a given period of time" (www.investordictionary.com); "an option to sell a specified amount of a security (as a stock) or commodity (as wheat) at a fixed price at or within a specified time" (www.merriam-webster.com/cgi-bin/dictionary).

PVGO: Present value of growth opportunities.

Recasting: Reorganization of financial statements to reflect different principles. Most financial statements in closely held firms reflect the current owner's attitudes and managerial needs. *Primary* recasting changes those statements to reflect normal professional practice, to put them in a form that allows routine comparison with similar firms. *Secondary* recasting restates the baseline data into the most useful framework for the potential buyer.

Return on assets (ROA): Profits earned divided by the business' total assets.

Return on continuing assets (ROCA): Same as ROA except non-operating assets, such as the owner/manager's resort condo and other perks that are likely to go with him or her into retirement, are subtracted out of total assets.

Return on equity (ROE): Profits earned over the book value of equity at the beginning of the time period.

Return on investment (ROI): Refers to the rate of return of a specific investment opportunity; defined as the profit divided by the investment.

Return on sales (ROS): An alternative method of estimating performance, especially useful when the firm uses few owned assets; profit is defined as the average gross margin, multiplied by the sales volume. Net ROS is defined as the profit, divided by the net sales volume.

Returns: *See* "Return on" entries above. *Excess returns*: any rate of return on invested capital that exceeds the required rate of return; sometimes also called monopoly rents. *Required rate of return (RROR)*: What one can expect to earn in the market by investing in securities of firms facing similar risks. It is usually based on a comparison to a diversified portfolio of the S&P 500 equities. If the S&P 500 has a long-term rate of return of 13%, ignoring inflation, then any business not earning that rate of return is not worth undertaking (or continuing) from a financial point of view. One would be better off selling the business and investing in the S&P 500. Another way to define RROR is the time value of money, usually estimated as the long-term government bond yield, plus a risk premium for the specific industry, and another illiquidity premium for being a closely held firm. For closely held firms, with little risk diversification and no market liquidity, a higher RROR should be expected, but it is difficult to define a precise level.

Risk, market: Refers to risk in investing in the overall securities market. Usually approximated as the standard deviation of the NYSE index.

Risk, political: Business risk caused by political changes or policy choices; most significant when regimes change and policies are reversed.

Risk, systematic: Systematic risk is usually measured by comparison with public markets. There are several kinds of risks associated with comparisons to public firms. The first is the overall value of the market, a systematic risk of the first order. The second would be the relative attractiveness of a particular sector at a point in time, that is, the rate at which capital is flowing in or out of that sector, relative to other sectors of the market. Then there's weighting between firms within the sector, with market-share leaders tending to grow in value at the expense of their competitors. Depending on which comparison group we use, we can produce quite different bases for these estimates of systematic risk. Usually referred to as beta.

Risk, unsystematic: Total risk of business minus the systematic risk.

SBA: Small Business Administration, U.S. federal agency charged with improving the opportunities and skills of smaller firms. Also a source of loan guarantees for early stage or expanding small firms. See www.sba.gov.

S corporation (Subchapter S corporation): U.S. corporation that has been granted Subchapter S status by the IRS, under section 1362 of the Internal Revenue Code. See www.access.gpo.gov/uscode/title26/subtitlea_chapter1_subchapters_.html.

Shareholder: Owner of equity shares in a company.

SME: Small and medium-sized enterprise. Actual definitions vary. Some organizations use "fewer than 500 employees" as the cutoff; others cut the group at 100 or 1,000 employees.

Stakeholder: Party with an interest (i.e., stake) in the performance of the firm. Includes shareholders, employees, customers, and suppliers.

Tax on contribution margin: Tax rate multiplied by Contribution margin from additional sales.

Trade credit: *Payables* are money owed by the firm, due to purchasing goods on credit. *Receivables* are money due from customers who purchased goods on credit.

Valuation: Process of establishing the market value of something, especially of a private firm.

Value: Used here in the specific meaning of estimated value of the firm. *See also* Present value.

Venture capital angels: Investors in early-stage or other small businesses; usually make direct investments of own capital, and take intense interest in the success of the investments. Also known as informal venture capital.

Venture capital funds: Organized firms that usually invest in high-growth potential, high-risk firms; based on capital contributions from high-net-worth firms and individuals, managed by investment professionals.

WACC: Weighted average cost of capital.

WIP: Work in process, or semi-processed inventories. This category of assets covers everything being prepared for sale to customers at a given point in time. WIPs reflect the value added by the firm to raw materials, but not yet completed or sold. They may include manufactured goods, consulting, or other service work.

Working capital: Current assets minus current liabilities.

Appendix 2

Useful Organizations and Web Sites

American Institute of Certified Public Accountants (AICPA): www.aicpa.org. See especially its Business Valuation and Forensic and Litigation Services (BVFLS) Center, designed to provide CPAs with an array of resources, tools, and information. The Center serves BVFLS practitioners, including business appraisal specialists and business valuation analysts, especially holders of the Accredited in Business Valuation (ABV) credential. http://bvfls.aicpa.org.

American Society of Appraisers: www.appraisers.org. Offers ASA and AM credentials.

Canadian Association of Family Enterprises: www.cafe.ca.

Dun & Bradstreet Credit Services, annually since 1982: *Industry Norms and Key Business Ratios*, available in many libraries. Also see www.dnb.com/us.

Edward Lowe Foundation, http://edwardlowe.org.

Ewing Marion Kauffman Foundation: www.kauffman.org

Family Firm Institute in Brookline, Massachusetts: www.ffi.org.

Fortune Small Business: www.fsb.com.

Institute of Business Appraisers: www.go-iba.org. Offers CBA, MCBA, BVAL, and AIBA credentials.

International Business Brokers Association: www.ibba.org.

Kauffman Center for Entrepreneurial Leadership: www.celcee.edu.

National Association of Certified Valuation Analysts: www.nacva.com. Offers CVA and AVA credentials

National Collegiate Inventors and Innovators Alliance (NCIIA): www.nciia.org.

National Network for Technology Entrepreneurship and Commercialization: www.n2tec.org.

Nation's Business (U.S. Chamber of Commerce): www.uschamber.com.

New Jersey Small Business Development Center Network: www.njsbdc.com.

Survey of Current Business (produced by the Bureau of Economic Analysis, U.S. Department of Commerce): www.bea.gov/bea/pubs.htm.

Wall Street Journal: www.wsj.com; see also the *Journal*'s early-stage site: www.startupjournal.com.

Appendix 3

Annotated Bibliography

The following classic references have been cited in this book. They are listed here for readers who may want to go back to the original sources.

Collins, J. C., *Good to Great: Why Some Companies Make the Leap and Others Don't* (New York: HarperCollins, 2001) An examination of mediocre companies who transformed themselves into growth companies, compared to those that didn't, and those that were unable to sustain a growth transformation. Focuses on leadership differences, technological change, strategic planning, and cultural change.

Collins, J. C., and J. I. Porras, *Built to Last: Successful Habits of Visionary Companies* (New York: HarperBusiness, 1994). What common factors are shared by the world's best long-term growth companies? See also:

Damodaran, A., *Investment Valuation* (New York: Wiley, 1996). Good summary of empirical studies. See subsequent studies by the same author: *The Dark Side of Valuation: Valuing Old Tech, New Tech, and New Economy Companies* (Upper Saddle River, NJ: Financial Times/Prentice-Hall [Pearson Education]), 2001), and *Damodaran on Valuation: Security Analysis for Investment and Corporate Finance* (Hoboken, NJ: Wiley Finance Series, 2006).

Fama, E., and K. French, "The Cross Section of Expected Returns," *Journal of Finance* 47 (June 1992): 427–64. Their three-factor model finds returns a positive function of systematic risk (betas), price/earnings ratio, and size.

Fisher, I., *The Theory of Interest* (New York: Macmillan, 1930). Still the foundation of ways we measure inflation and its effects.

Foster, R. N., and S. Kaplan, *Creative Destruction: From "Built to Last" to "Built to Perform"* (London: Financial Times/Prentice Hall [Pearson Education], 2001). How do companies successfully renew themselves, despite valued investments in products that are becoming obsolete all the time?

Gordon, M., *The Investment, Financing, and Valuation of the Corporation* (Homewood, IL: R. D. Irwin, 1962). Origin of the constant growth model that serves as the starting point for valuation techniques.

Hamada, R., "Portfolio Analysis, Market Equilibrium and Corporation Finance," *Journal of Finance* 24 (1969): 13–31. The basic method of analyzing risk, a version of which is presented in chapter 7 of the present book, was developed by Hamada.

Harrison, R. T., and C. M. Mason (Eds.), *Informal Venture Capital: Evaluating the Impact of Business Introduction Services* (London: Woodhead-Faulkner/ Prentice Hall, 1996). The first book that focused on reporting empirical research on the behavior of angel investors; it has a strong cross-national flavor, with studies from several European and North American countries.

Hitchner, J. R., *Financial Valuation: Applications and Models*, 2nd ed. (Hoboken, NJ: John Wiley & Sons, Inc., 2006). Used as the core text for AICPA and NACVA professional courses.

Ibbotson Associates, *Stocks, Bonds, Bills and Inflation: 1996 Yearbook* (Chicago: Ibbotson Associates, 1996). The standard reference for market return values. For more recent versions of this seminal discussion of the relationships between bond and stock markets, see www.ibbotson.com/content/product_lvl3_sort.asp?catalog = Products&category = Data%20Publications.

Lintner, J., "The Valuation of Risk Assets and the Selection of Risky Investments in Stock Portfolios and Capital Budgets," *Review of Economics and Statistics* 47 (February 1965): 13–37.

Lipper, A., III, *The Guide for Venture Investing Angels: Financing and Investing in Private Companies* (Columbia: Missouri Innovation Center Publications, 1998). A book designed to help angel investors improve their investment performance.

Litz, R. A., and A. C. Stewart, "Franchising for Sustainable Advantage? Comparing the Performance of Independent Retailers and Trade-Name Franchisees," *Journal of Business Venturing* 13.2 (March 1998): 131–50. Some solid empirical research about the kinds of strategies that have (and have not) worked for independent retailers facing competition from massive national or global competitors. See also, by the same authors:

Litz, R. A., and A. C. Stewart, "The Late Show: Small Retailers, Extraordinary Accessibility, and Selling beyond Sundays and Evenings," *Journal of Small Business Management* 38.1 (2000): 1–26.

Litz, R. A., and A. C. Stewart, "Where Everybody Knows Your Name: Extraorganizational Clan-Building as Small Firm Strategy for Home Field Advantage," *Journal of Small Business Strategy* 11.1 (2000): 1–13.

Long, Michael S., X. Wang, and J. Zhang. "Growth Options, Unwritten Call Discounts, and the Valuation of the Small Firm," working paper, Department of Finance, Rutgers Business School, Newark, NJ, 2006. Our source for the adjusted average returns used in chapter 7.

Markowitz, H. M., "Portfolio Selection," *Journal of Finance* 7 (March 1952): 77–91. Markowitz was later awarded the Nobel Prize in Economics for these ideas, shared in 1990 with Merton H. Miller and William F. Sharpe (see below).

Pratt, J., "Risk Aversion in the Small and in the Large," *Econometrica* 32.1 (January–April 1964): 122–36. A thorough discussion of risk aversion. Abstract: "This paper concerns utility functions for money. A measure of risk aversion in the small, the risk premium or insurance premium for an arbitrary risk, and a natural concept of decreasing risk aversion are discussed and related to one another. Risks are also considered as a proportion of total assets."

Sharpe, W., "Capital Asset Prices: A Theory of Market Equilibrium under Conditions of Risk," *Journal of Finance* 19 (September 1964): 425–42. This work was also the basis for a Nobel Prize, awarded in 1990, to Markowitz and Miller.

Shumway, T., and V. Warther, "The Delisting Bias in CRSP's NASDAQ Data and Its Implications for Size Effect," *Journal of Finance* 54 (1999): 2361–79.

Treynor, J. L., "Market Value, Time and Risk," in R. A. Korajczyk (Ed.), *Asset Pricing and Portfolio Performance: Models, Strategy, and Performance Metrics* (London: Risk Books, 1999). This is the classic 1961 paper on the management of investment risks, published after many underground years.

Appendix 4

How the IRS Views Valuation of Closely Held Firms

The Internal Revenue Service (U.S. government) has a strong interest in the valuation of closely held firms, especially at the time of transfer in their ownership, usually from founder to siblings either as a gift or inheritance.[1] This appendix reviews the IRS approach to valuation. This summary is based on the Gift and Estate Tax Section of the complete review of the valuation process published by the Bureau of National Affairs, entitled Tax Management Portfolio, in volume 831. The objective is to determine the fair market value of a property based on a hypothetical arm's-length transfer of the property between a willing buyer and a willing seller.

Unlike most IRS procedures that attempt to minimize the taxpayers' degree of flexibility in how to determine tax liabilities, the valuation process is based on IRS Revenue Ruling 59–60, which stated: "No formula can be devised that will be generally applicable to the multitude of difficult valuation issues."

Instead, the valuation process includes the following factors: the company's accounting net worth, its prospective earning potential and dividend-paying potential, goodwill associated with the business, the particular industry's economic outlook, the company's position in its industry, its management, the degree of control represented by the portion of stock being valued, the value of actively traded securities of corporations engaged in similar lines of business, any proceeds of life insurance policies that are payable to or for the benefit of the company, any restrictions or options on the sale of such securities, and "other relevant factors." This list represents a fairly exhaustive itemization of variables that might affect actual value.

The primary emphasis, when market valuation techniques are inapplicable, is based on a company's net worth, prospective earning power, dividend-paying capacity, and other relevant factors. The latter relate to industry growth,

[1] With arm's-length transactions with outsiders, the potential conflict is much lower because sellers want the greatest values and buyers want to pay the least. In these situations, the only real problems deal with structuring the deals merely to avoid taxes, usually by the sellers.

comparable firms' P/E ratios, general economic conditions, and so on. The reader of this book notices that net worth (actually, the Code requires a modified net worth) is similar to our liquidation value. The earning power and dividend paying capacity are similar to our value of a going concern. The confusing part is that a combination of values is usually used.

In its complete form, Revenue Ruling 59–60 provides that "all available financial data, as well as all relevant factors affecting the fair market value" should be considered in valuing the closely held firm. The Ruling also lists the following eight factors that should be considered: (1) the nature of the business and its history since inception, (2) the general economic outlook and condition and the outlook of the specific industry in particular, (3) the book value of equity, (4) the firm's earning capacity, (5) its dividend-paying capacity, (6) the existence (or absence) of goodwill and/or other intangibles, (7) the size of the specific block of stock being valued (courts have generally found minority shareholder discounts in the neighborhood of 20–30%, although they are sometimes much higher), and (8) the market prices of stocks of corporations engaged in the same or similar lines of business. The courts examine each of these factors, placing various weights on them depending on the specific business being valued.

Probably a more important consideration is that there can be substantial penalties for incorrectly valued businesses. It is clear that expert appraisals are a necessity in the valuation of any business interests. The appraisal does not necessarily avoid a penalty situation. However, the existence of a good appraisal offers the taxpayer the greatest opportunity for achieving the desired valuation, as well as the greatest likelihood of avoiding a penalty.

Appendix 5

Worksheets

A5.1: Likely Buyers Worksheet

- Customers
- Suppliers
- Competitors
  - Direct
  - Neighboring
  - Chains
- Strangers
  - Recent grads (and their families)
  - Early retirees (check corporate layoffs)
  - Strategic buyers from larger companies, including foreign firms
  - Recent immigrants
  - Prospective immigrants
- Companies wanting to enter market by acquisition of:
  - Product lines
  - Personnel
  - Location
  - Intellectual property
  - Access to key suppliers or accounts

A5.2: Valuation Scenarios

Items	Worst Case: Receiver Liquidation	Second Worst: Owner Liquidation	Option 1: ?	Most Likely: Reluctant Buyer	Best Case: Hungry Buyer
Assets					
Inventory	10%	50%		90% of cost	100% of cost
WIP	0	Completed		50% of profit value	100% of profit margin
Goodwill	0	Moral value only		½ year profits?	1 year of profits
Liabilities					
Secured creditors	50%	100%		Transferred	Cleared
Trade creditors; leases	Pull-backs only	Clean		Transferred	Cleared
Shareholders	0	Net		Net value of business	Net value of business
Costs to develop					
Search	Phone calls	0		Time and effort, expenses	Market leaders; portfolio
Agents	Bailiff, receiver	0		Business broker?	Self or broker
Advertising	$1,000	$2,500		Maybe; quiet?	?
WIP completion	?	At cost		By new owner	By current owner
Special items	Auction damage to reputation	Declining value; no recovery of sweat equity		Training and transfer period; cash preferred	Timing, selling, research, negotiation
Estimated net					
Terms and conditions					

A5.3 Valuation Worksheet

Items	Worst Case: Receiver Liquidation	Second Worst: Owner Liquidation	Option 1: ?	Most Likely: Reluctant Buyer	Best Case: Hungry Buyer
Assets					
Inventory					
WIP					
Goodwill					
Liabilities					
Secured creditors					
Trade creditors; leases					
Shareholders					
Costs to develop					
Search					
Agents					
Advertising					
WIP completion					
Special items					
Estimated net					
Terms and conditions					

Index

www.ingramcontent.com/pod-product-compliance
Ingram Content Group UK Ltd.
Pitfield, Milton Keynes, MK11 3LW, UK
UKHW021135160926
475595UK00020B/66

9 780195 301465